Europe, Hellas and Egypt

Complementary antipodes during Late Antiquity

Papers from Session IV.3, held at the European Association of Archaeologists Eighth Annual Meeting in Thessaloniki 2002

Edited by

Amanda–Alice Maravelia

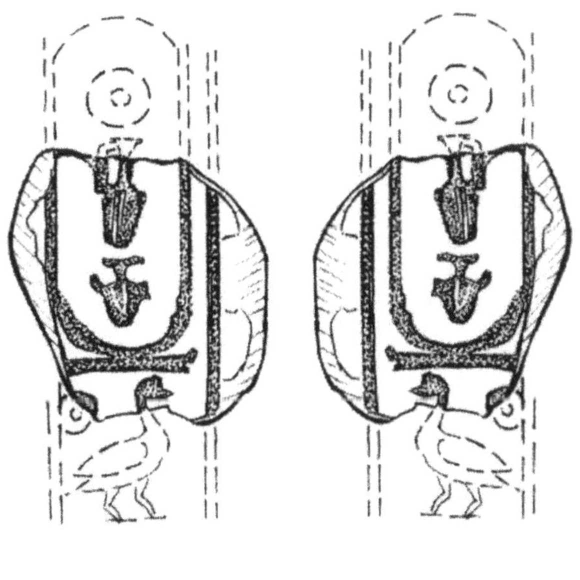

BAR International Series 1218
2004

Published in 2019 by
BAR Publishing, Oxford

BAR International Series 1218

Europe, Hellas and Egypt

COVER IMAGE Collage of a faience tile (B18.278) from the Benaki Museum Egyptian Collection, bearing the prenomen cartouche of Amasis II (570-526 BCE), a Saite pharaoh renowned friend of Polykratēs of Samos and of Hellenic States; also a generous donor to the Delphi Oracle [see Amanda—Alice Maravelia: 'Ancient Egyptian Inscribed Faience Objects from the Benaki Museum in Athens, 1', *JNES*, 61^2, 2002, 81-109 & fig. 7b; drawing by Katerina Mavragani].

ISBN 9781841715780 paperback
ISBN 9781407326290 e-book

DOI https://doi.org/10.30861/9781841715780

A catalogue record for this book is available from the British Library

This book is available at www.barpublishing.com

BAR Publishing is the trading name of British Archaeological Reports (Oxford) Ltd. British Archaeological Reports was first incorporated in 1974 to publish the BAR Series, International and British. In 1992 Hadrian Books Ltd became part of the BAR group. This volume was originally published by Archaeopress in conjunction with British Archaeological Reports (Oxford) Ltd / Hadrian Books Ltd, the Series principal publisher, in 2004. This present volume is published by BAR Publishing, 2019.

BAR
PUBLISHING

BAR titles are available from:

BAR Publishing
122 Banbury Rd, Oxford, OX2 7BP, UK
EMAIL info@barpublishing.com
PHONE +44 (0)1865 310431
FAX +44 (0)1865 316916
www.barpublishing.com

CONTENTS

Ashraf–Alexandre Sadek
Foreword iii

Amanda–Alice Maravelia and *Galina A. Belova*
Introduction v

Galina A. Belova
The Cretans (*Kfti.w*) in Egypt 1

Amanda–Alice Maravelia and *Eleni Cladaki–Manoli*
Among the Hidden Treasures of the National Archaeological Museum in Athens:
Searching for Forgotten Mummies, 1 5

Daniela Picchi
The Egyptian Collection of the Archaeological Museum in Bologna:
Past and Future 21

Sergej V. Ivanov
Ancient Egyptian Collections in Ukrainian Museums:
The Case of B.I. & V.N. Khanenko's Museum in Kiev 35

Ashraf Alexandre Sadek
La Musique Copte 43

Sophia Tsourinaki
Late Antique Textiles of the Benaki Museum with Bucolic and Mythological Iconography 51

Harry E. Tzalas
Fantastic Discoveries in Archaeology: The Case of the Tomb of Alexander the Great 67

Tatjana A. Sherkova
Egypt and the Great Silk Road 89

Helena G. Tolmatcheva
The Ancient Egyptian Roots of the Phoenix Myth: On the History of the Problem 93

AUTHORS & ADDRESSES

Galina A. Belova: Centre for Egyptological Studies, Russian Academy of Sciences; 12, Rozhdestvenka Str., RU–103 031, Moscow, Russia. [*e-mail*: cesras@online.ru]

Eleni Cladaki–Manoli: National Archaeological Museum; 1, Tositsa Str., GR–106 82, Athens, Hellas. [*e-mail*: cladaki@hotmail.com]

Sergej V. Ivanov: Center for Egyptological Studies, Russian Academy of Sciences; 12, Rozhdestvenka Str., RU–103 031, Moscow, Russia. [*e-mail*: cesras@online.ru]

Amanda–Alice Maravelia: Centre de Recherches en Sciences de l'Antiquité, Faculté des Lettres et des Sciences Humaines, Université de Limoges; 39E, Rue Camille Guérin, F–870 36, Limoges Cedex, France / Suite # 121; 24, Hagiou Iōannou Str., GR–15342, Hagia Paraskeuē; Athens, Hellas. [*e-mail*: a_maravelia@hotmail.com]

Daniela Picchi: Museo Civico Archeologico di Bologna; Via de' Musei 8, I–401 24, Bologna, Italia. [*e-mail*: Daniela.Picchi@comune.bologna.it]

Ashraf–Alexandre Sadek: Centre de Recherches en Sciences de l'Antiquité, Faculté des Lettres et des Sciences Humaines, Université de Limoges; 39E, Rue Camille Guérin, F–870 36, Limoges Cedex, France. [*e-mail*: a.sadek@club_internet.fr]

Tatjana A. Sherkova: Centre for Egyptological Studies, Russian Academy of Sciences; 12, Rozhdestvenka Str., RU–103 031, Moscow, Russia. [*e-mail*: cesras@online.ru]

Helena G. Tolmatcheva: Center for Egyptological Studies, Russian Academy of Sciences; 12, Rozhdestvenka Str., RU–103 031, Moscow, Russia. [e-mail: cesras@online.ru]

Sophia Tsourinaki: Benaki Museum; 1, Koumbari Str., GR–106 74, Athens, Hellas. [e-mail: tsourinaki@benaki.gr]

Harry E. Tzalas: Hellenic Mission in Alexandria, Hellenic Institute for Ancient and Medieval Alexandrian Studies; 94, Skra Str., GR–176 73, Kallithea, Athens, Hellas. [*e-mail*: htzalas@eudoramail.com]

FOREWORD

It is a real pleasure for me to write a brief Foreword for this volume, which is part of a wider project for conferences and publications dealing with Europe, Hellas and Egypt during (the Late) Antiquity. A previous volume called *Ancient Egypt and Antique Europe: Two Parts of the Mediterranean World,* edited by Dr A.–A. Maravelia (BAR International Series 1052, 2002), was already welcomed among Archaeologists and Historians. It is a very courageous step to underline the relationship between the two parts of the Mediterranean Sea, civilisations which put in touch three main continents: Africa, Europe and Asia. As we all know, ancient Egypt was a cradle of European civilization. Beginning with the historic times, Egypt was closely linked to the Mediterranean area, and the Egyptian culture had a great influence upon the growth of European civilization.

The country of the Pyramids always attracted the hearts and minds of Europeans not only because of its marvels and *savants*, but also due the fertility of its soil. The modern migration of the Hellenic Community towards Egypt during the 19th and 20th centuries also greatly contributed to the development of Modern Egypt. All these —among several other factors— make of our parallel histories to appear closely linked and illumine our future ...

First of all, we should be grateful to all the authors, who participated with their scientific contributions either in this volume or in the previous one mentioned above. The originality of their use of new material and data brings into light important aspects of the subject, even in the fields which had already been dealt with by previous researchers.

A very interesting aspect of these studies, both in the orientation of these symposia and in their published *Proceedings* is the contribution not only of Archaeologists and Historians but also of well qualified specialists in other scientific fields, like (for instance) Astronomy, Geography and Informatics.

From this project which links Ancient Orient and Europe, through this extraordinary ancient bridge of important culture, I mean Hellas, I am convinced that many positive results will arise and clarify for all researchers many original points, filling adequately the existing lacuna. Bravo to Dr A.–A. Maravelia, Dr G. A. Belova and Dr E. Cladaki–Manoli, for creating such an important source of studies. Their efforts in organising these symposia and publication of their *Acts* deserve strong support and encouragement.

Actually, Dr Maravelia —whose 2nd PhD Thesis in Egyptology I supervised— has convinced me by repeatedly attracting my attention on the importance of opening a new area of research to study the influences of Eastern and Western civilizations upon one another. Although I never really neglected this orientation, I had not intended to go as far as the present project. In fact, I edited a book on Alexandria, including several articles dedicated to the relationship between Hellas and Egypt: *Alexandrie, Perle de la Méditerranée* (= *Le Monde Copte*, **27-28**), Limoges 1997; my own contribution there being 'Alexandrie, fille de Rakotis' (see 7-20).

The present volume provides about ten high level contributions in which we can find the answers to many historical, artistic and archaeological questions, which were raised by scholars throughout their various research fields. Frankly it is a real success, deserving a warm welcome.

[Limoges, December 2002]

Ashraf–Alexandre SADEK

Cert. Professor of Egyptology & Coptology, University of Limoges, France
Director of the Journal *Le Monde Copte*

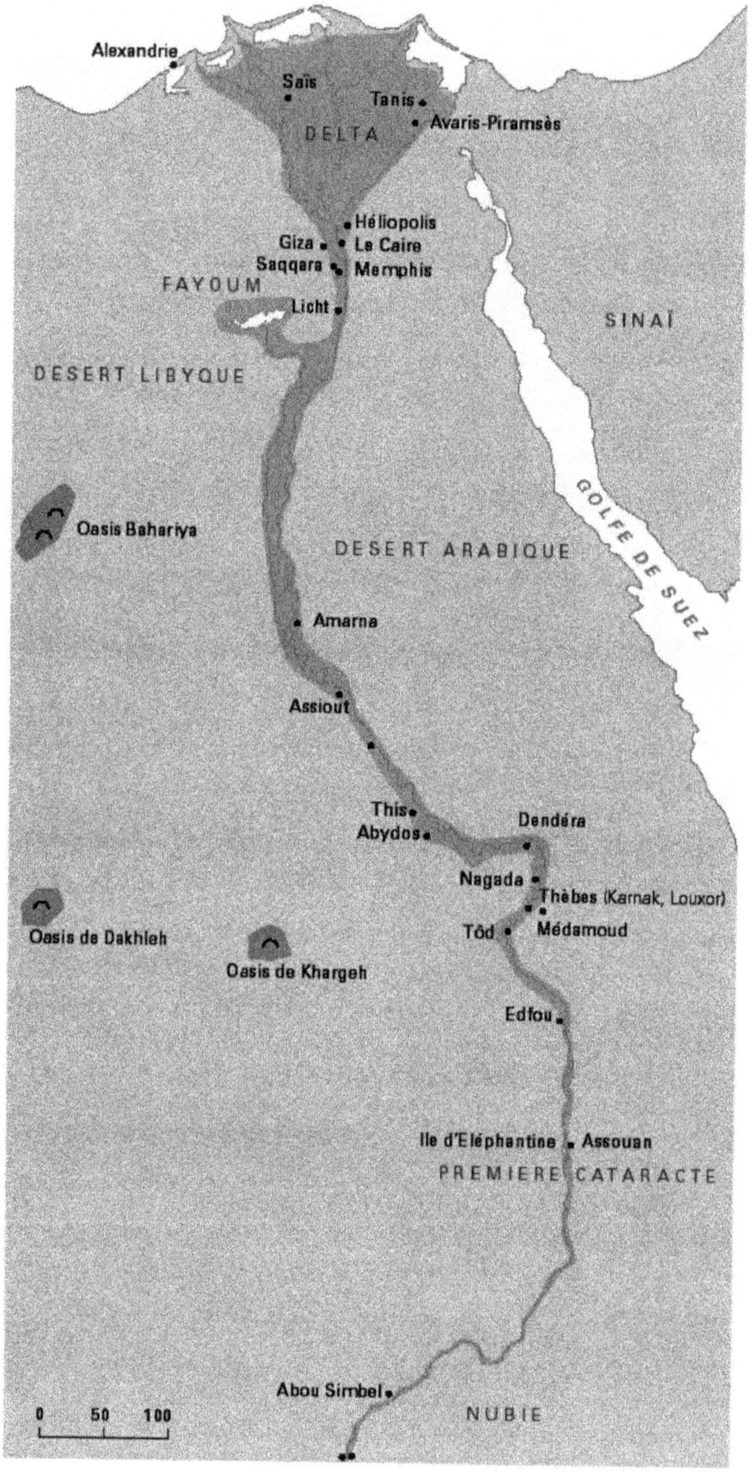

FIGURE: A simplified map of Egypt, featuring ancient and modern sites, some of which are mentioned in the papers of this volume.

INTRODUCTION

Ancient Egypt was a cradle of European civilization. From the beginning of historic times Egypt was closely linked to the Mediterranean area, and the Egyptian culture had a great influence upon the growth of European civilization. The country of pyramids always attracted Europeans not only because of its marvels and sages, but also because of the fertility of its soil. During Helleno–Roman and Byzantine times Egypt has been a granary for Europe, which moreover was strategically situated in the Middle East. That is why the historical destinies of Europe and Egypt were interlaced very closely, and at times portions of the European continent and Egypt were parts of one and the same empire. Especially during the Saitic renaissance, when Hellenic mercenaries were abiding in Egypt; when Amasis II and Polykrates of Samos were temporary allies; when Naukratis was the Hellenic emporium centre: during these times, the interactions of both nations were fruitful and deserve particular attention. With the advent of Alexander the Great, greeted by the priesthood of Amūn, and the reign of Ptolemies, Egypt enjoyed her last centuries of relative freedom and flourished. Then again, during the Roman occupation, the *enchorial* label was deliberately put on the autochtones, and the decline of purely Egyptian customs was completed, until they were nearly obsolete or highly transformed with the advent of Christianity during the Coptic era.

When an Egyptological session was officially incorporated for the first time in the agenda of the *European Association of Archaeologists*, during the EAA 7th Conference in Esslingen, we were not expecting such a warm welcome, even by non Egyptologists. Following this, the session organized by Amanda–Alice Maravelia, Galina A. Belova and Eleni Cladaki—Manoli during the EAA 8th Conference in Thessalonikē, Hellas, during September 2002, was intended as the second part of last year's project, and was focused to explore and discuss some of the themes, which would be mutually interesting both for Egyptologists and for specialists in European Archaeology. Emphasis was stressed on the Late Antiquity (after c. 660 BCE, including the Roman and the Coptic Period, until the Arab Conquest c. 640 CE), although studies concerned with earlier eras were also featured. The outcome of that fruitful session is contained in the pages that follow in the present book.

Furthermore, we are sure that the results of recent field investigations in Egypt would be very interesting to specialists in the field of European Archaeology and would give them an opportunity to identify themes of a mutual interest. The Thessalonikē egyptological session was planned and organized in connection with the former guidelines and concepts, in order to discuss the following topics:

1. The history of European Egyptology and European Museums holding Egyptian Antiquities today, together with the presentation of some (master) pieces of their collections.
2. The political, economic and cultural contacts between Europe, Hellas and Egypt especially during the LP, Helleno–Roman and Early Christian (Coptic) Periods.
3. The impacts of the advent of Alexander the Great, and the current excavations in Alexandria.
4. The links between populations of Egypt and Europe (especially Hellas) in ancient times.

We regret that some respected colleagues (e.g: Claude Obsomer, Alexei Krol) were not capable of giving us their contributions in order to be included in the present volume. We hope and wish that another time this shall become possible. Actually the quantity of papers in this book is small, but we do believe that the quality is high. In editing these *Proceedings* one of us (A.–A.M.) paid particular attention to correct and amend for many errors of a lesser or major character, sometimes adding relevant bibliography and footnotes. She also tried to make the texts more idiomatic in English. An attempt has been made, in order that the hosted papers follow some general common guidelines in format and appearance, although the principal traits of each and every one of them have been generally preserved. The editor corrected and checked for various erroneous or unclear points in them, although we wish to point out that for any specific error that might still exist it is only the author(s) of the corresponding articles that is(are) responsible. We should also like to thank: (i) the two referees (internationally distinguished colleagues in the field of Egyptology), that checked the papers and proposed some amendments for some of them, whose anonymity we keep here —respecting their desire— and whose help was valuable indeed; (ii) Prof. Dr Ashraf–Alexandre Sadek for his kind foreword.

Let us now take a closer brief look at the participants of this volume and their interesting contributions. The present book is characterized indeed by a uniformity and conciseness as to its contents, the main axis being Egypt and Hellas and the main temporal context being the Late Period.

♀ **Galina A. Belova**, head of the Russian mission in Cairo and of the newly inaugurated Institute there, director of CES/RAS and of GALEXYS egyptological database, reviews the latest achievements in the field of identification of the *Kfti.w* and proposes an interesting theory, according to which the Hellenic (Minoan and Aegean) presence in Egypt was considerably older than the LP (namely dating at least since the SIP). In 2001 the Center for Egyptological Studies of the Russian Academy of Sciences (CES/RAS) carried out archaeological exploration at the site of Kom Tuman (ancient Memphis). During the season there were found several terracotta figurines, which were presumably produced in Crete. Classical authors mention a small settlement of the Cretans, which already existed in Memphis during the reign of Pharaoh Apries (7th century BCE). The Egyptian records evidence the contacts between Egypt and Crete since ancient times. However, the localization of toponyms reordered in Egyptian inscriptions is rather problematic. In her original paper the author presents a new plausible interpretation and identification of toponyms, which were generally considered as corresponding to the island of Crete.

♀ **Amanda–Alice Maravelia and Eleni Cladaki–Manoli** offer a thorough study of five Egyptian sarcophagi and their inscriptions, which are kept in the storerooms of the National Archaeologial Museum in Athens. The Egyptian Collection of the National Archaeological Museum in Athens keeps most of its riches well hidden in the Museum's storing facilities. Among those, the authors have managed to rediscover some LP and Ptolemaic coffins with their mummies. All these particular anthropoid sarcophagi have been published in the Hellenic language in a rather elementary and concise way (with some erroneous points) more than a century ago by Tasos Neroutsos in *Ἀρχαιολογικὴ ἐφημερὶς* (Athens 1884). The author was a medical doctor who lived in Alexandria. Since then the coffins have fallen into oblivion, have never been exhibited in the Museum's showrooms (except one), and nobody else since the late Neroutsos cared to study them accurately. Now after so many years that have elapsed, the authors are trying to bring into light these forgotten and more or less unknown finds. These objects have been discovered in Egypt and were donated to the Hellenic Government during the late 19th century by wealthy Hellenic patriots who lived in Egypt. The purpose of this article is to remind both the Egyptologists and Egyptophili the presence of these forgotten mummies and to present a complete and precise study of some of these sarcophagi, dating from the Ptolemaic Period. Five out of these ten anthropoid coffins and their hieroglyphic inscriptions are thoroughly examined and presented in this paper, while the remainder five will be (also thoroughly) studied in a forthcoming paper.

♀ **Daniela Picchi**, curator of the Egyptian Collection in Museo Civico Archeologico di Bologna, gives an interesting account on the history of that very collection from the recent past until nowadays. In Bologna the initial interest in ancient Egypt derives from the 16th and 17th centuries, when a hundred Egyptian objects, whose origin and provenance are unknown, became part of the antiquities of the University Museum. However, it was only in the 19th century that interest in ancient Egypt became intense. Beginning in 1825, every third year the course of Archaeology in Bologna —at least in theory— had to be dedicated to the study of Egypt. In such a cultural *milieu* the Bolognese painter Pelagio Palagi (1775-1860) collated his Egyptian collection, which —on his death in Turin— included 3109 objects; in his will he donated it to his native town. In 1881 the objects housed in the University were added to this collection. Other collections of minor importance were also added in the following years, until in 1895 the *Museo Civico di Bologna: Catalogo di Antichità Egizie* by Giovanni Kminek–Szedlo was published. In 1987 another donation from a private collection consisting of 85 pieces was finally included. Today the Egyptian collection of the Archaeological Museum of Bologna, with its 3500 objects, is one of the richest in Italy and also in Europe.

♀ **Sergej V. Ivanov**, an Egyptologist specializing in Art History and Informatized Egyptology, vividly presents some nice pieces from modern Russian museums. His paper gives the results of the international project *The Databank of Eastern–European Egyptology*, carried out by the Center for Egyptological Studies of the Russian Academy of Sciences (CES/RAS, Moscow) and the Gnosarch Foundation (Basel), whose director is Edward Loring. The subject of his paper is the presentation of the Egyptian Collection kept in the B.I. Khanenko's Museum of Art (Kiev). It was gathered by Bogdan I. Khanenko, during his travels to Europe in the beginning of the 20th century. The collection includes fine pieces of private sculpture dating from Dynasty V up to the Ptolemaic Period. Coptic textiles form a large section of this collection. The author surveys the collection and an updated publication of several objects belonging therein is also given.

♀ **Ashraf–Alexandre Sadek**, a brilliant scholar and talented teacher whose love for Coptic Christianity is well known, also a Professor of Egyptology and Coptology at the University of Limoges (France), gives an original account of Coptic Music, its evolution and its relation to the ancient Hellenic musical ways of expression. Music is but a noble and gentle indicator of culture, expressing concisely the human psyche and also an intercultural medium of human contact. The relations between Music in Ancient Hellas and Egypt is definitely important and reciprocal, since it was the Coptic Music that consisted one of the most characteristic ways of communication between the Hellenic and the Egyptian civilization. The Hellenic influence on the Coptic Music is evident, mainly in the domain of language borrowing and the use of certain ecclesiastical hymns. The author aims at studying the reciprocal influence of Coptic onto the Hellenic Music, triggering the interest for such studies (which deserve to follow).

♀ **Sophia Tsourinaki**, a devoted specialist in ancient textiles, research associate at he Benaki Museum (a modern and living temple of archaeological studies, under the direction of Prof. Dr Angelos Delivorias) presents an original and well–written contribution on ancient textiles concerned with bucolic and mythological (Dionysian) iconographical patterns. The Benaki Museum possesses a collection of late antique textiles from Egypt, the iconography of which is strongly influenced by the Hellenistic style of Late Antiquity. In her paper attention is focused on a few rare examples, a loop pile hanging of Hēraklēs and a special group of tapestry woven elements. The designs including bucolic representations, hunting imagery and mythological scenes of Dionysian cult are comparable to designs in mosaic and metal work. From the compositional scheme and detailed analysis of the techniques, she attempts to determine more precisely that they form three stylistic groups. The naturalistically shaded loop pile weaves in polychrome wool derive from mosaics; the black–figured mythological textiles originated in the dark–silhouette tradition from vase painting; the textiles with simplified figures in muted colours derive from various literary manuscript illustrations.

♀ **Harry E. Tzalas**, director of the Hellenic Institute for Ancient and Medieval Alexandrian Studies and determined researcher, whose love for Alexandria is more than evident, offers a brief but interesting account on the efforts that have been made to detect the tomb of Alexander the Great. His contribution is important, since it discusses the idle tenacity of want–to–be–famous persons, otherwise irrelevant and incompetent in Archaeology. Even if academic degrees exist in some of their cases, the accompanying Alexandro–mania is enough by itself to create a background of false and tendentious interpretations of the facts, using even nationalistic (not to say fascistic!) 'arguments'. It is almost the same case with the various pyramidiots, esoterists and think–to–be–intelligent amateurs, who try to give ancient Egyptian historical facts a completely perverse and distorted image! The mythical and the fantastic as an attempt to interpret the remains of the human past have preceded Archaeology, which as a scientific discipline is no more than two centuries old. However, ignorance coupled with fertility of mind has often brought confusion to the uninitiated general public, when ruins are arbitrarily connected to legendary palaces of mythical kings and queens. This tendency, understandable for the Dark Ages, when knowledge was the prerogative of the few, continued even during the 19th and the 20th centuries, although education became available to greater numbers. Tellers of fantastic discoveries are then no longer ignorant peasants or illiterate burghers. The new breed is made up of superficially educated persons with a basic knowledge, who can read and often do read profusely books of history. They tend, however, to interpret arbitrarily the remains of the past. Because of their lack of scholarly background, and moved by exaggerated ambitions, they propose naïve interpretations, irresponsible theories, formulated in an unscientific manner. Often they resort to lies and hoaxes in their frenzy to make their cause prevail. These lovers of the past and amateur researchers are found at all levels of society, from workers and clerks, to medical doctors and retired military officers. The 'readings' of the disk of Phaestos and of the Runic inscription on the Marble Lion of Piraeus are only two of the fantastic interpretations of inscriptions that can be considered naïve at least, if not ridiculous. All means are mobilized: chance troves, secret maps, revelations in dreams and even 'psychic archaeology', a term that has lately been unashamedly advanced by a group of exalted visionaries, who nonetheless obtained permission to search in Alexandria for the tomb of Alexander the Great with the use of … mediums! In fact, it is on the alleged discoveries of the tomb of the Great Macedonian that the author focuses his attention and, more specifically, on the three most publicized and well–documented stories which have —for the last 150 years— created sensation. The dates for each story setting are different, the persons concerned have different occupations, and the sites of research vary; but the pattern followed by each of the instigators is the same. An interpreter in the Consulate General of Russia in Alexandria, in the mid–19th century, an Alexandrian waiter in the mid–20th century, an archaeologist at the end of that same century shared the same belief, with the same insistence and with the same lack of any scientific foundation. Apparently each initially believes to be the 'elected one' who will find the 'lost tomb'. As time passes, and although nothing substantiates it, the belief becomes certitude. Authorities are persuaded to grant permissions, but the visionary fails to prove his/her case and consequently further authorizations are refused. In despair the researcher claims being the victim of a 'plot' and is appalled that the authenticity (*sic*) of his/her discovery is questioned. As all these cases do not fall in the field of Archaeology, knowledgeable scholars react with either silence or laconic negations, and the confusion remains in the mind of everyday people who get their information through the newspapers, radio broadcasts and television programs. With the bad and sometimes dishonest use that is nowadays made of the private TV channels (especially in Hellas), one can easily understand the seriousness of the situation …

♀ **Tatjana A. Sherkova**, a bright Egyptologist and a really nice woman, vice–director of CES/RAS, guides us through later Antiquity and presents the connection of Egypt to the Great Silk Road in Asia, a route of international trade and a virtual funnel for cultural interactions. The wide popularity of Egyptian faience amulets among populations of different ethno–cultural background, belonging especially to the Helleno–Roman Period, presents a researcher with a considerable number of problems: the place of their production in Egypt itself and possible local copies; the semantics of images on these amulets outside Egypt; & c. These numerous objects make it possible to determine to a certain extent the character of continental trade and to reconstruct the meaning of the figurine for the Egyptian amulets outside Egypt. There is a notion that they were a kind of small change in the international trade. But in any case, by obtaining them the representatives of other cultures —besides their aesthetic attraction— also appreciated their magic protective abilities. At present there is a vivid interest in the Great Silk Road. This conception adds the importance, which is practically identical to the system of roads that linked the Mediterranean and the Black Sea regions with India and China. As to India it was in the sphere of sea–trade and its character differed from continental trade. Via Penjab and accordingly inner regions of Central Asia, Baktria was linked with Indian ports, through which a sea–trade with Egypt was taking place. The tracks of that trade are easily discernible, due to finds of art works of the Alexandrian School of art style. A collection of such artifacts was kept in the palace of the ruler of Capisa (the present Begram near Kabul in Afghanistan (a country highly suffered recently by the Islamic fanatics, especially the women) of the Kushan Empire, which was situated in Cenral Asia from the 2nd/1st century BCE to the 2nd/3rd century CE. In the sealed treasury these valuable objects —received as gifts or confiscated by the Customs— were placed together with Chinese carved ivory and lacquers. There were glass vessels of the famous Alexandrian glass–blowers and plaster medallions, bronze figurines, the representations of Harpocratēs and Hēraklēs–Serapis being among them. The works of art of the Roman Empire were not only gods, but also samples of many local articles as well as —especially— their image–bearing series. Kushan kings used the iconography of divinities of the Helleno–Roman pantheon representing personages of the local Indo–Iranian pantheon. In the representations of their divinities on reliefs of stupa and palaces, Helleno–Roman and Egyptian iconography of gods was borrowed by the Kushans much more extensively. This is a very interesting and original paper, featuring a multidisciplinary archaeological study.

♀ **Helena Tolmacheva**, a promising young Egyptologist of the CES/RAS team briefly discusses the issue of the mythical Phoenix, an ancient Egyptian Osirian and astronomical symbol, which passed into Hellenic Mythology as an archetype for rebirth and immortality. The author sheds light on the ancient Egyptian origins of the Hellenic myth. The classical myth of Phoenix has been under discussion since the midst of 16th century, when the humanists published a great number of authentic texts giving the possibility for the systematic studies of classical heritage. The Egyptian component of the myth was not clear until 1856, when Heinrich Brugsch proved that the Hellenic Phoenix have been known under the name of the Egyptian *bnw*–bird. Nevertheless the interests of the 19th century scholars were focused on Phoenix as the symbol of astronomical and chronological periods. That is why in the literature of those times this discussion is centered on such kind of correlations between the Egyptian *bnw* and the classical *Phoenix*. The image of *bnw*–bird had existed since the OK until the LP. During more than 2000 years it was transformed from the small bird demiurge worshipped in Heliopolis into a significant deity worshipped all over Egypt. The *bnw*-bird image was closely connected to other supreme gods, such as Atum, Rēʿ, and Osiris. In many aspects the modifications of its functions and symbolism could be explained by the position of these gods in Egyptian pantheon. At the time of the OK and MK Benu was identified with Atum–Rēʿ and had mainly solar and cosmogonical significance. On the contrary, during the NK the cult of Osiris attained its major expansion. Therefore, the *bnw* was popularized as one of the rulers of the Netherworld. Thus the components of the myth of Phoenix, which were emphasized by Adriana Belluccio, could have indeed an Egyptian origin. On the other hand the Hellenic elements should not be forgotten. The image of Phoenix known from classical sources was the result of the synthesis of the Oriental and the Hellenic cultural traditions; a synthesis that was so widespread during Hellenistic times. In Coptic sources and the Early Christian literature Phoenix was considered to be the symbol of resurrection and eternal life, of revival in general: of the Sun, Time, Christ, Virgin Mary. According to the Coptic authors, the Phoenix appeared during the time of the first sacrifice mentioned in the *Bible*. Another text says that during the Exodus from Egypt the Phoenix appeared in the temple of Heliopolis …

We do hope that the readers will find in the present volume some answers to several issues concerned with some aspects of the current egyptological research, especially with the fascinating domain of the cultural interactions and feedback between Egypt and Hellas (mainly during the Late Antiquity). We wholeheartedly wish them to enjoy their virtual trip towards the luminous *horizon of knowledge* (*ȝḫ.t n.t rḫ.t-ḫ.t*), at the threshold of three continents: Europe, Africa and Asia.

[Athens, June 2003]

Amanda–Alice MARAVELIA & Galina A. BELOVA

Papers Presented At The Session

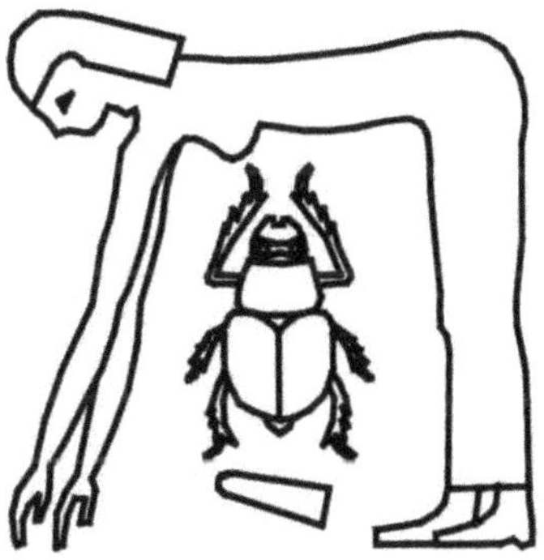

The Cretans (*Kfti.w*) in Egypt

Galina A. Belova

Abstract

In 2001 the Center for Egyptological Studies of the Russian Academy of Sciences (CES/RAS) carried out archaeological exploration at the site of Kom Tuman (ancient Memphis). During the season there were found several terracotta figurines, which were presumably produced in Crete. Classical authors mention a small settlement of the Cretans, which already existed in Memphis during the reign of Pharaoh Apries (7th century BCE). The Egyptian records evidence the contacts between Egypt and Crete since ancient times. However, the localization of toponyms reordered in Egyptian inscriptions is rather problematic. In this paper the author presents a new plausible interpretation and identification of toponyms, which were generally considered as corresponding to the island of Crete.

KEY WORDS: Egypt, Memphis, Kom Tuman, Crete, Cretans, Cretan Toponyms, Terracotta Figurines, Cultural Interactions between Cretans and Egyptians.

I. Introduction

The contacts between the Egyptians and the Aegean are known from Dynasty V (c. 2465-2323 BCE), as is evidenced by the finds of several objects and the appearance of certain motives in art as well[1]. Egyptian painters of the New Kingdom represented the inhabitants of Aegean islands as persons wearing long hair with a small lock above the front and an apron fixed with an unusual phallus pocket[2].

FIGURE 1. *Kftyw* represented in the tomb of Rekh–mi–Rē‘.

Most likely, the common expression 'the sea island', which is in particular recorded in the Middle Kingdom *Tale of Sinuhe*,[3], could also refer to Crete. The first text evident of the name *Kftyw* that is usually identified with Crete is found in the *Admonitions of Ipuwer*[4], but its dating —the second half of Dynasty XII— is not certain[5].

[1] Helck, W.: art. 'Ägäis und Ägypten', *LÄ*, **I**, 69-70.

[2] Helck: *op. cit.*, 71.

[3] Gardiner, A.H.: *Die Erzählung des Sinuhe und die Hirtengeschichte*, Leipzig 1909.

[4] Gardiner, A.H.: *The Admonitions of an Egyptian Sage*, Leipzig 1909, 6-10.

[5] Seters, J. van: 'A Date for the *Admonitions* in the Second Intermediate Period', *JEA*, **50**, 1964, 13-23.

II. The Cretans in Egypt

One century has now elapsed since the identification of the *Kfty.w* with the Cretans[6]. E. Brugsch was very likely the first who proposed this identification, which was later supported by Hall and Vercoutter[7]. The latter made a fundamental research on this problem: *L'Égypte et le monde égéen préhellénique*[8]. Vercoutter's point of view nowadays is generally accepted. The evidence is based on the reliefs of the vizier Rekh–mi–Rē‘, who flourished during the reign of Tuthmosis III (1479-1425 BCE). On the roof of the Rekh–mi–Rē‘ tomb (TT 100) there is a representation of a procession, some of the persons of which show Aegean features and physiognomies. Moreover their clothes and offerings permit us to suppose that they were Cretans. The accompanying inscription says[9]:

> *Ii.t m ḥtpw in wr.w n.w Kfty.w, iw.w ḥryw-ib n.w W3ḏ-Wr, m ks.w, m w3ḥ tp n b3.w Ḥm=f, Nsw-Bity Mn-ḫpr-Rᶜ* [...].

Which is translated as follows:

> *Coming in peace by the chieftains of Kfty.w, and of the islands in the midst belonging to the Sea, (humbly) bowing down (and) bending the head, because of the might of His Majesty, the King of Upper and Lower Egypt Men–kheper–Rē‘ (Tuthmosis III) [...].*

According to J. Vercoutter's opinion, the texts of the tomb of Rekh–mi–Rē‘ give us incontrovertible proof that the term '*Kfty.w*' should be linked with the islands of the sea, and this sea must be the Aegean.

A more striking argument to identify Keftiou with Crete is the base of the statue, found in the temple of Amenophis III (c. 1350 BCE) in Kom 'el-Heitan in Luxor[10]. On its front side there is a representation of two captives lying back to back and supporting the cartouche of Amenophis III

The royal cartouche is flanked by the topographical names, in such a way the Egyptians usually expressed their conceptions of symmetry and duality. Indeed we can see two rows of the topographical cartouches with the busts of captives on their tops. The left list is as follows: Amnisos, Phaistos, Kydōnia, Mycenae, Messēnē(?), Nauplia, Kythēra, Ilion(?), Knōssos, Amnisos (again), Lyktos. Some of these identifications are uncertain (only Kydōnia is localized definitely), but the geographical orientation of the lands is quite clear. On the right there are only two toponyms: *Kfty.w* and *Tinawi*.

[6] Panagiōtopoulos, D.: 'Keftiu in Context: Theban Tombs–Paintings as a Historical Source', *Oxford Journal of Archaeology*, **20**, 2001, 264.

[7] Vandersleyen, C.: 'Keftiou=Crète? Objections préliminaires', *GM*, **188**, 2002, 110-11.

[8] Vercoutter, J.: *L'Égypte et le monde égéen préhellénique: Étude critique des sources égyptiennes (du début de la XVIIIe à la fin de la XIXe Dynastie)*, (*BIE*, **22**), Le Caire (IFAO) 1956.

[9] Davies, N. de G.: *The Tomb of Rekh–mi–Rē‘ at Thebes*, **II**, New York 1943, Tab.16-23; cf. also *Urk.*, **IV**, 1098-99.

[10] Edel, E.: 'Die Ortsnamenlisten aus dem Totentempel Amenophis III', Bonn (*Bonner Biblische Beiträge*, **25**) 1966.

FIGURE 2. Kom Tuman: a general view of the site.

For many Egyptologists the order of the toponyms demonstrated that *Kfty.w* coincides with Crete: the Aegean lands are limited by *Kfty.w*.

Though, recently Vandersleyen studied thoroughly the texts mentioning the expression ‘*w3ḏ wr*’ (‘the Great Green’, that was usually interpreted as ‘the sea’), and has discovered that phrase ‘the islands of the sea’ can be also (should it be?) translated as ‘the islands of the Delta’[11]. This interpretation is rather well in agreement with the color of the Delta during annual Nile flood. A large number of branches generated from the Nile give life to numerous islets covered by bright green plants. According to Vandersleyen, the limitation of the right list of the above–mentioned base by two toponyms (*Kfty.w* and *Tinawi*) sums up preceding Asiatic names and has no connection with Crete[12].

So, we face two contradictions: **(i)** *W3ḏ-Wr* is ‘the sea’ ≠ *W3ḏ-Wr* is the Delta; **(ii)** *Kfty.w* were the inhabitants of Crete ≠ *Kfty.w* populated Asia. Only one thing we know for sure: the *Tinawi* were in very close contacts with *Kfty.w*: under the 42nd year of Annals of Tuthmosis III one can read that the *Tinayou* offered to the court of the Egyptian king ‘a vase of silver made in *Keftiou*’[13].

There are many known lists of foreign toponyms from Egyptian sources of the New Kingdom. Their identification always faces the problem of the order of toponyms and etnonyms in these lists. There are some names, which look like superfluous, i.e.: they have no place to be localized or identified with. We have a habit to explain their appearance ‘by a mistake of Egyptian writer’, but in reality the Egyptians were very precise in their word–lists.

The striking discovery of the Minoan frescoes by an Austrian team in Tell ’el-Dab‘a in 1992 demonstrated that we should pay more attention to the Delta in the field of relationship between the Aegeans and the Egyptians[14]. These frescoes are of pure Cretan style and date to the beginning of Dynasty XVIII (c. 1530 BCE). They were definitely made not by an Egyptian painter, but by a Cretan artist. This means that Cretans lived in the Delta at least for some time before, in order to be able to create these masterpieces. Perhaps some Cretan colonies were situated in the Delta? One of these colonies might be Memphis[15].

Beginning from the ancient times, Memphis was one of the most important administrative and religious centers of Egypt. It was founded in 3000 BCE by the legendary King Menes, who is traditionally considered to be the first king of Egypt. The city was called *The White Wall* (*Ỉnb-ḥḏ*), during Dynasty XVIII it got the name *Men–nefer* (*Mn-nfr*), the Hellenic form of which (*Memphis*) is assigned to the place until nowadays.

King Menes built a dam that protected the city from the Nile floods. The successor of Menes erected here one of the first Egyptian palaces. Bounding the Upper and Lower Egypt this city was never loosing its political, economic and religious importance. Foreigners often associated Memphis with the whole Egypt, and the name of the main Memphite temple *Ḥw.t-k3-Ptḥ* was transformed by the Hellens to *Aigyptos*, that

[11] Vandersleyen, C.: *Ouadj Our W3ḏ Wr: Un autre aspect de la vallée du Nil*, Bruxelles 1999.
[12] Vandersleyen, *op. cit.*, 110-11 (see n. 7).
[13] Sethe, K.: *Urkunden der 18. Dynastie*, Leipzig 1906-09, 731-32.
[14] Bietak M.: *Avaris, the Capital of the Hyksos: Recent Excavations at Tell ’el-Dab‘a*, London (BMP) 1996, 74-83 & pls. 4-7.
[15] See for instance and *LÄ*, **IV**, 1982, 24-41: art. ‘Memphis’.

became the name of the entire country. Memphis was always one of the main residences of Egyptian rulers; beginning with 197 BCE it became the place of coronation of the Macedonian/Ptolamaic kings.

Today Memphis is an almost completely destroyed city, the ancient ruins of which are disappearing under the pressure of growing villages and agricultural activity. Unlike the necropolis of Saqqara the biggest part of Memphis is not well investigated. The important quarters and constructions were only localized; at the same time most of the buildings that are known by numerous sources are not found yet.

According to Strabōn[16], Memphis During the Helleno–Roman times was considered in the second position after Alexandria. In the southern part of the city there were many temples; in the northern part, the royal palaces were erected. His description is very similar to the modern landscape of the site. The palace structures of Helleno–Roman time were situated close to the palace of Apries, and they were not studied by Archaeologists yet.

According to other Classical sources, the palaces were surrounded by living quarters, including settlements of foreigners (Hellenes, Persians, Syrians, Phoenicians, & c.), and they had their own shrines and civil infrastructure.

An unexcavated hill about 20 m high in Kom Tuman to the north of Memphis drew the attention of the hunters for treasures (or maybe they were persons who have had a high interest of history from the early beginning).

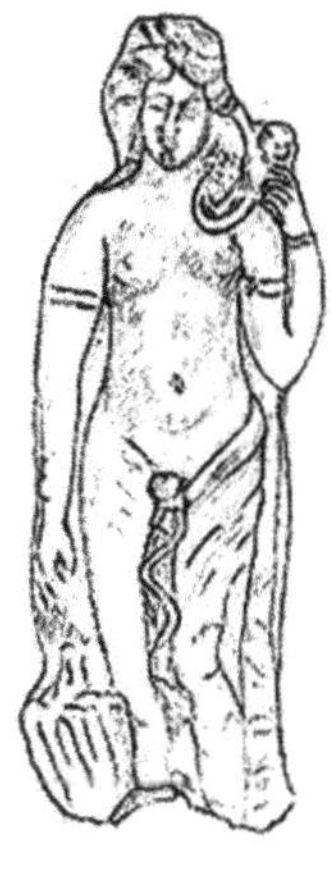

FIGURE 3. Figurine of a woman, carrying a jug in her right hand and a monkey on her left shoulder (terracotta).

In 1900–1901 A. Daninos Pasha[17] made a test cut in the northern part of a ruin field at a site which cannot be exactly determined today. He revealed a mud–brick building and a pit with a cache of bronze objects dated to Dynasties XXIII-XXVI.

In 1902 G. Daressy[18] reported that the objects must have come from Thebes, as only Theban deities are represented. In eight years G. Maspero[19] (1921) stated that Daninos' fragments were parts of decoration of several palanquins belonging to one of the last kings of Dynasty XXVI. It is possible that they were buried to save them from the Persians.

Memphis could also be the very place of the first Egyptian capital, the exact position of which was never defined. Some finds from the surface, like the cylindrical seal of Tuthmosis III, an offering table with the names of Tuthmosis IV, an embalming table of Amenophis III's time, found at a different time, prove that this region of Memphis was also rather important during the New Kingdom.

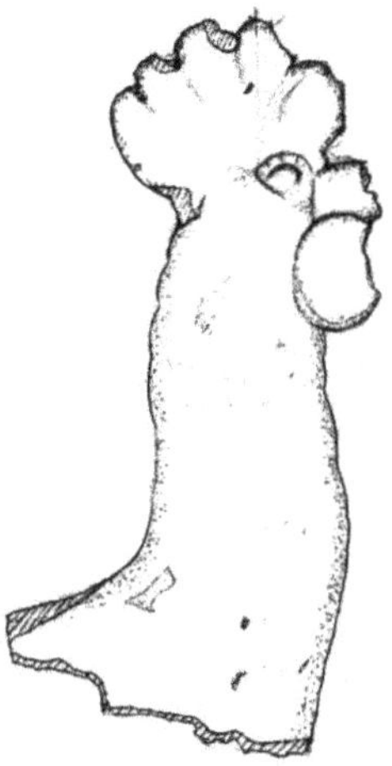

FIGURE 4. Fragment of vessel in the form of a cock (terracotta).

In the north–western part of Kom Tuman is situated the massive palace. It was build by the king of Dynasty XXVI Apries (VI century BCE) In 1909-1912 it was excavated by the English Archaeologist W.M.F. Petrie[20], who dated the palace to the Ptolemaic time (4th-1st centuries BCE). Unfortunately the high level of the water table stopped his excavation.

Thus, systematical studies on the territory in question were never carried out. In November 2001 the Center for Egyptological Studies of the Russian Academy of Sciences (CES/RAS) started its work at the site (Kom Tuman, to the north of Memphis). The result of the previous survey and the analyses of surface material are very promising.

The first season at Kom Tuman was concentrated on the topographical, geological and geophysical survey, which combined several methods: high–accuracy survey of the surface with the help of a satellite navigation system (GPS), magnetic geoelectrical and georadar study. The latter three methods allow for studying the geological structure of the site, determining the architectural structures and detecting possible ancient objects, covered by the soil. The high–accuracy topographical survey makes it possible to draw the details of landscape, which are not visible.

The surface area of 80 m by 100 m (Kom Tuman–West, central part) was thoroughly studied. The size of the cultural layer was defined to be approximately 12 m. The geophysical survey has detected the existence of subterranean structures, orientated from North to South and resembling the plans of palace structures and living quarters.

[16] Strabōn: *XVII.I*, § 32.

[17] Daninos Pacha, A.: 'Note sur le fouilles de Metrahyneh', *ASAE*, **5**, 1904, 142-43.

[18] Daressy, G.M.: 'Une trouvalle de bronzes à Mit Rahyneh', *ASAE*, **3**, 1902, 139-50.

[19] Maspero, G.: *Art in Egypt*, London 1921, 288.

[20] See *PM*, **III**^{2}, 831.

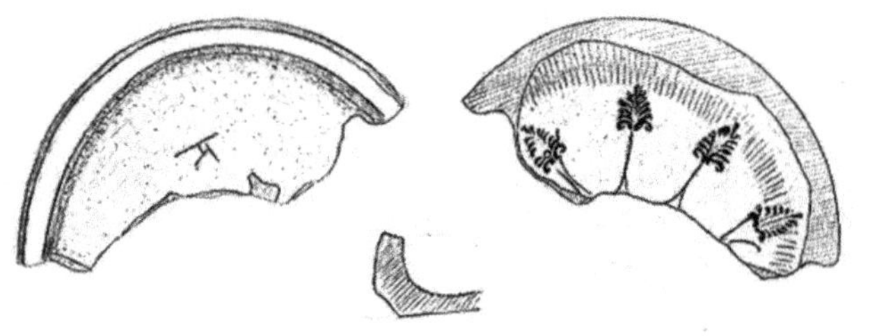

FIGURE 5. Fragment of a black polished vessel, decorated with palmettos and inscribed with a graffito.

Numerous accumulations as well as separate architectural fragments, spread all over Kom Tuman, Tell Aziz and Kom Dawbabi were examined and described. They include mud–brick and brick walls, limestone blocks, fragments of limestone cornices; bases, capitals and drums of columns made from granite and limestone; door–jambs, slabs, & c.

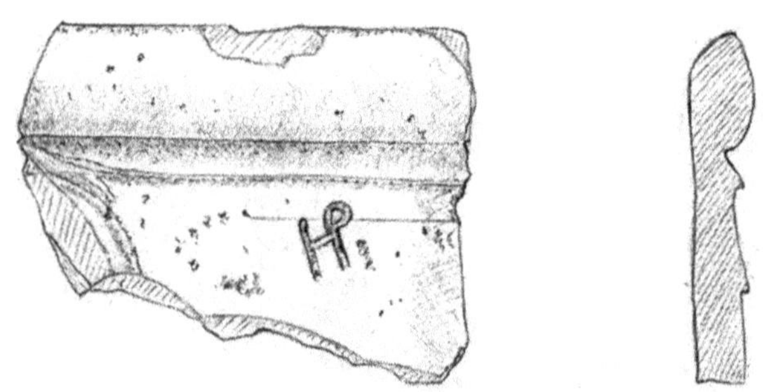

FIGURE 6. Fragment of a vessel, with a production mark (pottery).

The most important accumulations are situated at the south-eastern corner of Kom Tuman, which may be the remains of a large temple. This suggestion is proved by a number of fragments of cult vessels found there. Some of the limestone blocks bear the traces of reliefs. One of them contain the representation of a king (fragment of a royal kilt with uraeus decoration). The other important accumulations are located at the south–eastern part of Kom Dawbabi and along the eastern edge of Kom Tuman.

The central part of Kom Tuman is marked by a 1.8 m wide road, which was oriented from the east to the west. Its remains, 7 meters long, still have molded borders and a kind of drainage system (?).

In the central and northwestern parts of Kom Tuman, two ovens were discovered. One of them was detected because of a local magnetic anomaly; another one because of the characteristic vaulted top, which was partly unearthed at the time of our survey. There is a layer of charcoal in both ovens. Around the sites there were found numerous pieces of slag of different sizes, pieces of oxidized copper alloy and fragments of pottery covered by the same substance. These by–products may indicate that there were metallurgical activities.

A fragment of an amphora, damaged during firing, and pieces of cocked mass of glaze, point to the existence of ceramics and faience production at this region. There were also found samples of unfinished alabaster vessels, of the kind that was found here by W.M.F. Petrie during 1909-12, and pinpoint to the existence of an alabaster workshop located at Kom Tuman in Antiquity.

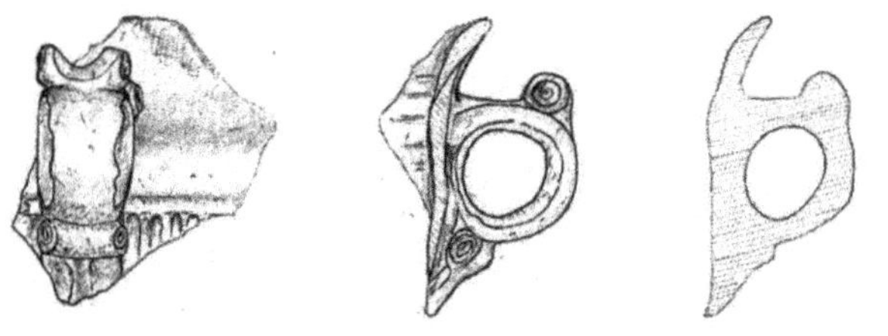

FIGURE 7. Fragment of a red–polished vessel.

Different kinds of ceramics dated to the Helleno–Roman Period were found here: amphorae, jugs, pots [Fig. 6], lids of vessels, several fragments of faience; black–varnished [Fig. 5] and red–polished [Fig. 7] pottery, as well parts of sandstone, limestone and granite dishes.

Some finds are pieces of round sculpture, the most significant of which is the unfinished head of a king of Dynasty XXV (a trial piece?) made of limestone. The others are: a terracotta figurine of a woman with a vessel in her right hand and a monkey on the left shoulder [Fig. 3]; and a fragment of a clay figurine of a naked woman (both dating to the Roman Period). Another interesting find is a fragment of a vessel in the form of a cock [Fig. 4], part of an Apis figurine.

Among the rest material is a fragment of home altar made of limestone; several weights of different values made of limestone and calcite, and a bronze Hellenic coin bearing the representation of an owl on the obverse and the profile of a king on the reverse.

To finalize the results of the previous survey we should agree with W.M.F. Petrie's conclusion that there were foreign quarters in Memphis, including the Hellenic one.

III. Conclusions

To sum up the archaeological data and the data of written sources, we can suppose the following:

(i) A Hellenic colony existed in Memphis during the time of Dynasty XXVI. **(ii)** Probably it was developed on the place of the Aegean settlement of Dynasty XVIII. **(iii)** There is no need to correct Egyptian topographical lists, if we agree that the foreign colonies were also included there; sometimes the Egyptians represented the names of foreign countries in cartouches decorated by fortified walls, which could be either small captured countries or colonies. **(iv)** The Egyptians had a habit to play with geographical names given to the places of similar significance: for instance, *ȝbw* was the name for Elephantine at the first Nile cataract and for the Egyptian fortress at the second cataract; both places definitely marked the frontiers of Egypt. **(v)** The name of the Aegean colony in the Delta might be *Kfty.w*; in this case this agrees concerning the localization of this toponym: it could define *both*, the metropolis at one of the Aegean islands and the colony in the Nile Delta.

We do hope and wish that the future excavations at Kom Tuman shall throw more light on this fascinating issue.

Among the Hidden Treasures of the National Archaeological Museum in Athens: Searching for Forgotten Mummies, 1*

Amanda–Alice Maravelia *and* **Eleni Cladaki–Manoli**

Abstract

The Egyptian Collection of the National Archaeological Museum in Athens keeps most of its riches well hidden in the Museum's storerooms. Among those, we have managed to rediscover some Late Period and Ptolemaic coffins with their mummies. All these particular anthropoid sarcophagi have been published in the Hellenic language in a rather elementary and concise way (with some erroneous points) more than a century ago by Tasos Neroutsos in *Ἀρχαιολογικὴ ἐφημερὶς* (Athens 1884). The author was a medical doctor who lived in Alexandria. Since then the coffins have fallen into oblivion, have never been exhibited in the Museum's showrooms (except one), and nobody else since the late Neroutsos cared to study them accurately. Now after so many years that have elapsed, a new generation of well qualified Egyptologists, with the Museum's collaboration, are trying to bring into light —once again— these forgotten and more or less unknown finds. These objects have been discovered in Egypt and were donated to the Hellenic Government during the late 19th century by wealthy patriots who lived in Egypt. The purpose of this article is to remind both the Egyptologists and Egyptophili the presence of these forgotten mummies and to present a complete and precise study of some of these sarcophagi, dating from the Ptolemaic Period. Five out of these ten anthropoid coffins and their hieroglyphic inscriptions are thoroughly examined and presented in this paper.

KEY WORDS: Museums: National Archaeological Museum, Egyptian Collections; Ancient Egypt: Anthropoid Coffins, Mummy Cases, Akhmīm (= Panopolis, Khemmis), Ptolemaic Period; Religion: Funerary Practices, Offering Formula.

I. Introduction

The National Archaeological Museum of Athens[1] owns a respectable number of anthropoid sarcophagi dated to the TIP, LP, Ptolemaic and Roman Periods. Ioannēs Dēmētriou has donated them to the Hellenic Government in 1884. He acquired ten of these sarcophagi from Akhmīm. They were found in 1884 in the necropolis of Khemmis[2]. Further information about the discovery of the sarcophagi and the circumstances that they were found is regrettably unknown.

Akhmīm, is an area on the east bank of the Nile opposite modern Sohāg. The ancient Egyptians called it *Ipu* (*Ỉpw*) or *Khent–Min* (*Ḫn.t-Mnw*). To the Copts it was *Khmin* or *Shmin* (ϣⲙⲓⲛ), and so the Hellēnes called it *Khemmis* (*Χέμμις*) or *Panopolis* (*Πανόπολις*) after the principal god of the city Min, who was called Pan[3] by them. It was once a great centre in Egypt and the capital of the 9th Upper Egyptian Nome (*Πανοπολίτης*). The ancient necropolis of Akhmīm and its large number of rock–cut tombs that belonged to different dates from the Sixth Dynasty[4] until the Ptolemaic Period, particularly at the 'El-Hawawīsh area, to the northeast of Akhmīm and at 'El-Salamūni, had never been scientifically excavated[5]. Percy Newberry[6] first made an attempt in 1912, but unfortunately most of the findings had been largely plundered during the 1880s. In fact he unearthed several tombs dating from the LP. More recently these tombs were re–examined and recorded by Professor Naguīb Kanawāti[7]. It seems plausible to suppose that the sarcophagi examined here originated from these very tombs, then dispersed into the antiquities' market, whereof they were all subsequently bought by Ioannēs Dēmētriou, who donated them —together with other items— to the National Archaeological Museum.

As was already mentioned, Dēmētriou granted the study of Museum's Akhmīm Sarcophagi to Tasos Neroutsos, before sending them to Athens. Neroutsos was a medical doctor living in Alexandria. He was most probably very interested in Egyptology and —as was the tendency in those years— he was self–educated on the subject. Some erroneous points in his reading and interpretation of the hieroglyphic inscriptions are discussed in the text. The five anthropoid sarcophagi that we present here are kept in the storerooms of the Museum's Egyptian Collection accompanying a few more that have been given to our government as a gift in the beginning of the 20th Century. These coffins have never been exhibited in the past

---

* Special thanks are due to Prof. Dr Naguīb Kanawāti for some information on the site of Akhmīm, as well as to Dr Mogens Jørgensen for reading our manuscript and for some information. Prof. Claude Obsomer, Prof. Willy Clarysse and Dr Mark Depauw, who provided useful information from *Prosopographia Ptolemaica*, are warmly acknowledged. Many thanks are also due to the director of the *National Archaeological Museum* of Athens, Dr N. Kaltsas, for permitting the study and publication of these sarcophagi; as well as to Mrs H. Tourna, in charge of the *Egyptian Collection*, and the staff of the Museum (especially Mrs E. Skamangouli, Mrs M. Apostolopoulou and Mrs H. Morati). Please send offprint requests to one of the authors (A.–A.M.) at her e–mail address: **a_maravelia@hotmail.com**.

[1] For a concise introduction to the Egyptian Collection at the National Archaeological Museum of Athens, see Maravelia, A.–A.: "Ὅτι πλεῖστα θωμάσια <Αἴγυπτος> ἔχει καὶ ἔργα λόγου μέζω παρέχεται πρὸς πᾶσαν χώρην ... Egyptian Collections in Hellenic Museums: A Brief History & Some Pieces', *Ancient Egypt and Antique Europe: Two Parts of the Mediterranean World. Papers from a Session held at the 7th Annual Meeting of the EAA in Esslingen 2001* (Maravelia, A.–A., ed.), Oxford (BAR Publishing, **S1052**) 2002, 15-29, where relevant bibliography is given.

[2] See Neroutsos, T.D.: 'Σημειώσεις ἐπὶ δέκα μομίαις ἑλληνο-ρωμαϊκῆς καὶ βυζαντινῆς (sic!) ἐποχῆς', *Ἀρχαιολογικὴ ἐφημερίς*, Athens 1884, cols. 171-80 & pl. 12.

[3] The god of fertility and master of the deserts between the Nile and the Red Sea. Min was associated to Pan, both being benevolent ithyphallic and/or fertility deities, personifying the male fecundity forces of Nature. See for instance, *BMD*, 1996, 187-88: art. 'Min'. Cf. also Ogdon, J.R.: 'Some Notes on the Iconography of Min', *BES*, 7, 1985-86, 29-41.

[4] See Browarski, E.J.: *Akhmīm in the Old Kingdom and First Intermediate Period*, Cairo 1985.

[5] See, for instance, McNally, S.: 'Survival of a City: Excavations at Akhmīm', *NARCE*, **116**, 1981-82, 26-30; cf. also Kuhlman K.P.: *Materialen zur Archäologie und Geschichte des Raumes von Achmīm*, Mainz 1983.

[6] See Newberry, P.E.: 'The Inscribed Tombs of Ekhmīm', *LAAA*, **4**, 1912, 101-20.

[7] See Kanawāti, N.: *The Rock Tombs of 'El-Hawawīsh: The Cemetery of Akhmīm*, **I-X**, Sydney 1980-92. Prof. Kanawāti (personal communication) believes that these coffins perhaps came from 'El-Salamūni, not far from 'El-Hawawīsh (which was the cemetery of Akhmim during the OK). In his opinion they are all Ptolemaic. He points out however that the area of Akhmīm contains many sites not yet excavated systematically and accordingly the whereabouts of earlier cemeteries, like the necropolis of the NK, is uncertain. For 'El-Salamūni and 'El-Hawawīsh, see also *PM*, **IV**, 17-20. For Akhmīm, see finally *LÄ*, **I**, 1975, cols. 54-55: art. 'Achmīm'.

because of the lack of space in the Museum's premises. The staff of the Egyptian Collection has recently restored the coffins. However the deficient knowledge in the maintenance of these sarcophagi, when they arrived in Hellas before 120 years, resulted in their bad condition and the splintering of some of their depictions. Regrettably parts of the inscriptions read by Neroutsos are completely destroyed today, but due to his readings we were able to re–synthesize them to the best of our knowledge. Only one of them is currently on display[8] (AIG 3340) in exhibition room # 40.

II. Study of the Sarcophagi and their Inscriptions

NAM, AIG 3340 *– Dēmētriou Collection.*
Object & Material: Anthropoid Coffin; Wood, Painted.
Owner: Hapy, aka Khor, son of Pamy (♂).
Date: Early to Mid–Ptolemaic Period (304-150 BCE).
Place & Date of Provenance: Achmīm 1884.
Dimensions: H = 1.83 m, L = 0.42 m.

'Black–ground' coffin, with a pedestal supporting the feet (see Figure 1a). The face is yellow. The head is decorated with the Egyptian blue–coloured wig. Attached to the chin is the ritual black beard. The chest is covered with a broad collar of blue and red beads. A big part of the upper lid is damaged. The mummy which is well kept inside the coffin and has never been medically examined is wrapped with bandages and adorned with multi–coloured cartonage, showing an excellent craftsmanship of mummification. The cartonage is holding in place the outermost shroud bandages, which are arranged in geometrical patterns. The head is confined in a gilded funerary mask and the blue wig. The partial coverage by cartonage and the golden mask of the body testify its dating from the early to mid–Ptolemaic Period[9]. The eyes are painted. A pectoral of a winged scarab decorates the chest as well as a multi–coloured large collar. Under the collar the goddess Ma'at enfolds the mummy with her winged arms. In her hands she holds the symbols of truth and justice, the ostrich feathers[10]. A long and narrow cartonage put vertically on the mummy's legs represents a lion bier with the mummy of the deceased outstretched. The bier is flanked by images of Isis and Nephthys, as mourners and protective divinities. Beside the mummy stands Anubis, the embalmer god, with hands stretched. In the next row a scarab is represented in the middle and two falcon heads crowned with the sun disk. There are three more rows beneath the previous one adorned with multi–coloured geometrical patterns, which are unfortunately partially damaged. The legs are covered with a cartonage fragment painted in light pink colour imitating the deceased's feet and dark red for his sandals. A hieroglyphic inscription runs in a vertical column from the chest of the cover of the coffin, ending at the feet. The hieroglyphs are written in black upon an orange–coloured ribbon, enclosed by a ceramic–redish rectangular frame. Almost one third of the inscription is currently severely damaged.

The hieroglyphic inscription on the coffin (see Figure 1b) reads as follows:

> *Ḥtp di nsw, ḥtp di Wsir, ḫnty-Ỉmn.tt {d} nṯr ꜥꜣ nb Ꜣbḏ.t* (read: *Ꜣbḏw*)*; Zkr-Wsir, ḥr-ib Ỉpw; Ỉnpw, nb tꜣ{.wy} ḏsr; Ỉs.t wr.t, mw.t nṯr<.w>, nb<.t> p.t*[11]*, ḥr-ib Ỉpw. Di=zn pr.t-ḫrw <m> t, ḥ<n>ḳ.t, kꜣ.w, ꜣpd.w, iḫ.t nb<.t> nfr.t, <n kꜣ n> Ḥpy, ḏd.f Ḫr, zꜣ Pm<y> <mꜣꜥ-ḫrw>.*

This text is translated as:

> *A funerary offering by the King to Osiris, foremost of the West, the great god, lord of Abydos; (and) to Sokaris–Osiris, who is in Khemmis; (and) to Anubis, lord of the holly land (i.e. the necropolis); and to Isis, the great mother of god(s), lady of the sky, who is in Khemmis*[12]*. (In order that) they (may) give invocation offerings (consisting of) bread, beer, oxen, fowl, and every nice thing, to the spirit (kꜣ) of Hapy*[13]*, called (lit.: said) Khor, son of Pamy (the justified).*

NAM, AIG 3341 *– Dēmētriou Collection.*
Object & Material: Anthropoid Coffin; Wood, Painted.
Owner: Ta–Redi–Bastet (♀).
Date: Early to Mid–Ptolemaic Period (304-150 BCE).
Place & Date of Provenance: Akhmīm 1884.
Dimensions: H = 1.67 m, L = 0.40 m.

Anthropoid coffin with mummy (see Figure 2a). The coffin is moderately preserved. The colour has been damaged and fractured in the surface of the coffin's lid. The coffin is painted creamy white. The head is covered with a yellow Egyptian wig, bearing blue stripes. The surviving part of the face is painted yellow. The left part is damaged. The eyebrows and the eye's contours are coloured black. A broad collar is decorating the chest and combines nine rows of similarly shaped beads of dark blue colour tucked together with red and dark green colour strings. Under the collar there is a representation of a ram–headed vulture bearing corkscrew horns[14], a scarab–

---

[8] For a colour photo of this sarcophagus, see Tzachou–Alexandri, O. (ed., *et al.*): *The World of Egypt in the National Archaeological Museum*, Athens (Kapon Editions / Ministry of Culture & Hellenic *ICOM*) 1995, 169: pl. LX. Cf. also Cladaki–Manoli, E. (*et al.*): 'Egyptian Thesauri in the *National Archaeological Museum of Athens*: § II.21. Anthropoid Inner Coffin of a Man with Mummy', *Ancient Egypt and Antique Europe*, *op. cit.*, 40-41 (see § II.21) & 56: pl. 15A.

[9] During the Ptolemaic Period the placement of shroud bandages on mummies reaches an artistic peak. Furthermore, the mummy is partially covered by decorated pieces of cartonage, bears a funerary mask, collar, amulets, a sheath at the feet, and such. Typical example is N 2627 from the Musée du Louvre, which dates from the same era as the coffins studied in this paper.

[10] For its symbolism, see Wilkinson, R.H.: *Reading Egyptian Art: A Hieroglyphic Guide to Ancient Egyptian Painting and Sculpture*, London (Thames & Hudson) 1992, 102-03.

[11] From this point onwards, the inscription is highly damaged and erased. Very few signs have survived, and in order to restitute this part use has been made of Neroutsos' rendering (see *op. cit.*, pl. 12: # 10). Let it be noted that in translating this and the rest of the inscriptions some auxiliary words or explanations (actually not occurring in the original) are put in parentheses to render the translation even more uniform.

[12] Isis is invoked as a city–goddess of Khemmis. This seems plausibly quite an indication that de Meulenaere was right about the possible Triad cult of Min, Isis and Horus in Khemmis; see de Meulenaere, H.: 'Prophètes et danseurs Panopolitains à la Basse Époque', *BIFAO*, **88**, 1988, 41-49 & pl. VI, especially 47.

[13] For several similar simple or composite names (*Ḥpy*), dating from various periods, see Ranke, H.: *Die ägyptische Personennamen*, **I**, Hamburg 1932, 237: 23-24 & 238: # 1-10.

[14] Syncretic deities of this type (cf. *Abrasax*, *Chnumis*) are common from the late LP onwards, especially during the Ptolemaic Period and later. For this, see for instance Pinch, G.: *Magic in Ancient Egypt*, London (BMP) 1994, 118, 165. The syncretic deity of this coffin has a solar nature and connotation, since it represents a vulture–winged ram headed creature, alluding to Chnum as the underworld nocturnal hypostasis of Rēꜥ. The head of the ram depicted is known as belonging to the species *ovis longipes palaeoegypticus*.

like body, extended wings, and grasping in its talons *šn*-signs[15]. To the right and left of the ram's head, which is crowned by a uraeus, there are two short hieroglyphic inscriptions, which seem to follow the curvature of the underside of the collar. A vertical column of a hieroglyphic inscription written with black colour prolongs under the protective ram–headed deity, ending at the feet. Between the inscription and the divine creature's body the winged tail of the hybrid deity continues, uniting it to the former, thus giving an official undertone. Both inscriptions are preserved in an almost excellent state. The vertical inscription, which is crowned by the hybrid divinity, is repeated on the cartonage of the corpse inside the coffin.

The hieroglyphic inscriptions on the coffin (see Figure 2b) read as follows:

1. Short Symmetric Inscriptions (in both Sides)[16]:

Nṯr ꜥ3 Bḥd.t.

This text is translated as:

The great god of Behdet (i.e. Horus of Behdet[17]).

2. Main Long Inscription:

Ḥtp di nsw, ḥtp di Rꜥ-Ḥr-3ḫ.ty, (Ỉ)tm, nb t3.wy, Ỉwnw. Di=f t, ḥ<n>ḳ.t, k3.w{t}, 3pd.w{t}, snṯr[18], n k3 n Wsir<.t> T3-Rdi-B3s.t<t> <m3ꜥ.t-ḫrw>.

This text is translated as:

A funerary offering by the King to Rē'–Horakhty (and) Atum, lord of the Two Lands (and) of On (i.e.: Heliopolis). (In order that he may) give bread, beer, oxen, fowl (and) insence to the spirit (k3) of the female Osiris Ta–Redi–Bastet[19] (the justified).

NAM, AIG 3342 *– Dēmētriou Collection.*
Object & Material: Anthropoid Coffin; Wood, Painted.
Owner: Thau, son of Ia'eh, born to Lady Ih (♂).
Date: Early to Mid–Ptolemaic Period (304-150 BCE).
Place & Date of Provenance: Akhmīm 1884.
Dimensions: H = 1.73 m, L = 0. 45 m.

The coffin lid is painted white and decorated on the chest with a multi–coloured pectoral (see Figure 3a). A black ritual beard with upturned end is attached to the chin. The face is painted red. The facial features, which are drawn in a traditional manner, are outlined in black colour. The distinctive Egyptian wig is covering the head. A winged scarab[20] painted with black colour, is decorating the top of the wig. The broad collar that covers the chest contains seven rows of beads (composed of different shapes) of red, green and black colour. A falcon's head adorned with a red solar disc is attached to both ends of the collar. Below this pectoral is an image of Nut, the sky–goddess. She wears the sun disk on her head, and her arms extend into wings, which wrap protectively around the mummy. Below the image of Nut, the four sons of Horus are represented flanking the hieroglyphic inscriptions, which are drawn in three vertical columns. The images of Imsety and Duamutef (on the right side) and of Qebehsenuef and Hapy (on the left side) are painted with black colour for the contour of the image, and red for the inside colour[21]. At the bottom of the coffin lid, decorating the pedestal, are two images of Anubis, the funerary god, portrayed as a jackal, painted with black and crouching on a red shrine–like stand. Finally, a hieroglyphic inscription arranged in three parallel vertical columns (starting from the middle of the coffin, and ending at the feet) is inscribed on the cover of the coffin (under Nut), significant parts of which are presently (regrettably) almost completely damaged[22].

The hieroglyphic inscriptions on the coffin (see Figure 3b) read as follows:

1. Right Column:

Ḥtp di nsw, ḥtp di Wsir, ḫn.tt-Ỉmn.tt, di=f k3.w{t}, 3pd.w{t} (read: *k3.w, 3pd.w*), *ḥ<n>ḳ.t*

This text is translated as:

A funerary offering by the King to Osiris, foremost of the West, (that) he (may) give oxen, fowl (and) beer.

2. Middle Column:

Di=f pr.t-ḫrw <m> ḳrz.t (read: *ḳrs.t*), *iḫ.t nb<.t> nfr.t wꜥb.t <n k3 n> Wsir Ṯ3[[.w,*

This text is translated as:

(That) he (may) give invocation offerings (consisting of a) burial, (and) every thing good and pure, to (the spirit of) Osiris Thau[23],

3. Left Column:
w]] z3 Ỉꜥḥ, ms <n> nb<.t>-pr Ỉh, z3.t{t} Ṯ3sw.t[24].

This text is translated as:
(the) son of Ia'eh[25], born to Lady Ih[26], (the) daughter of Thasut.

[15] For their symbolism, see Wilkinson, *op. cit.*, 192-93.
[16] These short inscriptions were omitted by Neroutsos (cf. *op. cit.*, pl. 12: # 6).
[17] The NE Delta site of Behdet acquired a cult of Horus. The symbol of this deity was the hawk–winged solar disc, which consisted a ubiquitous motif in temple decoration, as well as in gate lintels, reliefs and stelae. See for instance, Hart, G.: *A Dictionary of Egyptian Gods and Goddesses*, London (RKP) 1987, 94-95. For the possible Triad cult of Horus, Isis and Min in Panopolis, see n. 12, *supra*.
[18] At this point the reading of Neroutsos was incorrect, since he omitted the word *snṯr* (see *op. cit.*, pl. 12: # 10).
[19] Cf. a similar name [*T3-di(.t)-B3s.tt*; anc. Hellenic: *Τετόβαστις*] in Ranke, *op. cit.*, **I**, 373: # 3.
[20] For the symbolism of scarabs and their connection to the newly born solar deity (*Ḫprì*), see *LÄ*, **I**, 1975, cols. 934-40: art. 'Khepri', and *LÄ*, **V**, 1984, cols. 967-81: art. 'Skarabäus'.
[21] For the four sons of Horus, see Spencer, A..J.: *Death in Ancient Egypt*, UK (Penguin Books) ^{3}1986, 158-59.
[22] Almost the whole of the first column, a big part of the second column and the last half of the third column. We used again Neroutsos' rendering to restitute the hieroglyphic text (see *op. cit.*, pl. 12: # 9).
[23] For some similar names (*Ṯ3.w*), dating from the OK and MK, see Ranke, *op. cit.*, **I**, 388: # 15.
[24] For the rendering of this name in ancient Hellenic, Neroutsos (see *op. cit.*, col. 178), proposed *Αἰθοσώτην*.
[25] For some similar names (*Ỉꜥḥ*), dating from the MK and NK, see Ranke, *op. cit.*, **I**, 12: # 13.

NAM, AIG 3345 – Dēmētriou Collection.
Object & Material: Anthropoid Coffin; Wood, Painted.
Owner: Semen–Nefer, son of Pef–Nether–Heru and Lady Res–Pa–Menekh (♂, child).
Date: Late Ptolemaic Period (150-50 BCE).
Place & Date of Provenance: Akhmīm 1884.
Dimensions: H = 1.51 m, L = 0.37 m.

Anthropoid coffin in mediocre condition belonging to a child (see Figure 4a). The surface is white and the facial habitual Egyptian features are tinted with black colour on a yellow background. The mouth is painted red and in the nostrils a red nuance is visible. Trial of red can also be seen in both ears. The black Egyptian wig covers the head. The chest is decorated with a broad collar of rows separated by dark green, which contains red beads of different floral shape. At the middle of the collar a pectoral is hanging from a red string, representing the apotropaic *eye of Horus*[27] (*wḏꜣ.t*). On either side of the centered pectoral is a green bead. At the middle of the coffin lid, under the collar, the sign of the Thinite (8th) Nome of Upper Egypt is painted with red and dark green colour. A hieroglyphic inscription is written in two columns on either of its sides. At the bottom of the coffin lid, on the pedestal, facing each other and painted in black, there are two crouching Anubis jackals on shrine–like stands. On the basis of the style of decorations and of colours used, it seems plausible that this is the latest of all the coffins examined here. This fact allows us to assume that the cemetery where it was found (together with the rest of the coffins examined here) in Panopolis was used during the whole of the Ptolemaic Period for burials. Two vertical columns are depicted flanking the Thinite standard, bearing hieroglyphic inscriptions (starting at the middle of the coffin, and ending at the feet). Only fractions of them are damaged, permitting a better reading than in the case of some of the other mummies presented in this paper.

The hieroglyphic inscription on the coffin (see Figure 4b) reads as follows:

1. Right Column:

> *Ḥtp di nsw, ḥtp di Wsir, ḫnty-Ỉmn.ti, nṯr ꜥꜣ nb {Ỉ}bḏw* (read: *ꜣbḏw*); *Ptḥ-Z{g}r*[28]- (read: *Ptḥ-Zkr*)

This text is translated as:

> *A funerary offering by the King to Osiris, foremost of Amenthis, the great god, lord of Abydos; (and) Ptah–Sokaris–*

2. Left Column:

> *-Wsir, ḥr-ib ḳrst. Di=f t*[29]*, ḥnḳ.t <n kꜣ n> Smn-nfr, zꜣ Pf-nṯr-ḥrw, ms <n> nb<.t>-pr Rs-pꜣ-mnḫ*[30]*, <r> nḥḥ {nḥḥ} <ḥnꜥ> ḏt.*

This text is translated as:

> *–Osiris, who is in the burial. (In order that) he (may) give bread and beer to the (spirit of) Semen–Nefer, (the) son of Pef–Nether–Heru, born of Lady Res–Pa–Menekh. (For) ever (and) ever!*

NAM, AIG 3348 – Dēmētriou Collection.
Object & Material: Anthropoid Coffin; Wood, Painted.
Owner: The Ritual Dancer of Min, Lady Ta–Khered–Min, daughter of the Fourth Prophet of Min, Iret–Hor–Ru and Lady Isis–Nekhebut (♀).
Date: Early to Mid–Ptolemaic Period (304-150 BCE).
Place & Date of Provenance: Akhmīm 1884.
Dimensions: H = 1.75 m, L = 0.47 m.

'Black–ground'[31] anthropoid coffin with mummy (see Figure 5a). The face is painted white and the Egyptian style characteristics are outlined with black colour. A small part of the neck, which is shown, is depicted white. The traditional stripped wig is black with visible traces of yellow specks. A broad collar is decorating the chest. It contains eight rows of floral decoration imitating the multi–coloured necklaces of differently shaped beads. At the top of the collar the figure of Horus' head is depicted and outlined with black colour as are the rest of the collar's decorations. A big part of the coffin's surface starting at the chest level is fractured and damaged. The sky–goddess Nut is depicted under the collar, winged and crowned with the solar disc (bearing her name in hieroglyphs: *Nw.t*), protecting the dead (as the text of the shorter column inscriptions also states). Under that part two vertical columns of equal length are drawn with a hieroglyphic inscription. To adorn the inscriptions from left and right are narrower rows with black horizontal stripes. On the right side of the rows is a representation of a crouching Anubis jackal[32]. Most probably the same representation was adorning the other side as well, but now it is destroyed. Three shorter columns of hieroglyphic inscriptions, unequal in length, are flanking the main long columns by each side, as well as the depiction of Nut. All these hieroglyphic inscriptions are highly damaged and erased (a fact not shown on Figure 5b), few signs remaining intact[33].

The hieroglyphic inscriptions on the coffin (see Figure 5b) read as follows:

1. Main Long Columns, Right Side:

> *Ḏd-mdw in Wsir [ḫnty]-Ỉmn.tt, nṯr ꜥꜣ nb ꜣbḏw{.t}* (read: *ꜣbḏw*); *Wsir-Zkr, ḥr-ib Ỉpw. Di.tw ḳrs{.d}* (read: *ḳrs.t*) *nfr.t {f} nb{y}* (read: *nb<.t>*). *Pr.t-ḫrw <m> t, ḥtp.w n ḥ<n>ḳ.t, kꜣ.w, ꜣpd.w, snṯr, mnḫ.t, irp, ir.tt, iḫ.t nb<.t> nfr.t wꜥb[[.t*

---

[26] For some similar names (*Ỉhꜣ, Ỉhi*), dating from the LP, see Ranke, *op. cit.*, **I**, 43: # 30-32.

[27] For this, see Wilkinson, *op. cit.*, 42-43.

[28] The name of the syncretic divinity is damaged.

[29] The inscription is erased from here until the male taxogram (Gardiner's A1) of the name of the deceased.

[30] Name almost completely damaged. Use was again made of Neroutsos' reading (see *op. cit.*, pl. 12: # 5). It is to be noted that Neroutsos' translation of the final words was incorrect.

[31] For a similar to this coffin, see n. 48, *infra*. It is to be noted that in the funereal context black was considered as an Osirian colour (together with green), and was associated with regeneration and fertility. For the symbolism of colours, see Wilkinson, R.H.: *Symbol and Magic in Ancient Egyptian Art*, London (Thames & Hudson) 1994, 104-25.

[32] See for instance, Wilkinson, *Reading Egyptian Art*, *op. cit.*, 64-65.

[33] Our reading was partially based on Neroutsos' rendering (see *op. cit.*, pl. 12: # 3).

This text is translated as:

Words spoken by Osiris, foremost of Amenthis, (the) great god, lord of Abydos; and Osiris–Sokaris, who is in Khemmis. Every nice burial (will) be provided. Invocation offerings (consisting of) bread, beer libations, oblations of oxen, fowl, incense, dresses, wine, milk, (and) every thing good and pure;

2. Main Long Columns, Left Side:

.t]], ḥtp.w nb<.w> nfr<.w> nḏm<.w>, n Wsir nb<.t>-pr, Ỉhb.t-n-Mnw, nb Ỉpw, Tꜣ-ḫrd-Mnw, zꜣ.t{t} (read: *zꜣ.t*) *n ꜥnḫ-Ỉp<w>, ḥm-<nṯr> Ḥr-ꜣḫ.ty, {r} nfr ḫr ḥm-nṯr-4.nw n Mnw, nb Ỉpw, Ỉr.t-Ḥr-r-w*[34], *mꜣꜥ-ḫrw, ms <n> nb<.t>-pr Ỉs.t-nḫb.wt m{ꜥ}ꜥ<.t>-ḫrw* (read: *mꜣꜥ<.t>-ḫrw*).

This text is translated as:

every nice and pleasant offering, to the Osiris Lady, the Ritual Dancer of Min[35]*, lord of Khemmis, Ta–Khered–Min*[36]*, (the) daughter of the citizen of Khemmis, priest of Horakhty and honoured as the fourth prophet of Min*[37]*, (the) lord of Khemmis, Iret–Hor–Ru*[38] *the justified; born by Lady Isis–Nekhebut, the justified.*

3. Flanking Short Columns, Right Side, Col. 1:

Ḏd-mdw in Wsir, ḏd-mdw in Nw.t wr.t, ms

This text is translated as:

Words spoken by Osiris, (and) by the great Nut[39]*, mother (lit.: who born)*

4. Flanking Short Columns, Right Side, Col. 2:

nṯr.w. Pšš.t ḏnḥ<.w=s> [[ḥr=

This text is translated as:

of the gods. She, who spreads her wings upon

5. Flanking Short Columns, Right Side, Col. 3:

ḥr]]={k} (read: *=ṯ*), *Wsir nb<.t>-pr, Ỉhb.t*

This text is translated as:

you, the Osiris Lady, Ritual Dancer

6. Flanking Short Columns, Left Side, Col. 1:

n Mnw, nb Ỉp{.t} (read: *Ỉpw*), *Tꜣ-ḫrd-*

This text is translated as:

of Min, (the) lord of Khemmis, Ta–Khered–

7. Flanking Short Columns, Left Side, Col. 2:

-Mnw; n[ṯṯ] ir.t n

This text is translated as:

–Min; who was created on behalf of

8. Flanking Short Columns, Left Side, Col. 3:

Mnw, <in.t> n ꜥnḫ r=f; nt{k} (read: *nṯṯ*) *pr m-ḥꜣ.t{y}* (read: *m-ḥꜣ.t*) *Mnw.*

This text is translated as:

Min, (brought) at life to him; you[40] *who proceed in front of Min.*

III. Conclusions

The large Egyptian Collection at the National Archaeological Museum in Athens features significant masterpieces and has a long story. Presumably it is the 4th largest in Europe — comprising about 7000 pieces— out of which only 310 are currently exhibited[41]. In the present article we examined thoroughly five anthropoid coffins belonging to it. One of us (E.C. M.) performed a stylistic analysis, and one of us (A.–A.M.) studied the hieroglyphic inscriptions, compiled the footnotes and conclusions, and edited the whole paper. This is the first part of a project, which aims in studying the mummies of the Egyptian Collection. The second part will be published later, and hopefully it will be followed by the study of all the sarcophagi and other funerary implements.

The coffins are characteristic of the early–Ptolemaic until mid–Ptolemaic Period relatively rich anthropoid sarcophagi, and bear the typical offering formula inscriptions and funerary liturgical spells. Chthonic gods (like Osiris or Osiris–Sokaris–Ptah) are invoked, but also heavenly and solar deities (Rēʿ, Horakhty, Nut, Atum), as well as local and other gods (like Min, Horus of Behdet and Isis[42]) are praised, in order to

[34] For the same name, cf. an elaborate LP sarcophagus at the Musée de l'Évêché in Limoges, belonging to a royal butcher who had the same name, in Sadek, A.I.: 'La Collection Égyptienne du Musée de l'Évêché de Limoges: le Sarcophage de Iret–Hor–erou', *GM*, **115**, 1990, 85-98 (especially 92-93).

[35] For a discussion on this and a similar title (*iḥb-knd*), see de Meulenaere, *op. cit.*, 47 ff. Another instance of this title (*Ỉḥb.t-n-Mnw*), with Gardiner's B47 as a possible taxogram, is found on un unpublished funerary stele of the LP (see l. 5 of hieroglyphic text, near the bottom), coming from Panopolis, namely # 6–19880 of the Phoebe Hearst Museum of Anthropology, in Berkeley, CA, which will be eventually published by one of us (A.–A.M.).

[36] For this name, see de Meulenaere, *op. cit.*, 46 : # 18; cf. also *op. cit.*, n. 29 for another reference in Lieblein, J.: *Dictionnaire de noms hiéroglyphiques*, # 2445.

[37] For this somehow free rendering we based on Gardiner (see *EG*, [10]1988, 128, § 167: 1). Probably more correctly: 'honoured (lit.: *happy*) with the 4th prophet … '. For the sacerdotal office of Fourth Prophet of Min and of the Panopolitan clergy, see Gauthier, H.: *Le personnel du dieu Min*, Le Caire 1931; cf. also n. 35, *supra*.

[38] For some similar names [*Ỉr.t-n(.t)-Ḥr-ir.w*, anc. Hellenic: *Ἰνάρως*], dating from the LP, see Ranke, *op. cit.*, **I**, 42: # 11. For some additional instances of the same name (in the *milieu* of the ritual dancers of Min), dating from the same period and originating from Panopolis, see de Meulenaere, *op. cit.*, 48: # (c), (e), (l).

[39] Nut is also depicted in the Limoges sarcophagus: (i) as winged, crowned with the solar disc, holding *ꜥnḫ*–signs, and protecting the deceased (see Sadek, *op. cit.*, 87, 92); (ii) as well as a woman, holding an *ꜥnḫ*–sign and an *wꜣs*–sceptre (*op. cit.*, 89). For a colour photograph of this sarcophagus, see the collective catalogue *Visages d'Égypte*, Limoges (Musée Municipal de l'Évêché/Musée de l'Émail) 1998, 22.

[40] Independent personal pronoun, 2nd person female singular, used as subject. See *EG*, [10]1988, 53-54: §§ 64-65.

[41] See nn. 1 and 8, *supra*.

[42] For the cult of these deities in Panopolis and the plausible correctness of de Meulenaere's assumptions, see nn. 12 & 17, *supra*. Let it be noted that

offer the spirit of the deceased humans rich libations of beverages and oblations of food. Anthropoid coffins depict the deceased with the face of a living human and the bandaged/embalmed body of a mummy. This hybrid entity, called the *sꜥḥ* (var.: *zꜥḥ*), was considered to partake of both the divine and the human hypostases. The *sꜥḥ*–status was achieved through a religiously correct burial, where the corpse was mummified, and provided with a mummy mask and a special coffin, in order to stride in the territory of the *lightland* (*ꜣḫ.t*) of the blessed and of incorruptibility[43]. Additionally, the correct preparation of the body and its provision with the anthropoid coffin would allude and magically provoke the acquisition of this very blessed status. On the other hand, the presence of liturgical inscriptions, like the offering formula, or excerpts from the *Book of the Dead* (and other underworld ritual texts), could be considered as a magical funerary practice, which would be sympathetically capable of virtually creating the necessary afterlife victuals and provisions, thus safeguarding the immortality of the deceased humans, providing sustenance for their *spirits* (*kꜣ.w*).

Typologically, the sarcophagi studied here belong (more or less) to the *Swollen Type of Coffin*[44], which is typical of the period c. 650 to 150 BCE. This emerged during the beginning of the Saitic Dynasty and remained in use with numerous variations until the middle of the Lagid Dynasty. It was made of either wood or stone. The coffin's head was often unnaturally placed deeply between the shoulders, and two decorative features, the *plinth* and the *back pillar* were practically obligatory. The deceased was depicted wearing a wig, ceremonial cosmetic lines, and frequently a symbolic chin–beard[45]. Finally, the mummiform body was often decorated with a broad collar, inscriptions[46] and images of various divinities[47]. During the last three centuries BCE, traditional pharaonic styles of burial were considerably and increasingly influenced by the classical motifs[48]. The coffins studied here can be considered as representative of the final stages of development of the mid (see for instance NAM: AIG 3341, AIG 3342, AIG 3345) and higher status (see for instance NAM: AIG 3340, AIG 3348) burials of the pharaonic type, before the adoption of foreign (Hellenic and Roman) elements. The five anthropoid coffins studied here in their component parts (lids, mummies, cartonages, & c.), as well as in the choice of decoration and inscriptions, constitute a purely Egyptian assemblage.

Finally, it is to be noted that all the studied coffins contain embalmed corpses, which have never been examined medically, anatomically or radiologically. It would be an interesting idea to be studied by medical experts and X–ray scanned, in order to gain some insight on the physical condition of the deceased persons, their possible causes of death, diseases and degree of preservation of bodily tissues, bones, internal organs and the like[49]. The use of modern techniques of anatomical mapping could also be used, in order to resynthesize the facial characteristics of these ancient individuals[50], who lived during the swan song era of the Egyptian Empire.

---

the composite Hellenic name *Μενάρητις* presumably derives from the junction of the names *Μῖν* + *Ὧρος* + *Ἶσις*.

43 See for instance *Wb.*, **IV**, 52; Faulkner's, *CD*, 214-15; Budge's, *Hieroglyphic Dictionary*, **II**, col. 646. For this blessed status, see Schneider, H.D.: *Shabtis*, Leiden (Rijksmuseum van Oudheden te Leiden) 1977, 65 ff, *passim*. The gilded cartonage mask placed on the face of the deceased, provided an idealistic image of him/her as eternally young and equipped with the golden skin and curled beard characteristic of a divine being.

44 See Jørgensen, M.: *Catalogue EGYPT III: Coffins, Mummy Adornments and Mummies from the TIP, LP, Ptolemaic and Roman Periods (1080 BC – AD 400)*, Copenhagen (Ny Carlsberg Glyptotek) 2001, 18. For a typical example of a limestone coffin originating from Akhmīm, see *op. cit.*, 268-69.

45 For the liturgical and magical symbolism of the wigs, cosmetic lines, chin–beards, collars, pectorals and amulets, plinths, back pillars, wreaths of flowers, and other funerary embellishments and tools, see Jørgensen, *op. cit.*, 23-28.

46 See the coffin of Petosiris (JE 46.592) at the Egyptian Museum in Cairo, bearing elaborate hieroglyphic inscriptions, in Lefebvre, G.: *Le tombeau de Petosiris*, **III**, Le Caire 1924, pl. 58; cf also *PM*, **IV**, 174.

47 See for instance the deities on the coffin of Nespam'ai (ÄMB 12/66 A-B), in the catalogue *Ägyptisches Museum Berlin*, Berlin 1967, # 868; and in Fay, B.: *Egyptian Museum Berlin*, Berlin (SMPK) [5]1992, 150: # 75.

48 See Walker, S. & Bierbrier, M.: *Ancient Faces: Mummy Portraits from Roman Egypt*, London (BMP) 1997, 29. A very elaborate nice coffin, similar to that of Lady Ta–Khered–Min (and particularly to NAM, AIG 3347, which is not studied here), characteristic of the same transitional period, is that of the priest and dignitary Hornedjitef, dating from c. 250 BCE and coming from Thebes West ('Asāsīf); for this, see *op. cit.*, 29-30 & fig. 1. Various coffins dating from the Late Ptolemaic and Helleno–Roman Period, found at Akhmīm, are kept in the British Museum. For some additional Ptolemaic coffins, see Berlev, O. & Hodjash, S.: *Catalogue of Monuments of the Ancient Egypt*, Freibourg (University Press / *OBO*, **17**) 1998, 35-36: # 48-50, 53 & 55.

49 See for instance Cocburn, A. & Cocburn, E.: *Mummies, Disease and Ancient Cultures*, Cambridge (Cambridge Univeristy Press) 1980. For the radiographs of royal mummies, see Harris, J.R. & Wente, E.F.: *An X–Ray Atlas of the Royal Mummies*, Chicago (University of Chicago Press) 1980.

50 For this topic, see Germer, R.: 'La momification', *L'Égypte: Sur les traces de la civilisation pharaonique* (Schulz, R. & Seidel, M., eds.), Cologne (Könemann) 2000, 465: fig. 69-70, where a mummy from Akhmīm, dating from c. 300 BCE and kept in the Provincial Museum at Hanover (LMH 7849) is referred to. Cf. also Partridge, R.: *Faces of Pharaohs: Royal Mummies and Coffins from Ancient Thebes*, London (BMP) 1994.

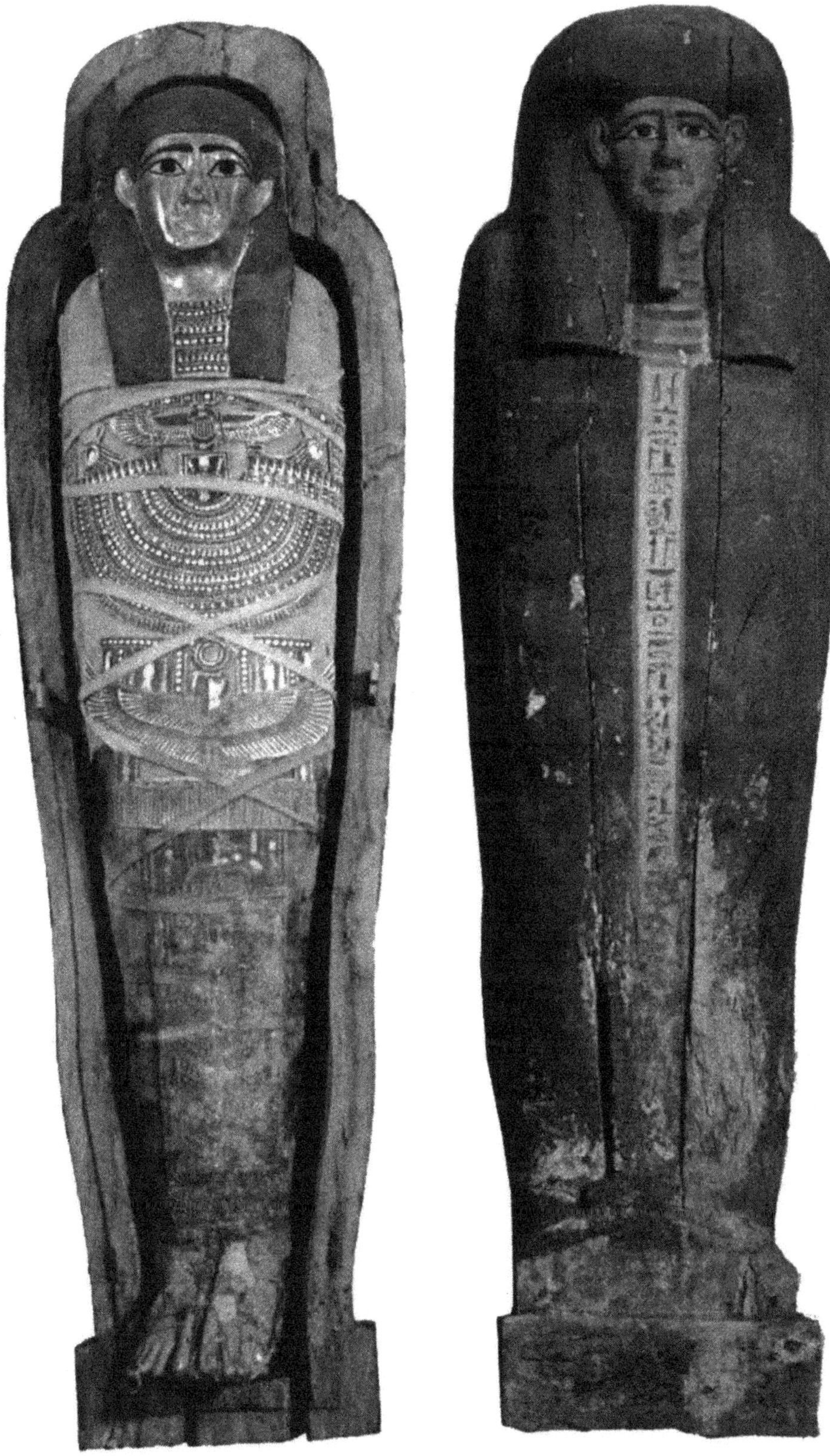

Figure 1(a): The wooden anthropoid coffin belonging to Hapy (NAM, AIG 3340), featuring its interior with the mummy (left) and its lid (right).

NAM, AIG 3340

Owner: Hapy, aka Khor, son of Pamy (♂).
Date: Early to Mid–Ptolemaic Period (304-150 BCE).
Place & Date of Provenance: Achmīm 1884.
Dimensions: H = 1.83 m, L = 0.42 m.
Material: Wood, Painted.

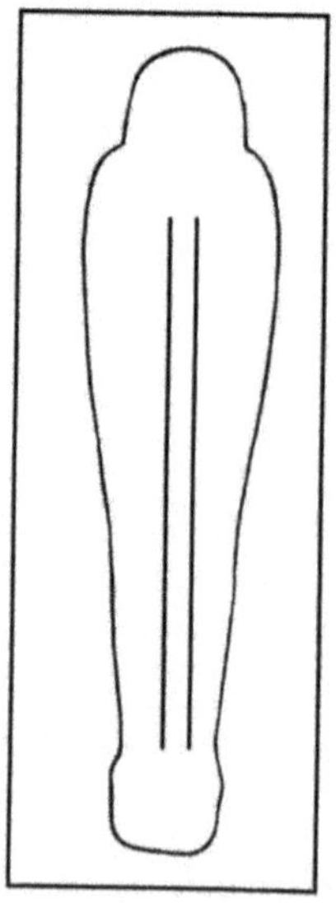

Figure 1(b): The hieroglyphic inscription of the previous anthropoid coffin (NAM, AIG 3340) and its relative position.

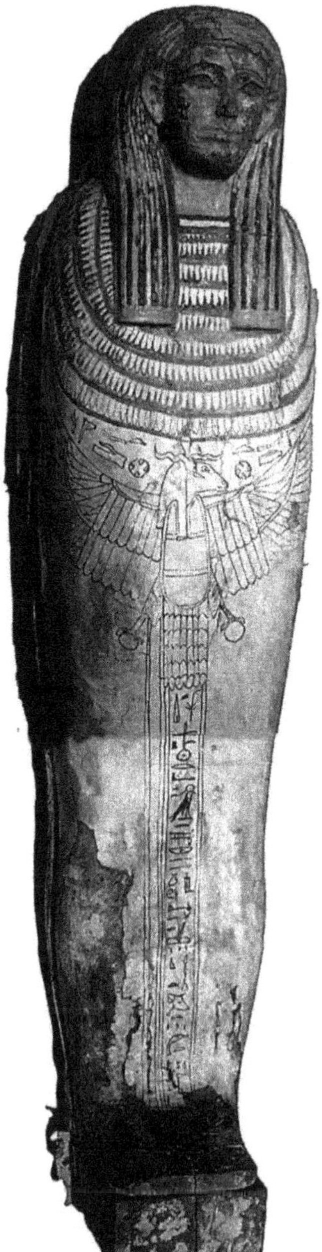

Figure 2(a): The wooden anthropoid coffin belonging to the Lady Ta–Redi–Bastet (NAM, AIG 3341).
© Copyright & Courtesy of the National Archaeological Museum, Athens, Hellas, 2003.

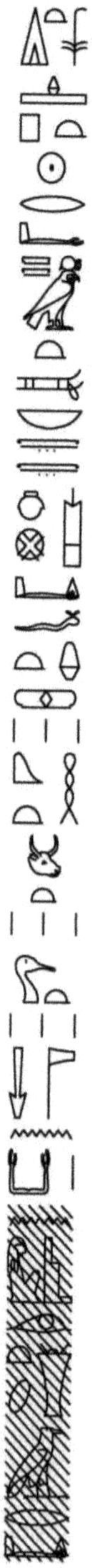

NAM, AIG 3341

Owner: Ta–Redi–Bastet (♀).
Date: Early to Mid–Ptolemaic Period (304-150 BCE).
Place & Date of Provenance: Akhmīm 1884.
Dimensions: H = 1.67 m, L = 0.40 m.
Material: Wood, Painted.

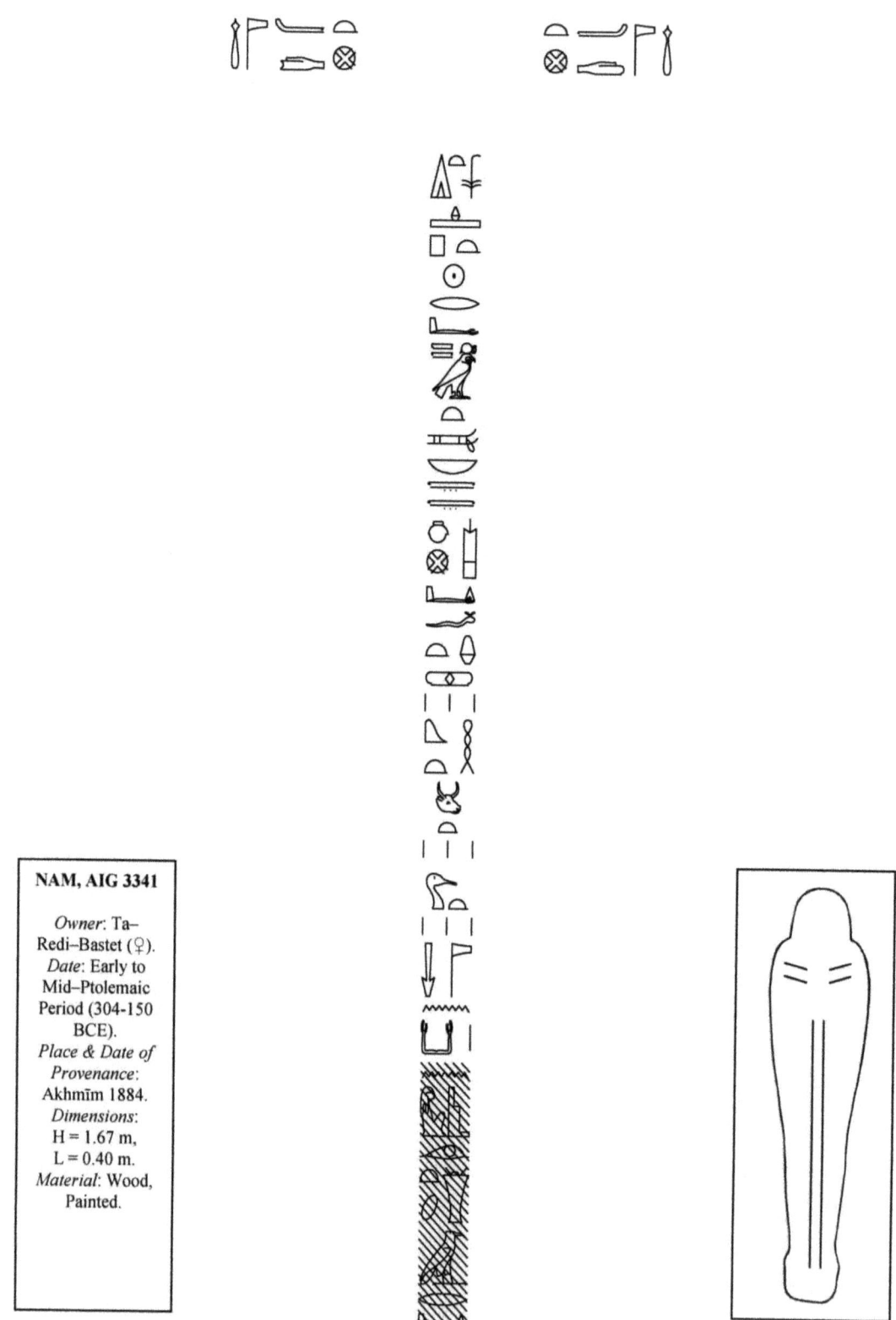

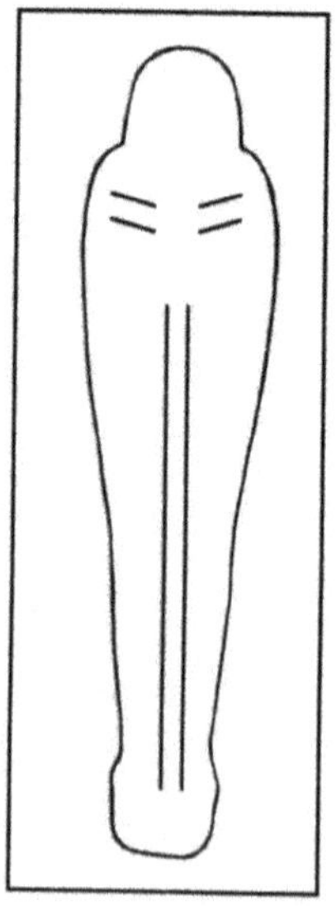

Figure 2(b): The hieroglyphic inscriptions of the previous anthropoid coffin (NAM, AIG 3341) and their relative position.

Figure 3(a): The wooden anthropoid coffin belonging to Thau (NAM, AIG 3342).

NAM, AIG 3342

Owner: Thau, son of Ia‘eh, born to Lady Ih (♂).
Date: Early to Mid–Ptolemaic Period (304-150 BCE).
Place & Date of Provenance: Akhmīm 1884.
Dimensions: H = 1.73 m, L = 0. 45 m.
Material: Wood, Painted.

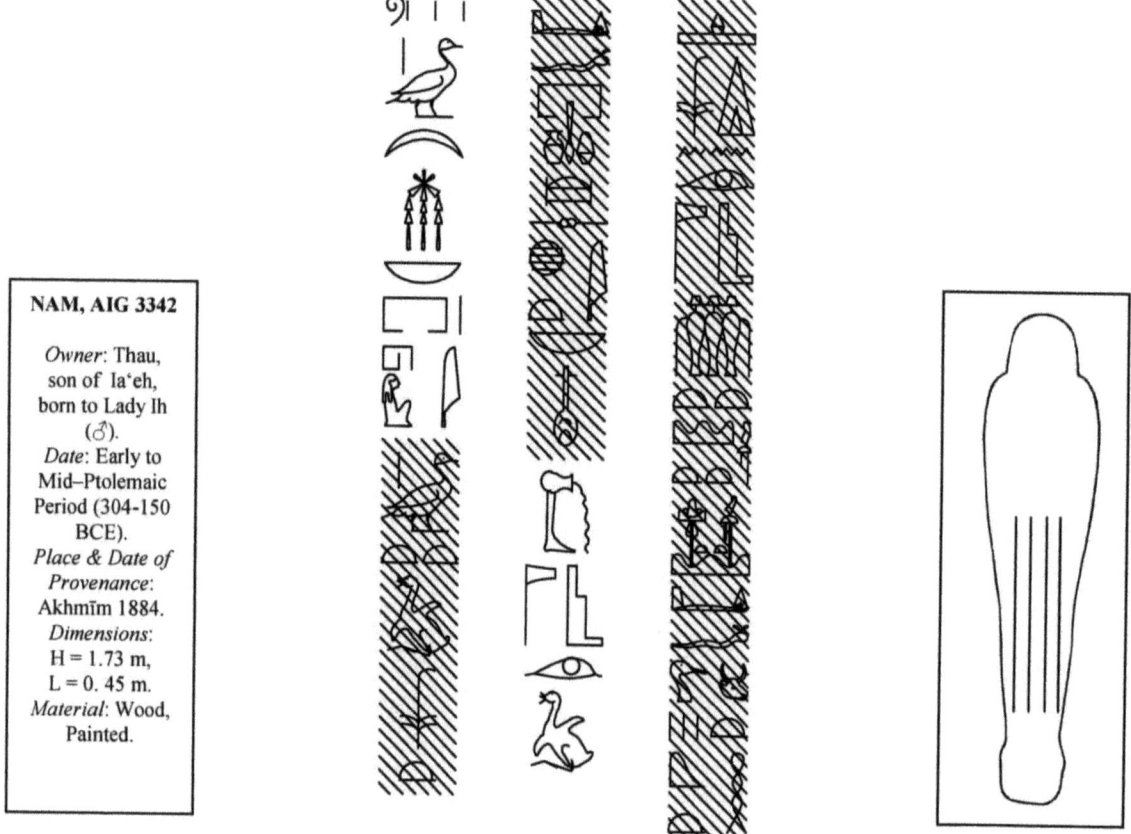

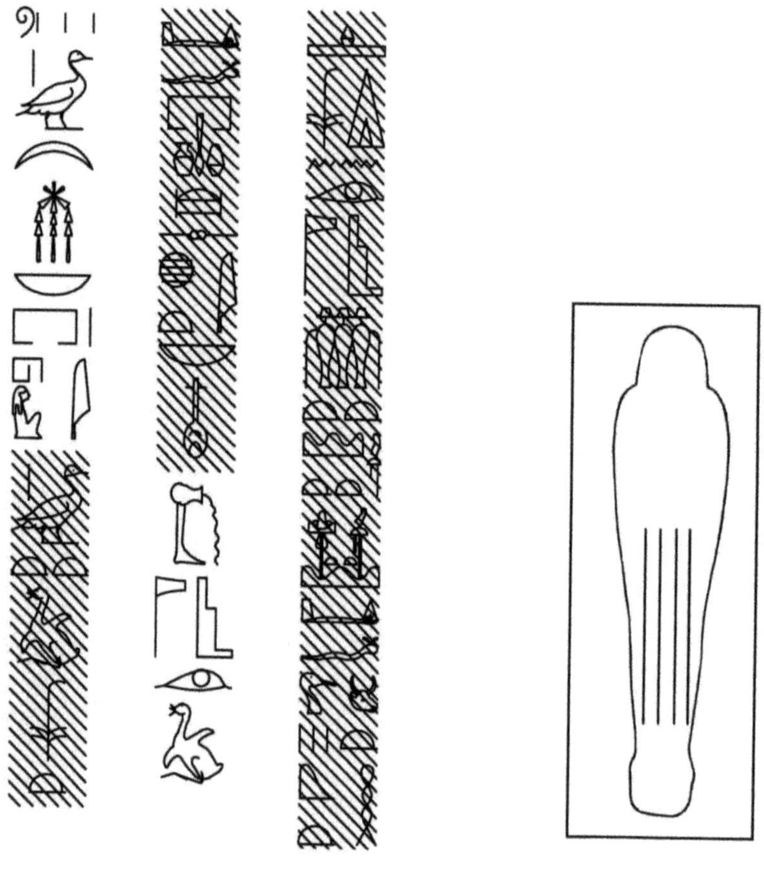

Figure 3(b): The hieroglyphic inscriptions of the previous anthropoid coffin (NAM, AIG 3342) and their relative position.

Figure 4(a): The wooden anthropoid coffin belonging to the boy Semen–Nefer (NAM, AIG 3345), featuring the lid (left) and the lower part of the sarcophagus (right).

NAM, AIG 3345

Owner: Semen–Nefer, son of Pef–Nether–Heru and Lady Res–Pa–Menekh (♂, child).
Date: Late Ptolemaic Period (150-50 BCE).
Place & Date of Provenance: Akhmīm 1884.
Dimensions: H = 1.51 m, L = 0.37 m.
Material: Wood, Painted.

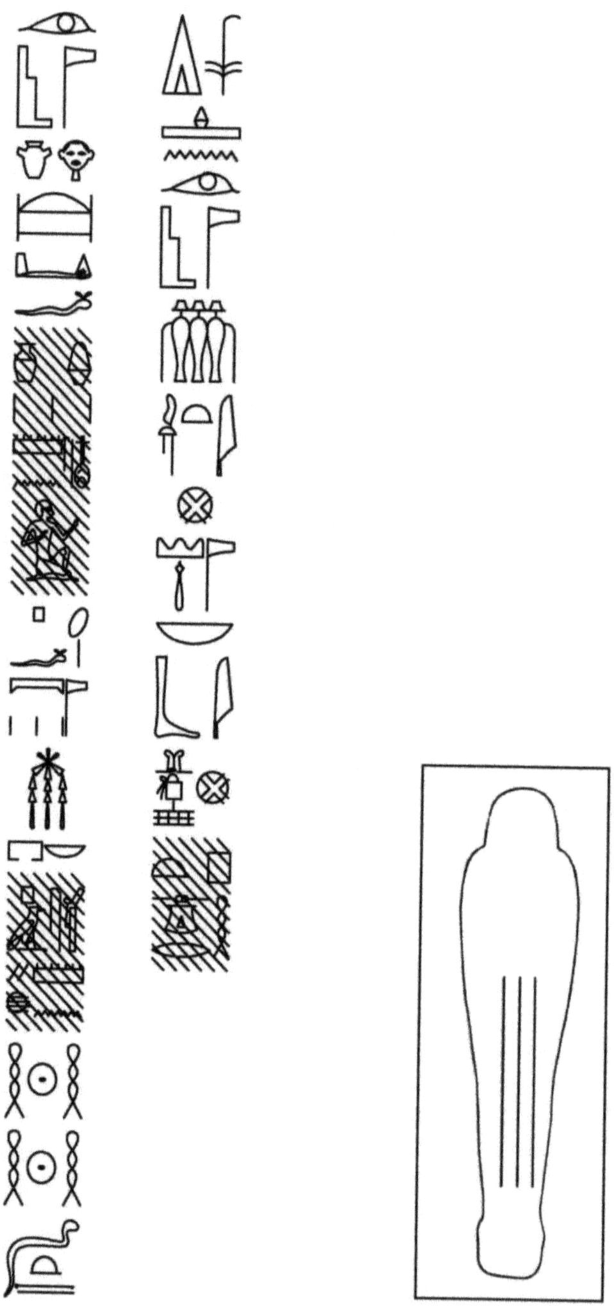

Figure 4(b): The hieroglyphic inscriptions of the previous anthropoid coffin (NAM, AIG 3345) and their relative position.

Figure 5(a):): The wooden anthropoid coffin belonging to the Lady Ta–Khered–Min, the Ritual Dancer of Min from Panopolis (NAM, AIG 3348).

NAM, AIG 3348
Owner: The Ritual Dancer of Min, Lady Ta–Khered–Min, daughter of the Fourth Prophet of Min, Iret–Hor–Ru and Lady Isis–Nekhebut (♀).
Date: Early to Mid–Ptolemaic Period (304-150 BCE).
Place & Date of Provenance: Akhmīm 1884.
Dimensions: H = 1.75 m, L = 0.47 m.
Material: Wood, Painted

Figure 5(b): The hieroglyphic inscriptions of the previous anthropoid coffin (NAM, AIG 3348) and their relative position.

The Egyptian Collection of the Archaeological Museum in Bologna: Past and Future*

Daniela Picchi

Abstract

In Bologna the initial interest in ancient Egypt derives from the 16th and 17th centuries, when a hundred Egyptian objects, whose origin and provenance are unknown, became part of the antiquities of the University Museum. However, it was only in the 19th century that interest in ancient Egypt became intense. Beginning in 1825, every third year the course of Archaeology in Bologna —at least in theory— had to be dedicated to the study of Egypt. In such a cultural *milieu* the Bolognese painter Pelagio Palagi (1775-1860) collated his Egyptian collection which, on his death in Turin, included 3,109 objects; in his will he donated it to his native town in 1860. In 1881 the objects housed in the University were added to this collection. Other collections of minor importance were also added in the following years, until in 1895 the *Museo Civico di Bologna: Catalogo di Antichità Egizie* by Giovanni Kminek–Szedlo was published. In 1987 another donation from a private collection consisting of 85 pieces was finally included. Today the Egyptian collection of the Archaeological Museum in Bologna, with its 3500 objects, is one of the richest in Italy and also in Europe.

KEY WORDS: Egyptian Collections, Archaeological Museum of Bologna, Modern Museology, Pelagio Palagi, Bologna.

I. Introduction

The Egyptian collection of the Archaeological Museum in Bologna [Fig. 1], with its more than 3500 objects, is one of the richest in Italy and also in Europe. It consists, like other important parts of the Museum, of objects mostly originating from the Bolognese painter Pelagio Palagi's collection of antiquities, who donated it to the city council of his native town.

II. The Egyptian Collection

The initial interest in Bologna for ancient Egypt derives from the 16th and 17th centuries, when a fragmentary stone with a hieroglyphic inscription was found in the area of S. Stefano's church (1664)[1], as well as a few Egyptian funerary or votive items —shabtis, amulets, parts of mummies, small wooden furniture and bronzes— whose origin and provenance are unknown, were situated in the private Museums of Ulisse Aldrovandi and Ferdinando Cospi.

Ulisse Aldrovandi (1522-1605)[2] [Fig. 2] kept the first chair of Natural History (*lectura philosophiae naturalis de fossilibus, plantis et animalibus*) at the University of Bologna from 1561 to 1600. During his life, he collected about 18000 different objects including *naturalia* (minerals, fossils, stuffed and dried animals, plants, & c.) and *artificialia* (archaeological and ethnographical items, and other artifacts) for scientific and didactic purposes. After his death, the entire collection was transferred from his private residence to the Town Hall, where they were arranged in five rooms at the ground-floor (1617). Some years later, in 1648, Bartolomeo Ambrosino, curator of the Museum, published *Ulyssis Aldrovandi Patricii Bononiensis Musaeum Metallicum in Libros IIII Distributum (De Metallis, De Terra, De Succis Concretis, De Lapidibus)*, which is, together with the Aldrovandi's manuscripts, well preserved in the University Library of Bologna (BUB)[3], a very important text for understanding why[4] and what kinds of Egyptian artifacts had been bought by this famous Bolognese; but it is not precise enough to identify the ones that still survive in the Egyptian collection of the Archaeological Museum.

The Marquis Ferdinando Cospi (1606-1686)[5] became a collector as a young man living at the Medicean court in Florence. From then on, he constantly acquired beautiful and selected different types of objects aiming at creating a flourishing museum. His collection, one of the most significant Italian *Wunderkammern*[6] [Fig. 3], was first arranged inside the family palace in the center of Bologna and opened to distinguished visitors, such as Cosimo III de' Medici, and later, while Cospi was still alive, exhibited in a sixth room of the Town Hall (1657-1660), close to Aldrovandi's Museum. About twenty Egyptian antiquities[7], often well described or drawn according to the antiquarian taste of the period in the fifth part of the book written by Lorenzo Legati and printed by Giacomo Monti in Bologna (1677), *Museo Cospiano annesso a quello del famoso Ulisse Aldrovandi e donato alla sua Patria dall' Illustrissimo Signor Ferdinando Cospi Patrizio di Bologna e Senatore Cavaliere Commendatore di S. Stefano, Balì d'Arezzo e March. Di Petriolo*[8] [Fig. 3], reveal the marquis's atten-

* The author wishes to thank Dr. Cristiana Morigi Govi, director of the Archaeological Museum of Bologna and the Museum staff. All photographs have kindly been made available by the Museum of Bologna.

[1] This fragment was considered, together with the inscription *Dominae Isidi Victrici* (*CIL*, **XI**, 695) walled up in the northern side of the same church, an important evidence confirming the existence of a Roman *Iseum* in that area. See Pernigotti, S.: 'L'iscrizione egiziana di Santo Stefano: pagine di storia antica e moderna', *Atti e Mem. Dep. Romagna*, XXXI-XXXII, 1980-1981, 1-28; *Idem*: 'Ancora sull'iscrizione egiziana di S. Stefano, con *Postilla* di Gina Fasoli', *Atti e Mem. Dep. Romagna*, XXXV, 1984, 37-46; Cesaretti, M.P.: 'Sull'ubicazione dell'Iseo bolognese', *Stefaniana: Contributi per la storia del complesso di S. Stefano in Bologna* (Fasoli, G., ed.), Bologna 1985, 15-26.

[2] See Brizzolara, A.M..: 'Il museo di Ulisse Aldrovandi', *Dalla Stanza delle Antichità al Museo Civico: Storia della formazione del Museo Civico Archeologico di Bologna* (Morigi Govi, C. & Sassatelli, G., eds.), Bologna 1984, 119-24.

[3] See in particular the final part of BUB, ms. Aldr. 46, vol. II, entitled *Elenchus alphabeticus rerum omnium quae in eius musaeo spectantium oculis obiiciuntur*.

[4] Together with the other *artificialia*, these were considered to be significant examples of the primeval human use of natural raw materials.

[5] See Gualandi, G.: 'Il Museo delle 'meraviglie' di Ferdinando Cospi', *Dalla Stanza delle Antichità* (Morigi Govi, C. & Sassatelli, G., eds.), 1984, 125-30; Brizzolara, A.M., Medica, M., Morigi Govi, C.: 'Ferdinando Cospi e l'antico', *L'antichità del mondo: Fossili, Alfabeti, Rovine* (Tega, V., ed.), Bologna 2002, 25-31.

[6] Very famous was his collection of pictures including works by Reni, Domenichino, Sirani, Andrea del Sarto, Tiziano, Veronese, Bronzino, Brueghel.

[7] Recently, on the occasion of a temporary exhibition organized by the University of Bologna in collaboration with the Archaeological Museum and entitled *L'antichità del mondo: Fossili, Alfabeti, Rovine*, the author of this paper has identified other Egyptian antiquities belonging to Cospi's Museum. See Picchi, D. in *L'antichità del mondo, op. cit.*, 2002, 35.

[8] Actually the fifth part of this book was written by Silvestro Bonfioli or Bonfiglioli. In order to define how many Egyptian antiquities were in the Cospi's collection, see also Legati, L.: *Inventario semplice di tutte le materie*

tion toward this original Near–Eastern culture and, in particular, its religious conception[9].

In 1742-1743 both these collections, which had been donated by their owners to the Municipality of Bologna during the previous century, were transferred to the Science Institute in Palazzo Poggi, which featured the *Antiquities Room*; there they were enriched with the objects coming from the Luigi Ferdinando Marsili's collection (1658-1730) and enhanced by the donations of other collectors[10], as well as by some purchases.

The Bolognese Ferdinando Marsili[11] [Fig. 4], well known in Europe as a soldier and a diplomat[12], was an acute observer, a pragmatic scholar and a restless collector of books, codes, maps, drawnings, instruments, *naturalia* and *artificialia*[13]. In 1709 he expressed a wish to put these objects at the community's disposal[14], so that they could be used by the University of Bologna to test theoretical knowledge by means of direct experience. The Science Institute, including its *Antiquities Room*, was successively founded (1711)[15], organized and inaugurated (1714) thanks to Marsili's firmness [Fig. 5]. His collection, donated to the Institute in 1712 and accurately described in *Instrumentum donationis illustrissimi, et excellentissimi viri Domini Comitis Aloysii Ferdinandi de Marsiliis favore illustrissimi et excelsi Senatus, et civitatis Bononiae in gratiam novae in eadem Scientiarum Institutionis*[16], was very rich of antiquities; 185 of them were depicted with oil–colours by an anonymous author in two volumes entitled *Copia delle Anticaglie, de' Marmi, di Porfido e di Bronzo et altre Pietre ritrovate in più parti raccolte dall'Illustrissimo Signor Conte Luigi Ferdinando Marsiglii Generale di Sua Santità, donate all'Illustrissimo Regimento di Bologna sua Patria per ereger l'Instituta Marsigliana e fedelmente poste in Pittura*[17], and for this reason, it is possible to identify many of them.

By browsing the pages of these books, his interest in the ancient world clearly emerges; it was specifically dedicated to listing the classical Greek and Roman civilizations, without nevertheless disregarding the more ancient and exotic pharaonic culture. Unfortunally Marsili was not able to carry out his project of a journey to Egypt[18]; yet, his scientific curiosity about Egypt, its *res miltares*, art and religion, surfaces from the following manuscripts: *Aegyptiorum, Etruscorum, Romanorum militaris suppellex ex sculptis gemmis, nummis, marmoribus atque picturis vetustissimis recollecta ad agnitionem eorum Methodi militandi*[19]; *Rottolo di dissegni di più Idoli egizii fatti fare dal Conte Marsili su gli originali o di legno o di Mettallo, o di pietra Bisalto della grandezza che erano, che trovò in più gabinetti di Curiosi di Marsilia e Lione per formare un trattato dell'Idolatria egizia*[20]; *Anotationi sopra le divinità d'Egypto* and, at last, *Proietto per l'esame della Mumia anatomicamente, phisicamente, eruditamente*[21]. In 1727, when the *Index suppellectilis quae asservatur in Museo antiquitatis*[22] was drawn up, the Egyptian artifacts acquired by Marsili[23] were about thirty, all of modest historical importance but of great antiquarian relevance[24].

Following the Napoleonic suppression in 1796, the *Antiquities Room*, which had been reorganized in wider spaces, was turned into the University Museum (1810-1878)[25], which was directed by Filippo Schiassi, the professor in charge of Archaeology from 1803 to 1836. Under his direction[26] and under his successor, Francesco Rocchi (1847-1875), the city's interest in ancient Egypt became more factual.

It is important to remember that the Napoleonic expedition to Egypt (1798-1799), the publication of *Description de l'Égypte*, edited in Paris between 1803 and 1813, and the decipherment of hieroglyphs by J.–F. Champollion (1822)[27] gave birth to Egyptology as a science. Consequently it became a subject taught in Universities. From 1825 onwards, every three years, the Archaeology course held at the University of

---

esattamente descritte che si trovano nel Museo Cospiano, Bologna (Monti, G.) 1680, *passim*.

9 See the interesting chapter entitled 'De gli Dii dell'Asia, e dell'Egitto', *Museo Cospiano* (Legati), 1677, 459-86 & *passim*.

10 Pope Benedictus XIV (1740-1758) donated four big mummies —one of which black and without bandages (Inv. № KS 1979)— and the famous relief of Nectanebo I, XXX Dynasty, 380-62 BCE (Inv. № KS 1870), to the Science Institute of his native town. This relief, a masterpiece of the LP featuring the king in the act of offering jewels and precious objects to various guardian deities, was originally an architectural element located between two columns in the temple of the god Atum in Heliopolis. Transported from Egypt to Italy during the Roman Period, it was found in Rome in 1709. See Schiassi, F.: *Guida del Forestiere al Museo delle Antichità della Regia Università di Bologna*, Bologna (Lucchesini, G.) 1814, 92-95.

11 See Brizzolara, A.M.: *Le sculture del Museo Civico Archeologico di Bologna: La collezione Marsili*, Bologna 1986, 9-31; *Idem*: 'Le *Antiquitates* di Luigi Ferdinando Marsili', *L'antichità del mondo, op. cit.*, 2002, 48-53.

12 From 1682 to 1704, he was at the service of Leopold I of Austria and, later, of the Papal States.

13 Marsili' activity is well documented by his monumental work, finished in 1704 and published only a few years later, *Danubius Pannonico–Mysicus Observationibus Geographicis, Astronomicis, Hydrographicis, Historicis, Physicis Perlustratus et in Sex Tomos Digestus*, Hagae Comitum – Amstelodami 1726.

14 State Archives, Bologna (ASBo), Magistrates' Office, *Atti*, 1708-710, c. 130 v.

15 See 'Le costituzioni dell'Istituto delle Scienze', *Atti legali per la fondazione dell'Istituto delle Scienze, ed Arti liberali per memoria degli Ordini ecclesiastici, e secolari che compongono la città di Bologna*, Bologna (Stamperia bolognese di San Tommaso d'Aquino) 1728, XXI-XXXI.

16 See 'Instrumentum donationis', *Atti legali per la fondazione dell'Istituto delle Scienze*, 1728, III-XII.

17 The two volumes, unfortunately *sine data*, are preserved at the Archaeological Museum.

18 See BUB, cod. 1044 n. 96 E: *Proietto per l'esame naturale ed artificiale per tutto l'Egitto* e *Memorie dell'Egitto cavate da Diodoro Siculo*.

19 BUB, cod. 1044 n. 1.

20 BUB, cod. 1044 n. 25. He visited Marseille and Lyon in the period between 1706 and 1708.

21 BUB, cod. 1044 n. 25.

22 BUB, cod. 1044, n. 85 H.

23 From 1712 until his death, Marsili continued to supplement the 'Antiquities Room' of the Institute with new donations. Thus, in 1715 he donated a 'Testa della dea Iside di marmo basalto con piedistallo piccolo d'alabastro ed un altro di giallo brecciano grande' to the Institute; see Archaeological Museum of Bologna, Archives, Universitary Museum, Cart. 61, lett. M.: *Donativi fatti alla stanza della Erudizione antica dell'Instituto delle Scienze*.

24 See Picchi: *L'antichità del mondo, op. cit.*, 2002, 56-57. During this exhibition the author has identified a few Egyptian objects of the Marsili's collection, which until then were generically defined as being part of the University's collection; see *Ibid.*, 56.

25 Brizzolara, A.M.: 'Il Museo Universitario (1810-878)', *Dalla Stanza delle Antichità* (Morigi Govi & Sassatelli, eds.), 1984, 159-66.

26 Some of the objects removed in 1796 by the Frenchmen, among which the fragmentary feet of an Egyptian statue dating from the Roman Period (Inv. № KS 1837), were found in Paris and returned to the University. The first guide of the Museum was published: Schiassi, F.: *Guida del Forestiere al Museo delle Antichità di Bologna*, Bologna (Tipografia di Lucchesini, G.) 1814, (the second of the seven rooms described in the book was devoted to the Egyptian collection).

27 Champollion was in Bologna in 1825.

Bologna was to be dedicated in theory to the study of Egypt[28]. At the same time the rising interest in ancient Egypt gave birth to a flourishing antique market. During the first half of the nineteenth century monarchs, governments and a few rare individuals acquired Egyptian collections, which later contributed to the establishment of the greatest European Museums.

In such a cultural *milieu*, the Bolognese painter Pelagio Palagi (1775-1860) [Fig. 6], one of the most open Italian artists to the various impulses coming from the Neoclassical and Romantic culture[29], put together his great collection of antiquities[30]. Sharing the fervour for Archaeology and for the re–discovery of the classical world, which also deeply influenced his artistic activity, starting from 1813, he created a collection broadly representative of the dominant archaeological tendencies of those years, with a particular attention not only to the classical ancient civilizations, but also to more remote cultures such as the Egyptian one.

In 1831 he bought the majority of his Egyptian objects from the Triestine Giuseppe Nizzoli, chancellor at the Austrian Consulate in Egypt from 1817 to 1828, who sold him another smaller part some years later[31]. Nizzoli was not unfamiliar with such a trading activity; he already owned two important collections, the first one forming the central core of the Egyptian collection of the Kunsthistorisches Museum in Vienna[32] and the second one bought by Leopoldo II the Grand Duke of Tuscany in 1824 and now part of the Archaeological Museum of Florence[33]. Nizzoli obtained the antiquities that Palagi had acquired through purchases and exchanges in the antique market of Cairo as well as through some excavations, among which those carried out in the necropolis of Saqqara —entrusted to his nineteen years old wife, Amalia— are especially significant[34].

When the Bolognese artist and collector died in Turin in 1860, he donated his 'Museum of art objects and antiquities, medals, drawings and books ... ' to his native town, his 'diletta patria', for an almost nominal payment of 213,876 Italian lire in his heirs' favour. The Egyptian collection consisted of 3109 artifacts, including the famous reliefs from the Horemheb's tomb, statues, architectural elements, funerary stelae, sarcophagi, mummies, papyri, shabtis, bronzes, almost 2000 amulets and scarabs, necklaces and jewellery, funerary equipment of different provenances and periods, objects remarkable for their uniqueness and value mainly dating from the NK and the XXVI Dynasty (LP). The collection included artifacts that were almost always of great historical significance and beauty, but contrary to the requirements of modern scientific research these objects were very often detached from their archaeological context.

After the donation of the Pelagio Palagi's collection (1860), in 1871, on the occasion of the 5th Congress of Prehistoric Anthropology and Archaeology, the city council of Bologna organized its first exhibition in five rooms of Palazzo Galvani (ex Death Hospital), directly connected to the Library of Archiginnasio. Two halls hosted the Palagi collection, which had in the past attracted illustrious scholars on account of its historic importance. Francesco Rossi, vice–director of the Egyptian Museum of Turin, was its curator[35].

Over the next ten years, following numerous archaeological findings in Bologna, the city council had to build a larger museum. When in 1881 the Archeological Museum of Bologna was inaugurated in the renovated Palazzo Galvani, the objects coming from the University Museum were added to this collection[36]. Both the Egyptian collections were almost entirely displayed in three halls (III, IV and V) at the first floor decorated according to the taste of the period with frescoes showing Egyptian–like motifs, such as lotus flowers, papyri and a female divinity[37]. Stelae and funerary reliefs were displayed in the 3rd hall, sarcophagi, mummies and funerary objects were put in the 4th hall, the 5th one hosted statues of Kings, bas–reliefs and the rich collection of scarabs and amulets. The objects, contained in large glass cupboards, were ordered according to their typology without considering their chronology. The arrangement and massing of these objects did not allow for a full understanding of their historical and artistic development. This arrangement —apart from slight changes— has remained unchanged until today [Fig. 7].

Other collections of minor importance were also added in the following years until in 1895 the *Catalogo di Antichità Egizie* by Giovanni Kminek–Szedlo, first curator of the Egyptian collection[38], was published in Turin. Among those which are worth mentioning are those by Giuseppe Ferlini, donated to

28 This course had never included on–site archaeological research until October 1993 when a joint archaeological expedition organized by the Bologna and Lecce Universities led the first excavation campaign in Kom 'Umm 'el-'Atl, a site in the north–eastern area of the Fayum oasis, where the ancient town of Bakchias was once located.

29 Pelagio Palagi worked in the main Italian artistic centres of his time including Bologna, Rome, Milan and Turin. See *Pelagio Palagi artista e collezionista* (Morigi Govi, C. & Grandi, R., eds.), Bologna 1976; *Pelagio Palagi pittore: Dipinti dalle raccolte del Comune di Bologna* (Poppi, C., ed.), Bologna 1996.

30 Tovoli, S.: 'La collezione di Pelagio Palagi', *Dalla Stanza delle Antichità* (Morigi Govi & Sassatelli, eds.), 1984, 191-99.

31 Nizzoli, G.: *Catalogo dettagliato della collezione di Antichità Egizie*, Alessandria d'Egitto 1827; *Idem*: *Catalogo di una raccoltina di Antichità Egiziane*, *S. d.*: BCAB, Sez. Mss. e Rari, F. S. Palagi, Cart. 31, fasc. 2, lett. C, n. 5.

32 This first Egyptian collection was sold by Nizzoli to Ernst August Burghart in 1821. See Satzinger, H.: 'Der Werdergang der Ägyptisch–Orientalischen Samlung des Kunsthistorischen Museums in Wien', *L'Egitto fuori dell'Egitto: Dalla riscoperta all'Egittologia* (Morigi Govi, C. & Curto, S. & Pernigotti, S., eds.), Bologna 1994, 367-82; *Idem*: *Das Kunsthistorische Museum in Wien: Die Ägyptisch–Orientalische Sammlung*, Mainz 1994.

33 See Del Francia, P.R.: 'I Lorena e la nascita del Museo Egizio fiorentino', *L'Egitto fuori dell'Egitto* (Morigi Govi, Curto & Pernigotti, eds.), 1994, 159-90.

34 Amalia Nizzoli wrote an interesting diary during her stay in Egypt from 1819 to 1828, i.e. *Memorie sull'Egitto e specialmente sui costumi delle donne orientali e gli harem, scritte durante il suo soggiono in quel paese (1819-1828)*, Milano 1841.

35 Morigi Govi, C.: 'Il Museo Civico del 1871', *Dalla Stanza delle Antichità* (Morigi Govi & Sassatelli, eds.), 1984, 259-67; Tovoli, S.: 'Il Museo Archeologico Comunitativo e il progetto di unificazione delle collezioni comunali e universitarie (1860-1871)'; *Ibid.*, 211-15.

36 Some of the most important historical and artistic monuments of the whole Bolognese collection, such as the statue of the King Neferhotep I (Inv. № KS 1799) and the statue of the scribe Ahmose (Inv. № KS 1823), can be found among the approximately one hundred Egyptian objects which were until then exhibited in Palazzo Poggi, besides the above mentioned relief of Nectanebo.

37 The painter was the Bolognese Luigi Busi; see Poppi, C.: 'Luigi Busi', *Dall'Accademia al Vero: La Pittura a Bologna prima e dopo l'unità*, Bologna 1983, 191-93; Sassatelli, G.: 'La 'Galleria della pittura etrusca' nel salone X', *Dalla Stanza delle Antichità* (Morigi Govi & Sassatelli, eds.), 1984, 365-70.

38 Curto, S.: 'A ricordo di due egittologi dimenticati: Giuseppe Acerbi e Giovanni Kminek–Szedlo', *Atti del convegno: La Lombardia e l'Oriente*, Milano 1963, 89-128; *Atti del colloquio su Giovanni Kminek–Szedlo (Bologna, 7 Maggio 1987)* (Pernigotti, S. & Piacentini, P., eds), Pisa (*SEAP*, 2) 1987.

the Museum in 1843[39], by Pietro Neri Baraldi in 1881[40], by Federico Amici after 1883[41] and by Cesare Fava in 1893[42]. Starting from the 1960's, there has been a revival of the scientific interest in the Egyptian collection, which was almost exclusively known through the publication of Kminek–Szedlo catalogue (1895). The objects were restored, studied and displayed in temporary exhibitions[43]; a guide to the collection was published[44], and the writing of scientific catalogues, which is still under way, was begun[45].

More recently numerous studies about single monuments and about the history of the collection have become the basis for the elaboration of the new Egyptian section [Fig. 8], which was inaugurated in 1994 in five halls at the underground of the same palace[46] [Fig. 9]. It is divided into three sections.

After an introduction dedicated to the history of the collection [Fig. 10], in the new presentation the reliefs of the Memphite tomb of Horemheb are displayed together with those coming from Saqqara. The Archaeological Museum of Bologna has also produced a graphic computerized video[47] on the Saqqara tomb of General Horemheb and its reliefs [Figs. 11-12] for this section. During the reign of Tut'ankhamun, Horemheb, the commander in chief of the Egyptian army, commissioned a personal tomb in the Saqqara necropolis, next to Memphis. In the early 19th century merchants of archaeological antiquities emptied the tomb: some of the reliefs that decorated its walls were taken away and sold to various European and North–American museums. Five of these are now in the Archaeological Museum of Bologna and are the most important part of the Egyptian collection due to their high artistic quality. They are carved in perfect Amarna style and portray Horemheb in his life in the Underworld: while at work in the Heaven; and in different moments of his military life. During the years following its first discovery the tomb was newly covered by the desert sand and it was found again only in 1975 by Geoffrey Martin[48]. The publication on these excavations enabled experts to develop a hypothesis for the tomb reconstruction, which has been subsequently reproduced in our video, allowing visitors to enter Horemheb tomb 'virtually' and to understand the meaning of the most significant scenes carved on the reliefs [Figs. 13-14]. This reconstruction can be considered to be another step in the education activity that the Archaelogical Museum of Bologna has started since 1973.

This first section is followed by objects and sculptures, displayed in chronological order, which illustrate aspects of Egyptian art from the OK until the LP. The last hall, which has a didactic purpose, is dedicated to relevant themes of the collection such as the funerary equipment[49] [Fig. 15], the writing, the amulets and scarabs[50].

In 1994 the Archaeological Museum of Bologna also started the computerized cataloguing of its Egyptian collection. At present the text data–base includes more than 3500 catalogue and inventory records developed by means of the File Maker Pro Software by Claris. Each record is subdivided into different specific fields in order to functionally use the data–base and to obtain better results in data processing and in carying out research[51]. The work is still in progress; in the immediate future the text data–base will be supplemented with the image data base thanks to a software created for the management and consultation of the numismatic data and image banks of the Museum[52].

Furthermore, since 1995 the Museum has developed its own web site within the *Iperbole Project*, one of the first Italian municipal Internet–based networks. The site has an articulated structure (today it comprises about 300 HTML pages). It is subdivided into different sections among which the Egyptian one[53], being the first one that was inaugurated and that will be updated over the next months.

III. Conclusions

To sum up, let us briefly summarize what we have already discussed above. In Bologna the initial interest in ancient Egypt derives from the 16th and 17th centuries, when a hundred Egyptian objects, whose origin and provenance are unknown, became part of the antiquities of the University Mu-

[39] In 1837 this Bolognese doctor sold the greatest part of his collection to the Glyptotek of Munich and in 1843 another smaller part of it to the Museum of Berlin; during those same years he also donated two stones, some mummy cartonnages, two vases made by means of galvanoplasty, several close copies of jewels and a wooden model of pyramid to the Archaeological Museum of Bologna. See Ferlini, G.: *Nell'interno dell'Affrica, 1829-1835* (Boldrini, F., ed.), Bologna 1981; Curto, S.: 'Giuseppe Ferlini', *Oriens Antiquus*, XXII, 1-2, 1983, 141-43; Davoli, P.: 'Un rilievo meroitico 'ritrovato'', *SEAP*, **12**, 1993, 39-47; *Idem*: 'Una tavola per offerte meroitica del Museo Civico Archeologico di Bologna', *SEAP*, **18**, 1998, 23-32.

[40] Among his three gifts there was the head of royal statue in micro gabbro of high artistic value, probably representing Apries, XXVI Dynasty (589-570 BCE) = Inv. № KS 1801.

[41] He donated about ninety objects of modest historical importance: amulets, scarabs, shabtis, funerary cones, & c. For further information about the collectors of Egyptian antiquities in Bologna see Cesaretti, M.P.: 'L'Egittologia a Bologna', *SEAP*, **2**, 1987, 19-39.

[42] The *nemes* and the sacred cobra uraeus suggest that the head donated to the Museum by Cesare Fava was part of a statue of micro diorite featuring a king, Ptolemaic Period (second half of the 3rd century BCE) = Inv. № KS 1803 bis.

[43] *Ori e argenti dell'Emilia antica* (Alfieri, N. *et al.*, eds.), Bologna 1958; *L'Egitto antico nelle collezioni dell'Italia Settentrionale* (Curto, S., ed.), Bologna 1961.

[44] Bresciani, E., *La collezione egizia nel Museo Civico di Bologna*, Ravenna 1975.

[45] Pernigotti, S.: *La statuaria egiziana nel Museo Civico di Bologna*, Bologna 1980; Bresciani, E.: *Le stele egiziane del Museo Civico Archeologico di Bologna*, Bologna 1985; Jaeger, B.: *Les scarabées à noms royaux du Museo Civico Archeologico di Bologna*, Bologna 1993.

[46] See Morigi Govi, C. & Pernigotti, S.: *Museo Civico Archeologico di Bologna: La collezione egiziana*, Milano 1994.

[47] The video was made by Antonio Gottarelli, Te.m.p.l.a. Multimedia Technologies for Archaeology, University of Bologna, Cultural Heritage Conservation Department 'Techniques for Documentation, Classification and Publishing'.

[48] Martin, G.T.: *The Memphite Tomb of Horemheb Commander–in–Chief of Tut'ankhamon: I. The Reliefs, Inscriptions, and Commentary*, London 1989; and also Schneider, H.D.: *The Memphite Tomb of Horemheb Commander–in–Chief of Tut'ankhamon: II. A Catalogue of the Finds*, Louvain 1996.

[49] This funerary equipment is typical of the LP and includes materials belonging to different owners: sarcophagi made out of painted wood, and the mummy of Usai, who lived in Thebes during the 26th Dynasty, bandages and net, papyrus sandals, headrests, canopic jars and shabtis.

[50] The last section also includes a group of 85 pieces, which are remarkable due to the written material, that was donated to the Museum in 1987. See Pernigotti, S.: *Una nuova collezione egiziana al Museo Civico di Bologna*, Pisa (*SEAP*, *Series Minor*, **6**) 1994.

[51] The electronic cataloguing and filing of the Egyptian collection is directed by Daniela Picchi.

[52] The electronic cataloguing and filing of the Numismatic collection is directed by Paola Giovetti (filing–card system) and by Antonio Gottarelli (electronic storing system) with the collaboration of Daniela Picchi and Massimo Bozzoli.

[53] Our Web site address is the following: **http://www.comune.bologna.it/Musei/Archeologico/egitto_e.htm**.

seum. However, it was only in the 19th century that interest in ancient Egypt became intense. Beginning in 1825, every third year the course of Archaeology in Bologna —at least in theory— had to be dedicated to the study of Egypt. In such a cultural *milieu* the Bolognese painter Pelagio Palagi (1775-1860) collated his Egyptian collection which, on his death in Turin, included 3109 objects; in his will he donated it to his native town in 1860. In 1881 the objects housed in the University were added to this collection. Other collections of minor importance were also added in the following years, until in 1895 the *Museo Civico di Bologna: Catalogo di Antichità Egizie* by Giovanni Kminek–Szedlo was published. In 1987 another donation from a private collection consisting of 85 pieces was finally included. Today the Egyptian collection of the Archaeological Museum in Bologna, with its 3500 objects, is one of the richest in Italy and also in Europe.

FIGURE 1. The courtyard of the Archaeological Museum of Bologna.

FIGURE 2. Lead medal with Ulisse Aldrovandi's portrait by Timoteo Refati (16th century). Archaeological Museum of Bologna, University Collection, Inv. № 9900.

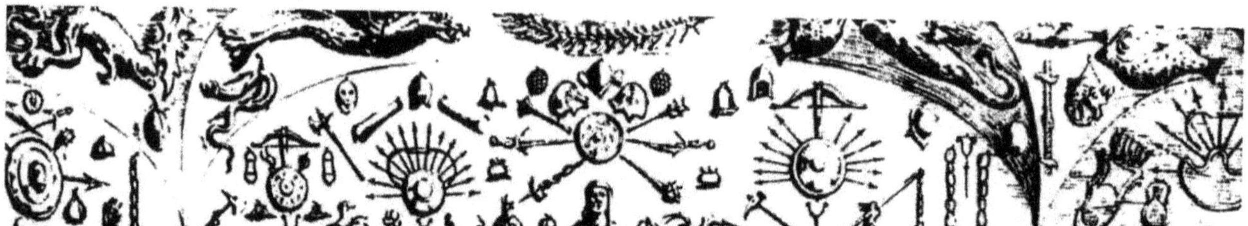

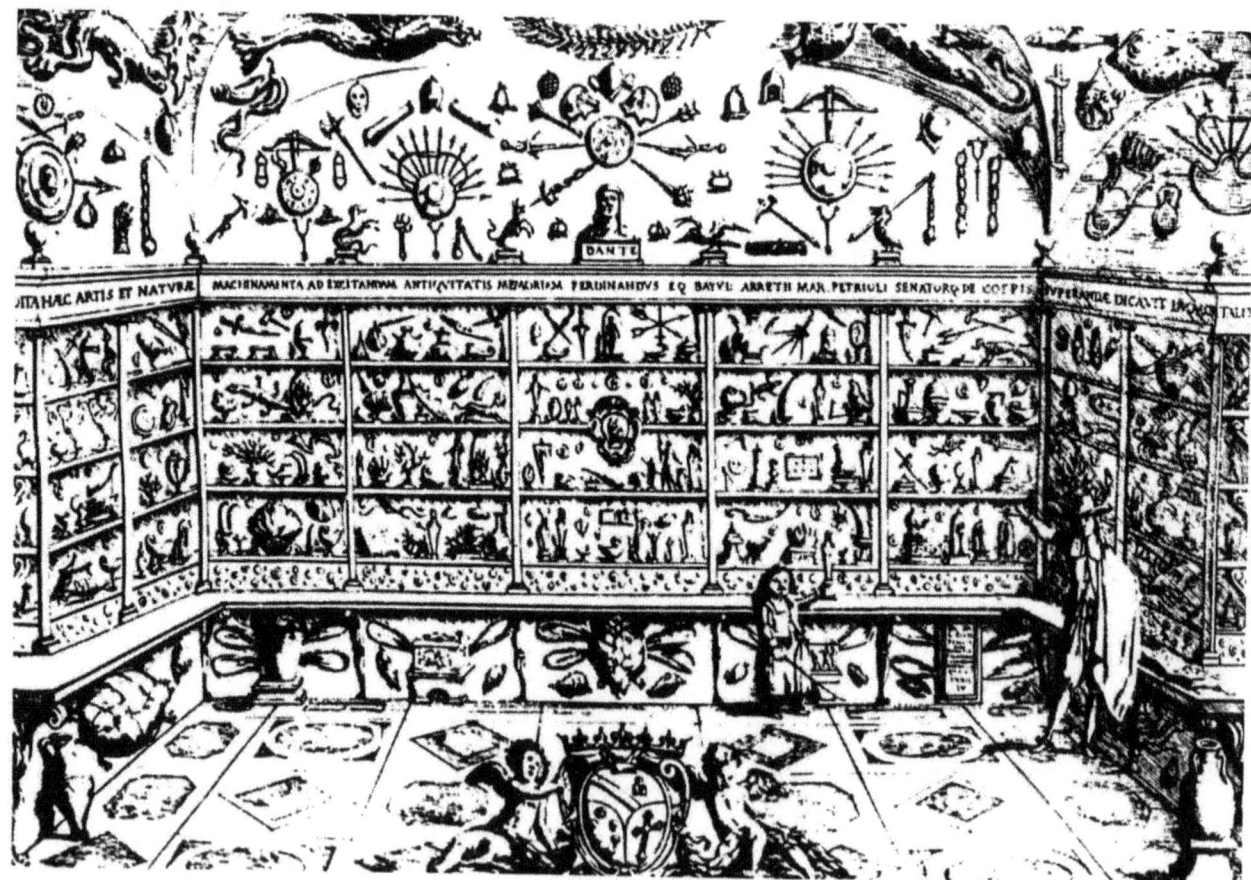

FIGURE 3. The *Wunderkammern* of Ferdinando Cospi. Engraving by G.M. Mitelli from Legati's book *Museo Cospiano*.

FIGURE 4. Silver medal with Luigi Ferdinando Marsili's portrait by F. de Saint Urbain (1731).
Archaeological Museum of Bologna, Salina Collection (?), Inv. № 11033.

FIGURE 5. Bronze medal showing Palazzo Poggi, seat of the Science Institute by Ermenegildo Hamerani (1720).
Archaeological Museum of Bologna, Universitary Collection, Inv. № 3803.

FIGURE 6. Portrait of the Italian painter Pelagio Palagi.
© Copyright & Courtesy of Museo Civico Archeologico di Bologna, Bologna 2003.

FIGURE 7. The picture shows the previous arrangement of the Museum, dated back to 1881, no longer suitable to host and preserve more than 3500 items.
© Copyright & Courtesy of Museo Civico Archeologico di Bologna, Bologna 2003.

FIGURE 8. Decorative panel of King Zehibrē‘, logo of the new Egyptian Section. Wood, 25,5 x 15 cm. Unknown provenance, XXIII Dynasty, reign of Zehibrē‘ (832-716 BCE). Palagi (Nizzoli) Collection, Inv. № KS 289.

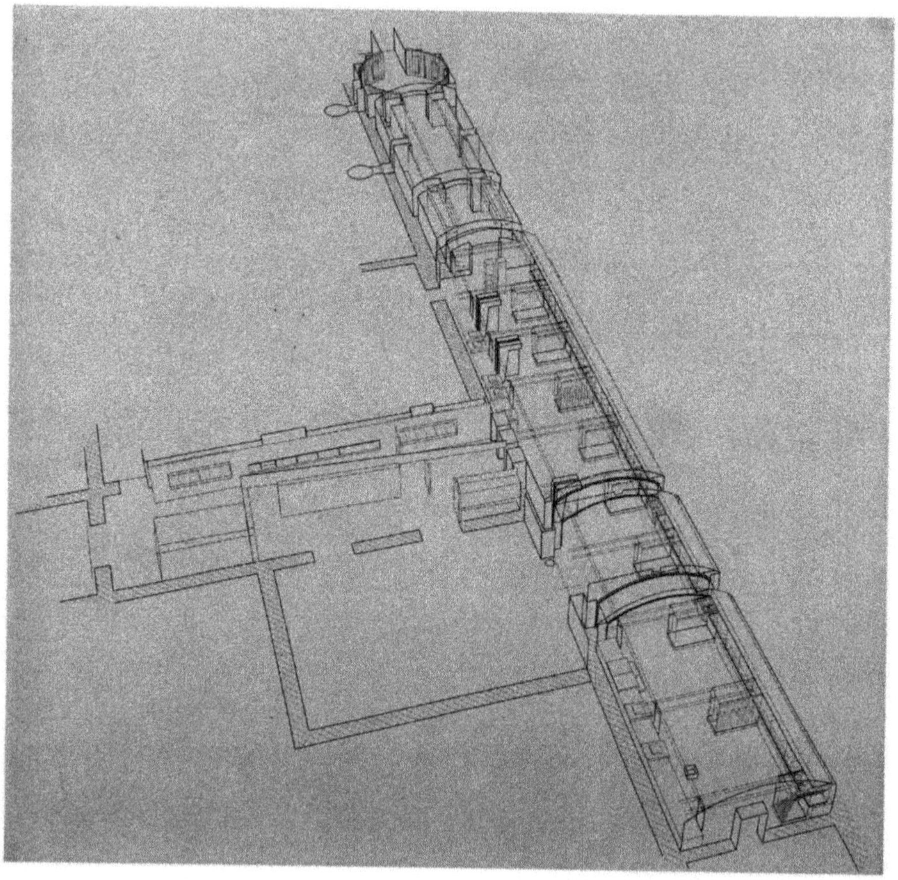

FIGURE 9. The new Egyptian section of the Museum.
© Copyright & Courtesy of Museo Civico Archeologico di Bologna, Bologna 2003.

FIGURE 10. The first hall of the new Egyptian section.
© Copyright & Courtesy of Museo Civico Archeologico di Bologna, Bologna 2003.

FIGURE 11. Part of the relief from the tomb of Horemheb. depicting Nubian prisoners. Limestone, 62.5 cm x 85 cm. Saqqara, XVIII Dynasty, reign of Tut'ankhamun (1332-1323 BCE). Palagi (Nizzoli) Collection, Inv № KS 1869 = 1887.

FIGURE 12. Section of the relief from the tomb of Horemheb depicting a military camp. Limestone with traces of colour, 62 cm x 126.5 cm. Saqqara, XVIII Dynasty, reign of Tut'ankhamun (1332-1323 BCE). Palagi Collection, Inv. № KS 1889.

FIGURE 13. A virtual reconstruction image of the tomb of Horemheb at Saqqara.
© Copyright & Courtesy of Museo Civico Archeologico di Bologna, Bologna 2003.

FIGURE 14. A virtual reconstruction image of the tomb of Horemheb at Saqqara
© Copyright & Courtesy of Museo Civico Archeologico di Bologna, Bologna 2003.

FIGURE 15. The reconstruction of a typical funerary equipment of the LP.
© Copyright & Courtesy of Museo Civico Archeologico di Bologna, Bologna 2003.

Ancient Egyptian Collections in Ukrainian Museums: The Case of B.I. & V.N. Khanenko's Museum in Kiev*

Sergej V. Ivanov

Abstract

This paper presents the results of the international project called *The Databank of Eastern–European Egyptology*, carried out by the Center for Egyptological Studies of the Russian Academy of Sciences (Moscow) and the Gnosarch Foundation (Basel). The subject of this article is the Egyptian collection, kept in Bogdan I. & Varvara N. Khanenko's Museum of Western and Eastern Art in Kiev. The major part of the collection was gathered by Bogdan I. Khanenko, who purchased Egyptian objects in European auctions during the 1910s. The collection includes objects dating from the Pre–Dynastic Period until the Medieval Epoch: a vessel, private sculpture, funerary figurines and different specimens of textiles. This paper is a survey of the collection and an updated publication of several objects belonging therein.

KEY WORDS: Museums: B.I. & V.N. Khanenko's Museum of Western and Eastern Art, Egyptian Collection; Art: Shabti, Sculpture–in–the–Round; Ancient Egypt: Ramesside Period, Third Intermediate Period, Late Period; Religion: Cult of Amun, Cult of Monthu, Cult of Thoth, Funerary Practices.

I. Introduction

From the early antiquity Egyptian civilization was one of the main sources that influenced European culture. The legacy of Egypt is huge: Egyptian artifacts were spread all over the world, and every important museum has a set of Egyptian or Egyptianizing objects. Taken out of their original context, destroyed by time and (sometimes barbarian) humans —wherever they are displayed— Egyptian objects still draw our attention. There are a lot of reasons for this; but there is also a fact that no one can deny: the Egyptian culture that formally does not exist for at least two thousand years, is still virtually alive. It penetrates into an alien (in our case, European) culture and becomes an indispensable part of it.

After the Egyptian campaign of Napoleon the European culture experienced the waves of Egyptomania, in many features similar to those that took place during Roman times. From the end of the 18th until the beginning of the 19th century CE, collecting Egyptian artifacts became a significant element of modern culture. Many tourists charmed by the mysterious land of the pyramids sought after bringing or purchasing on local markets a souvenir from Egypt. With time these small acquisitions became a considerable part of modern museum collections.

II. The Collection

This was the case of the Kiev Museum of Western and Eastern Art, which was founded by Bogdan I. and Varvara N. Khanenko. From his childhood Bogdan Khanenko was particularly interested in art. After entering the Faculty of Law at the Moscow University, he obtained the first pieces of his collection. Khanenko used to visit antiquarian shops, the major European auctions, and in two decades he already owned a very considerable collection: ancient and medieval ceramics, a collection of early Christian crosses and many other objects. But the real pride of Khanenko was his collection of paintings, which included some works of D. Velásquez, P. Brügel, F. Zurbarán, J. Reynolds (and others), and was considered to be the best private picture gallery in the Russian Empire. After his death Khanenko left all his collections, a huge library and a private residence to the city of Kiev, in order to build a Museum named after him and his wife, who passed away five years later, in 1922. Unfortunately after the October revolution all archives related to Khanenko's Museum have disappeared.

Among the collections of B. Khanenko, who felt a special interest for the ancient Egyptian culture, there is a set of about 30 Ancient Egyptian objects. During the Soviet Period the Museum received a number of objects from other institutions, mostly from the Kiev State Historical Museum, and now its collection includes 38 Egyptian objects. Among them are a Pre–Dynastic bowl, four funerary figurines, three pieces of sculpture–in–the–round, a bronze figurine of the god Amūn, a trial piece (stele), a funerary mask of a woman, and different specimens of Coptic textiles.

Despite the small size of the collection it was studied by different scholars[1]. In 1999 the Center for Egyptological Studies of the Russian Academy of Sciences carried out a new survey within the framework of the project *The Databank of Eastern–European Egyptology*[2]. During the study some inaccuracies of the previous publications were revealed. Besides, the epigraphic material —which was generally published only in translations— was properly copied.

For these reasons it seems necessary to present again several of the objects here, as well as to share some observations concerning the Egyptian collection, kept on the B. & V. Khanenko's Museum of Western and Eastern Art in Kiev.

II.1. Funerary Figurines [Figs. 1-2]

Inv. № BV–1331 and BV 1332.
Material: Terracotta, Painted.
Dimensions: H = 15.1 cm (BV–1331) & 15 cm (BV–1332).
Provenance: Unknown.
Date: XIX-XX Dynasties.

* The author would like to thank Galina I. Bilenko and Inna A. Mezian, curators of the Museum, for granting the permission to study the collection and for their kind help during his survey.

[1] Hodjash, S.I. & Etingof, O.E.: *Ancient Egyptian Monuments from the Museums of the USSR* (in Russian), Moscow 1991; Berlev, O.D. & Hodjash, S.I.: *Catalogue of the Monuments of Ancient Egypt from the Museums of the Russian Federation, Ukraine, Bielorussia, Caucasus, Middle Asia and the Baltic States*, Freibourg (*OBO SA*, **17**) 1998.

[2] Detailed information about this project can be found in Ivanov, S.V. 'Databank of Eastern–European Egyptology: The Project and its Prospects', *Ancient Egypt and Antique Europe: Two Parts of the Mediterranean World* (Maravelia, A.-A., ed.), Oxford (*BAR International Series*, **1052**), 2002, 79–81 (for bibliography, see p. 81).

This pair of funerary figurines represents the deceased in the form of a mummy with the unsleeved hands crossed on the chest right over left. The figurines held a hoe in each hand; but due to the poor preservation of objects these implements are not clearly seen. The deceased wears a composite duplex wig (upper part striated, lower part echeloned). The breast of the figurines is decorated with an *wsḫ*–collar in relief; the hands are represented with painted bangles.

The figurines still bear traces of paint, covering the faces (brown), wigs (gray), hoes and armlets (red). The figurines are almost complete. The loses include rubbing of the facial features of BV–1331, as well as a small dent on the right elbow of BV–1332.

Judging by the typical wig and stylistic characteristics of BV–1332 the figurines can be dated back to the Ramesside Period. Despite the absence of inscriptions, it seems most probable that these objects come from the same set of funerary equipment.

Bibliography:

* Berlev & Hodjash: *Catalogue ...* , 117;
* Schneider H.D.: *Shabtis: An Introduction to the History of Ancient Egyptian Funerary Statuettes with a Catalogue of Shabtis in the National Museum of Antiquities at Leiden*, **I-III**, Leiden 1977.

II.2. Statue of Nesnebnetheru [Figs. 4–5]

Inv. № SK–128.
Material: Greywacke.
Dimentions: H = 43 cm, W = 24 cm.
Provenance: Thebes.
Date: XXV Dynasty.
History: Kept in the Collection of K. V. Didenko until 1951.

The statue of Nesnebnetheru is one of the finest pieces of the Museum's collection. It was ordered by an official, who was a chamberlain of the God's wife and also the Ambassador of the Divine Adoratrice in the Land of Nubia.

Nesnebnetheru is represented as a kneeling theophorous, carrying a figure of Osiris. The official is dressed in priestly kilt and wears a composite plain wig.

The base of the statue is inscribed with two offering formulae, beginning at the front and going towards the opposite direction to the back [right side]:

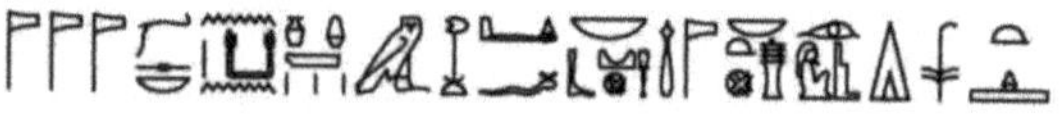

Whose transliteration is:

> *Ḥtp di nsw, ḥtp di Wsir nb Ḏdw{.t}* (sic), *nṯr ꜥꜣ nb ꜣbḏw; di=f ḫꜣ m t ḥnk.t n kꜣ n Ns-nb-nṯr.w [mꜣꜥ ḫrw]*.

The translation of this text is the following:

> *A boon, which the king gives to Osiris, Lord of Busiris, the Great God, Lord of Abydos, (that) he (may) give thousands of loafs and beer to the spirit (kꜣ) of Nesnebnetheru (the justified).*

The left side bears the following inscription:

Whose transliteration is the following:

> *Ḥtp di nsw, ḥtp di Wsir ḫnty-Ỉmn.tt, nṯr ꜥꜣ nb ꜣbḏw; di=f pr.t-ḫrw [m] t, ḥnk.t, kꜣ.w, ꜣpd.w, n kꜣ n Ns-nb-nṯr.w, mꜣꜥ ḫrw.*

The translation of this text goes like this:

> *A boon, which the king gives to Osiris, Foremost of the West (Amenthis), the Great God, Lord of Abydos, (that) he (may) give invocation offerings (consisting of) bread, beer, oxen and fowl to the spirit (kꜣ) of Nesnebnetheru, (the) justified*

The inscription of the back pillar runs as follows:

> *Ỉmꜣḫy ḫr nṯr niw.ty=f, imy-ḫn.t Ḥm.t-Nṯr, Ỉpwty n Dwꜣ.t-Nṯr r Tꜣ-Sti, Ns-nb-nṯr.w*

Whose translation is:

> *Honoured by his city–god, the chamberlain of the God's Wife, the Ambassador of the Divine Adoratrice to the Land of Nubia, Nesnebnetheru.*

The upper part of the Osiris figure is inscribed with two inscriptions [right & left], arranged in two columns:

Right side:

> (1) [*jmꜣḫy ḫr*] *Wsir nb Ḏdw{.t}* (sic) (2) *Ỉmy-ḫn.t Dwꜣ.t-Nṯr, Ns-nb-nṯr.w*

Whose translation is the following:

> (1) *Honoured by Osiris, the Lord of Busiris,* (2) *the chamberlain of the Divine Adoratrice, Nesneb Nesnebnetheru*

Left side:

> (1) [*Ỉmꜣḫ.y ḫr*] *Wsir, Ḫnty-Ỉmn.tt,* (2) *ipwty n Ḥm.t-Nṯr r Tꜣ-Sti, Ns-nb-nṯr.w* (?)[3]

Which is translated as:

> (1) *Honoured by Osiris, Foremost of the Westerners,* (2) *the Ambassador of the God's Wife to the Land of Nubia Nesnebnetheru* (?)

The shoulders of Nesnebnetheru bear two short inscriptions:

Left

Right

[3] The name of Nesnebunetheru is spelled differently here. Oleg D. Berlev suggested that it is a cryptogram, with the signs for 'Thoth' read as '*Nj-sw*', that for 'Amūn' read as '*nb*', and the one for 'stars' written for '*nṯr.w*' (cf. Berlev & Hodjash: *Catalogue ...* , 1998, 60).

Ḥm.t-Nṯr (Dwꜣ.t-Nṯr)[4] *Ỉmn-ỉr-dỉ=s, mꜣꜥ[.t] ḫrw*

Translated as :

The God's Wife (The Divine Adoratrice) Amenirdis, the justified.

Such kind of theophorous statues was exclusively produced during the XXV-XXVI Dynasties[5]. The exact dating can be deduced by the cartouches of Amenirdis I, who was the daughter of Kashta, a ruler of the XXV (Kushite) Dynasty. At the time of the statue's manufacture Amenirdis I was already dead, hence this object can be dated to the reign of Taharqa.

Judging by the inscriptions Nesnebnetheru was a person in attendance of the God's Wife and surely he was given commissions to fulfil in her homeland. Keeping in mind the role that Nubia played in Egyptian politics during the LP, and especially during the XXV Dynasty[6], it is plausible to suggest that Nesnebnetheru was one of the most prominent politicians of his time.

Bibliography:

* Hodjash & Etingof: *Ancient Egyptian Monuments*, 53;
* Berlev & Hodjash: *Catalogue ...* , 60;
* Moss: 'The Statue of an Ambassador ... ', 1960, 269–271.

II.3. Shabti of Dieskhonsu [Fig. 3]

Inv. № BV–1268.
Material: Faience, Pale Blue.
Dimensions: H = 7.3 cm.
Provenance: Theban Necropolis.
Dating: XXVI Dynasty.
History: Discovered in the Village Stavichi (Kiev Region); Kept in Kiev State Historical Museum until 1958.

Though this object was found not far from Kiev, it originates from Thebes, where its owner, Dieskhonsu, served as a prophet of the local god Monthu. The figurine represents the deceased in the form of a mummy with sleeved and curved hands, holding a hoe and a bag, typical of the Saite shabtis[7]. The deceased wears a plain wig with plaited beard, common for the figurines of that same Period[8]. The figurine is incomplete: the legs are broken off.

There is an inscription, beginning on the back of the head (3 horizontal lines) and continued in six (plus one or two) horizontal lines on the body; the latter are separated by a plain back pillar. The inscription runs as follows:

(1) *Ḏd-mdw ỉ[n] Wsỉr* (2) *ḥm-nṯr Mnṯw, nb* (3) *Wꜣs.t, sḥḏ Dỉ=s-Ḫnsw:* (4) *Ỉ wšb.tyw* (5) *ỉpn! Ỉr [ỉ]p.tw{w} Wsỉr Dỉ=s-Ḫnsw*[9] *ỉ* (6) *ỉr.t kꜣ.wt*[10] *n ỉr.t=sn ỉm m* (7) *ḫr.t-nṯr ỉs.tw*[11] *nr sḏb*[12] *ỉm* (8) *=s r.t rtw=f mk.wỉ kꜣ* (9) *=tn ỉp r nw(y) rꜥ-nb…*

Which is translated as:

(1) *Words, said by Osiris* (2) *the Prophet of Mothu, Lord* (3) *of Thebes, the illuminated*[13] *Dieskhnonsu:* (4) *O, these shabtis!* (5) *If Osiris Dieskhonsu is reckoned* (6) *to do the works that have to be done there, in* (7) *the necropolis, indeed, there are obstacles implanted* (8) *(by) a man at his duties. 'Behold, (here) I am!', you shall say,* (9) *(when) you are reckoned; in the course of every day!*

Here is the inscription on the shabti of Dieskhonsu:

Bibliography:

* Hodjash & Etingof: *Ancient Egyptian Monuments*, 60;
* Berlev & Hodjash: *Catalogue ...* , 96;
* Schneider: *Shabtis*, **I-III**, 1977.

II.4. Statue of Thoth as a Cynocephalus [Fig. 6]

Inv. № SK–44.
Material: Basalt.
Dimensions: H = 52 cm, W = 27 cm, L = 26 cm.
Provenance: Unknown.
Dating: LP.
History: B.I. Khanenko's Collection, bought in Paris.

B. Khanenko was especially interested in the sacred knowledge of the ancient Egyptians. That is why this statue of Thoth in the form of a baboon was his favorite piece.

The divine animal is presented in the usual iconography, sitting with his hands on his lap. The high level of craftsmanship and the treatment of the surface are typical of the LP statuary.

---

[4] R. Moss did not mark the difference between the cartouches (Moss, R.: 'The Statue of an Ambassador to Ethiopia at Kiev', *Kush*, **VIII**, 1960, 270); O. Berlev read *ḥm.t-nṯr* as *Rꜥ.t* (?) (cf. Berlev & Hodjash: *Catalogue*..., 1998, 60.

[5] Bothmer, B.: *Egyptian Sculpture of the Late Period 700 BC to AD 100*, NY 1960, 3–4.

[6] Kitchen, K.A.: *The Third Intermediate Period in Egypt (1100–650 BC)*, Warminster [2]1995, 378-98; Myśliwiec, K.: *The Twilight of Ancient Egypt: First Millenium B.C.E.*, Ithaca & London 2000, 68–109.

[7] Schneider: *Shabtis*, **II**, 1977, 171ff.

[8] Schneider: *Shabtis*, **II**, 1977, 165ff.

[9] The spelling of this line is rather unusual; the suggested reading is the typical formula *ỉr ỉp.tw Wsr N*. Cf. Schneider: *Shabtis* , **III**, 1997, fig. 5 (VII.A).

[10] The *ỉ*, beginning the line, seems to be superfluous.

[11] The last sign of the group *ỉs.t(w)* is not clear.

[12] Note the use of *nrỉ* instead of *ḥwỉ*.

[13] Oleg Berlev has missed the *sḥḏ* signs in his translation (cf. Berlev & Hodjash: *Catalogue*..., 1998, 96).

The breast and the belly of the baboon are concave as if a round object (like a vessel or may be a clepsydra[14]) was put in front of the baboon. There is one more peculiarity, which is worth mentioning here. The frontal part of the base (as well as the baboon's feet) is broken off. The chip is marked with two round cavities, measuring about 1 cm in diameter and 2.5 cm in depth. These might be done to attach the round object mentioned above. On the other hand, these penetrations could have been made for some other reason at a much later era.

There is an exact copy of this figure kept in the Museo Gregoriano Egizio Vaticano (Inv. № 193)[15]. The statue is made in the same manner, though it is put on a much thinner base. Most probably these statues come from the same set ordered as a donation to the temple of Thoth.

Bibliography:

* Turaev, B.A.: *A Description of Egyptian Monuments in the Russian Museums and Collections* [in Russian: *Тураев Б.А.* Описание египетских памятников в русских собраниях // Записки Одесского общества истории и древностей], *Zapiski Vostochnogo Otdelenija Imperatorskogo Russikogo Archeologicheskogo Obschestva*, **XII**, St. Peterburg, 1900, 217;
* Hodjash & Etingof: *Ancient Egyptian Monuments*, 58;
* Berlev & Hodjash: *Catalogue* ... , 77–78.

II.5. Electrotype Copies

During the study of the collection of bronzes, kept in the Museum of Western and Eastern Art, it was found out that three out of four bronze figurines turned to be electrotype copies. The replicas of two figurines of Osiris (Inv. № BV–1336 and BV–1338)[16], as well as the statuette of Ptah (Inv. № 1356)[17], were probably ordered by B.I. Khanenko from some of the European collections.

III. Conclusion

In 1998-2002 the Center for Egyptological Studies has performed surveys of 14 Egyptian collections kept on the territory of the former Soviet Union. All the data were processed in the Databank of Eastern–European Egyptology. The main goal of the databank is to provide the information necessary for scientific research and study. We hope that in the nearest future the Databank will become a network, joining different institutions and scholars. This paper presents the results of the international project called *The Databank of Eastern–European Egyptology*, carried out by the Center for Egyptological Studies of the Russian Academy of Sciences (Moscow) and the Gnosarch Foundation (Basel). The subject of this article was the Egyptian collection, kept in Bogdan I. & Varvara N. Khanenko's Museum of Western and Eastern Art in Kiev. The major part of the collection was gathered by Khanenko, who purchased Egyptian objects in European auctions during the 1910s. The collection includes objects dating from the Pre–Dynastic Period until the Medieval Epoch: a vessel, private sculpture, funerary figurines and different specimens of textiles. This paper is a survey of the collection and an updated publication of several objects belonging therein.

[14] ***Editor's Note:*** This seems indeed a good guess; for similar objects, see for instance Pogo, A.: 'Egyptian Waterclocks', *Isis*, **25**, 1936, 403-25.

[15] This observation was first made by B. Turaev (Turaev: *Description* ..., 217) with reference to Massi, J. *Description des Musées de sculpture antique*, Rome 1891, 217. The most recent publication of the Vatican piece is can be found in Botti, G. & Romanelli, P.: *Le sculpture del Museo Gregoriano Egizio Vaticano*, Vaticano 1951, 48 & tav. XLII.

[16] Berlev & Hodjash: *Catalogue* ... , 1998, 73 & tab. 100, 101.

[17] Berlev & Hodjash: *Catalogue* ... , 1998, 76.

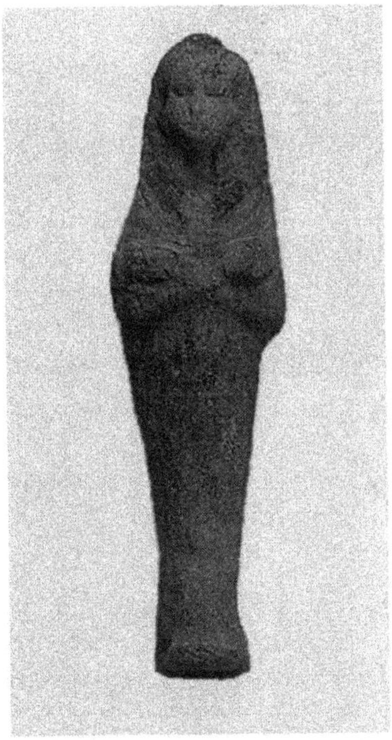

FIGURE 1. Funerary figurine Inv. № BV–1331 [photo by the author].

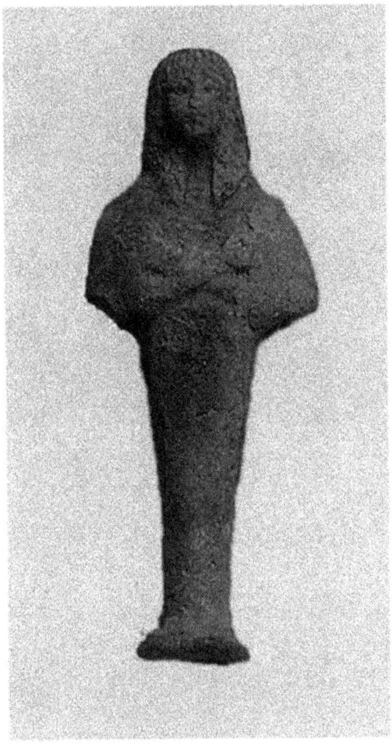

FIGURE 2. Funerary figurine Inv. № BV–1332 [photo by the author].

FIGURE 3. Shabti of Dieskonsu Inv. № BV–1268 [photo by the author].

FIGURE 4. Statue of Nesnebnetheru, Inv. № SK–128 [photo by the author].
© Copyright Dr S.V. Ivanov, 2003.

FIGURE 5. Statue of Nesnebnetheru, Inv. № SK–128 [photos by the author].

FIGURE 6. Statue of the god Thoth in the form of baboon, Inv. № SK–44 [photo by the author].
© Copyright Dr S.V. Ivanov, 2003.

La Musique Copte

Ashraf–Alexandre Sadek

Abstract

Si nous présentons ici un article sur le thème assez général de la musique Copte[1], c'est parce qu'elle est l'un des lieux de communion entre la culture hellénique et la culture égyptienne antiques, et qu'elle manifeste entre elles une influence réciproque et harmonieuse, comme un chant responsorial. Si l'influence hellénique, en particulier au niveau du langage et de l'usage de certaines hymnes, est évidente, il reste à étudier de façon approfondie l'influence Copte sur la musique hellénique. Nous espérons que cet article, en rappelant les données de base en ce domaine, incitera des chercheurs et musiciens à développer ces recherches.

KEY WORDS: Coptic Era, Coptic Egypt, Coptic Music, Coptic Church, Ecclesiastical Hymns, Musical Instruments, Ancient Pharaonic Music.

I. Introduction

I.1 L'Église Copte Orthodoxe

Évangélisée au premier siècle par Saint Marc, l'Égypte fut l' un des premiers pays christianisés. L'*Église d'Alexandrie* (également appelée *Église Copte*[2] ou *Église d'Égypte*), *Copte* signifiant *égyptien*, a joué un rôle essentiel dans l'histoire de la chrétienté: sur le plan théologique, à travers l'Ecole d'Alexandrie et la littérature Copte et copto–arabe du Moyen Age, et sur le plan spirituel par la naissance et l'extraordinaire expansion du monachisme. Elle a donné à la chrétienté de très grands saints, de remarquables théologiens et pères de l'Église, ainsi que de nombreux martyrs.

L'Église Copte orthodoxe appartient au groupe des anciennes Eglises orientales non–chalcédoniennes. Son *Credo*, défini en 325 au Concile de Nicée, est celui de saint Athanase (devenu par la suite 20ème Pape–Patriarche d'Alexandrie), et elle professe depuis les origines sa foi en la divinité et en l'humanité de la personne unique du Christ, Dieu fait homme. Après avoir subi sous Dioclétien (245-313 BCE) des persécutions telles que son calendrier débute avec l'avènement de cet empereur (284 CE) et porte le nom d'*ère des martyrs*, l'Église d'Égypte, à la suite d'une controverse théologique et de différends politiques, a connu à nouveau des persécutions, cette fois de la part de l'Église Byzantine, et un certain isolement par rapport au reste de la chrétienté. La conquête musulmane en 641 a marqué le début de nouvelles persécutions, la régression du christianisme au profit de l'islam, l'interdiction progressive de la langue Copte, l'instauration d'un statut de *dhimmis* (= citoyens de seconde zone, *dhimmis* signifiant *protégés* et désignant les non–musulmans); en dépit de tout cela, l'Église d'Égypte s'est maintenue à travers les siècles sous la souveraineté musulmane, et demeure encore de nos jours la plus importante communauté chrétienne dans un pays dont la religion d'état est l'islam.

Cette situation d'isolement et d'autarcie a fait de l'Église Copte un véritable conservatoire cultuel, linguistique et musical: elle utilise encore de nos jours dans sa liturgie des rites extrêmement anciens, notamment la langue Copte, qui est une forme de l'égyptien pharaonique transcrite en caractères helléniques et une musique qui a, elle aussi, véhiculé des éléments de la musique et des traditions musicales de l'Égypte ancienne des pharaons.

I.2. La Langue Copte

Dès le 2ème siècle avant notre ère, les Egyptiens transcrivirent leur langue écrite en hiéroglyphes en caractères helléniques, y ajoutant sept caractères correspondant à des sons purement égyptiens. C'est donc (aussi) en étudiant le Copte parlé, auprès d'un prêtre Copte rentré à Marseille avec l'expédition de Napoléon, que Champollion a pu trouver la clé du déchiffrement des hiéroglyphes. La langue Copte a été parlée en Égypte jusqu'au 13ème siècle; il existe une riche et abondante littérature Copte, actuellement en cours d'étude. Grâce à sa grande fidélité à ses origines, l'Église Copte a maintenu la pratique de cette langue, tout en introduisant dès le 10ème siècle des éléments de liturgie en arabe.

Langue très musicale, le Copte se prête de façon remarquable aux mélodies liturgiques, au point que Ragheb Moftah, l'ancien directeur du département de musique à l'Institut des Études Coptes a pu dire: «Si le français est la langue de la poésie et l'italien la langue de la musique, le Copte, lui, est la langue de la prière ».

I.3. La Liturgie Copte

L'Église d'Égypte utilise le plus souvent la liturgie de Saint Basile et, certains jours de fête, la liturgie de Saint Grégoire; la liturgie de Saint Cyrille, la «plus égyptienne» des trois, a été en partie perdue. Ces liturgies sont entièrement chantées: le prêtre officiant, le diacre et le chœur (composé également de diacres, et accompagné de l'assemblée) se répondent. Seul le *Credo* et le *Notre Père* sont généralement récités. Ces liturgies sont précédées du rite de l'élévation de l'encens, rite qui est propre à l'Église Copte et qui se déroule le matin. En arabe ce rite est appelé *Raf'Bukhur Bakir*.

Outre la Divine Liturgie, la communauté Copte possède un riche patrimoine spirituel et musical grâce à la *Prière des Heures*, ouvrage qui est aussi nommé *Hōrologion* (*Agbeya* en arabe). Il s'agit des sept offices quotidiens qui règlent la journée des convers et des moines, offices qui existent aussi en Occident. Les moines y ajoutent une prière: la prière du voile. Durant ces offices, des psaumes attribués à chaque jour sont récités mais certains y incluent des hymnes appelées *Psalmōdia* (ou *Psalies*) chantées en langue Copte. Ces hymnes sont chantées par des laïcs, qui se mettent face à face des deux côtés du sanctuaire et se répondent: c'est un chant res-

[1] C'est grâce à l'insistance du père André Gouzes et de Michel Wolkowitsky, de l'Abbaye de Sylvanès, que j'ai fini par rassembler les notes que j'avais accumulées sur ce sujet, et qui ont abouti à cet article; qu'ils soient remerciés ici! Je remercie aussi particulièrement Mademoiselle Emmanuelle Lemasson pour la relecture de cet article et pour ses suggestions de musicienne, également étudiante en Égyptologie.

[2] Cf. MALATY, 1993 (voir bibliographie).

ponsorial. Les célèbres *Théotokies* Coptes (louanges à la Vierge Marie) appartiennent à la *Psalmōdia*. Dans les monastères la *Psalmōdia* est quotidienne; elle n'est qu'hebdomadaire pour les laïcs et a lieu en général le Samedi soir. En plus de ces psaumes la liturgie comporte vingt-et-un cantiques tirés de la *Bible* ou des écrits *Apocryphes*, qui sont chantés à certaines occasions, en particulier le soir du Vendredi Saint; deux de ces cantiques sont en Copte: le *Chant de Moise* (*Ex.*, 15: 1-21) et le *Chant des trois jeunes gens dans la fournaise* (*Dn.*, après 3: 1-67); les dix-neuf autres cantiques sont en arabe.

II. La Musique Copte

La musique Copte est une musique sacrée, essentiellement composée de chants liturgiques.

II.1. Une Musique trop longtemps Ignorée

La musique liturgique Copte n'a été étudiée que très récemment, seulement depuis une cinquantaine d'années, et pourtant elle a été connue en Occident dès le 18ème siècle, grâce à l'expédition d'Égypte de Bonaparte, qui se déroula durant les années 1798-99. Bonaparte emmena avec lui en Égypte toute une équipe de savants dont Guillaume–André Villoteau (1759-1839). Villoteau a écrit sur la musique Copte dans *La Description de l'Égypte*, parue à Paris de 1809 à 1826. Pour lui cette musique n'était qu'une succession de voyelles et de sons étranges qui la rendaient affreusement désagréable à son oreille[3]. Il relate d'ailleurs le fait qu'il ne reconnut pas un «Alleluia» qu'avait chanté un moine, il essaya néanmoins d' en faire une transcription qui se révéla par la suite être fausse. L'incompréhension de Villoteau face à la musique Copte eut pour conséquence de mettre dans l'ombre pendant plus de 50 ans la musique Copte. Certains tentèrent de la faire sortir de l'ombre comme Joseph Fétis (1784-1871) qui a essayé de comprendre la musique d'Égypte; il a notamment mis en valeur l'utilisation des vocalises dans les chants coptes[4].

Il a fallu attendre le 20e siècle pour voir de nouvelles études sur cette musique si riche et si ancienne. La musique fut étudiée de façon plus approfondie, grâce à la création de l'Institut des Hautes Etudes Coptes, dont le Département de musicologie fut dirigé par Ragheb Moftah de 1954 à sa mort durant l'année 2000. Cet érudit passa sa vie à faire découvrir, enregistrer et préserver ce patrimoine musical unique au monde. Il le fit notamment avec le musicologue anglais Newland-smith. Ils entreprirent dans les années '30 de noter et d'enregistrer, selon la méthode du musicien hongrois Béla Bartòk, les chants liturgiques coptes; méthode que Béla Bartòk avait mise au point en enregistrant les chants populaires des paysans à l'aide d'un phonographe. Les musicologues se sont servis de sa méthode pour écouter plus lentement les chants afin de pouvoir noter ce que les Occidentaux appellent des ornementations, mais qui (dans la musique Copte) est l'un des traits caractéristique des chants.

Aujourd'hui toute la liturgie de saint Basile a été transcrite en écriture occidentale dans un certain ouvrage[5].

II.2. La Musique Liturgique Copte et ses Instruments

Dans le monde hellénistique et alexandrin la musique n'était pas considérée seulement comme un divertissement mais comme un pan important de l'éducation[6]. Les pères de l'Église, dont beaucoup furent en contact avec les courants de pensée alexandrins, ont réfléchi sur les diverses formes de musique et leur rôle liturgique.

Certains pensaient, comme Clément d'Alexandrie, que l'usage liturgique de la *lyra* et la *kithara* (la cithare) était rendu légitime par le fait que le roi David les utilisait dans le chant de ses psaumes. Clément d'Alexandrie n'admettait pas en revanche l'usage d'instruments qui, d'après les recherches, étaient utilisés en Égypte ancienne comme les trompettes, les tambourins, les timbales ou les flûtes. D'autre part, il considérait la voix humaine comme étant la seule capable et digne de communiquer parfaitement avec Dieu: «Il chante lui, mon Eunome[7], non pas selon les modes Phrygien, Lydien ou Dorien, mais selon le mode éternel de la nouvelle harmonie, qui porte le nom de Dieu ... »[8].

Origène (185-254) accordait à chaque instrument une spiritualité différente: pour lui, la trompette était le Verbe de Dieu, le tambourin luttait contre la luxure et les cymbales exprimaient l'esprit d'amour du Christ.

Basile de Césarée, comme Clément d'Alexandrie, place la voix humaine au-dessus des instruments, et donne à cela une raison théologique: «Comme l'Esprit Saint porte dans son souffle le Verbe de Dieu, de même le chant est ce souffle qui, par sa douceur transcendante, introduit la Parole dans le cœur des hommes ... Seule la voix humaine est digne de répondre au Verbe de Dieu, et le chœur qui chante «d'une seule âme» est la plus adéquate expression du peuple de Dieu uni au chœur des anges».

Désormais seulement deux instruments seront utilisés dans la liturgie de l'Église d'Égypte: les *cymbales*[9] et le *triangle*; les chrétiens d'Ethiopie, enfants de l'Église Copte, ont également gardé l'usage des ces instruments, avec —en plus— le *sistre*.

II.3. Influences et Origines

Trois grandes traditions musicales ont pu contribuer, à des degrés divers, à la formation de la musique Copte.

II.3.1. Influence Juive

Elle se situe plus au niveau de la liturgie et des textes que de la musique; de nombreux textes de l'Ancien Testament, en particulier le Psautier, le Sanctus et peut-être la bénédiction juive, sont utilisés par les Coptes. Sur le plan mélodique en revanche, aucune filiation n'a pu être établie à ce jour, mais il semble en revanche que l'Égypte ait musicalement influencé la liturgie juive.

II.3.2. Influence Hellénique

L'Ecole d'Alexandrie, l'un des centres du monde hellénistique, a produit parmi les Egyptiens hellénisés, de grands théo-

---

[3] Cf. GILESPIE, 1978: 230.

[4] *Ibid*, 231.

[5] *The Coptic Orthodox Liturgy of St Basil*, Cairo (The AUC Press) 1998.

[6] Cf. BELIS, 1999: 15-16.

[7] Chanteur.

[8] Clément d'Alexandrie, *Proteptique*, I, § 2-3, dans Valentin, 64-65.

[9] Mentionnées en *Ps. 150* et *I Cor.* 13, 1.

riciens et enseignants de la musique: Didyme d'Alexandrie, le Pseudo–Dimitri de Phalème, Claudius Ptolémée, Alypios d'Alexandrie. Les plus anciens manuscrits helléniques de notation musicale ont été retrouvés en Égypte. C'est le cas des premiers chants chrétiens et pré–chrétiens. Le plus ancien manuscrit contenant un chant pré–chrétien est actuellement conservé au musée du Caire: il date du milieu du 3e siècle BCE; il s'agit du *Papyrus Zēnōn N° 59532*. Un autre texte a aussi été retrouvé en Égypte, datant du milieu du 3ème siècle CE: le *Papyrus Oxyrhynchus 1786*. C'est le plus ancien exemple connu d'une mélodie chrétienne. Il est possible qu' un répertoire commun entre les Eglises Hellénique et Copte ait pu exister; là encore, si de nombreux textes sont certainement communs comme le *Trisagion*, les mélodies, elles semblent avoir préservé des traditions bien distinctes. Ce domaine d'étude est encore peu exploré.

II.3.3. Influence de la Musique de l'Égypte Ancienne

La clé du mystère de la musique pharaonique se trouve dans une bonne édition de la musique ecclésiastique Copte en usage de nos jours (Abbé et Égyptologue Étienne Drioton).

Nous savons avec certitude que la musique de l'Égypte ancienne[10] [Fig. 1] continuait à être pratiquée dans les temples pharaoniques et les zones rurales d'Égypte bien après le début du christianisme, malgré une forte influence hellénique dans les milieux urbains.

Des liens ont été établis par les chercheurs entre certaines prières chrétiennes comme le *Kyrie* ou les litanies des saints, et des prières de l'Égypte ancienne. D'après Baumstark[11], une forme litanique trouvée dans une prière à Isis contenue dans le *Papyrus Oxyrhynchus 1380* ressemblerait à certains chants litaniques; dans des textes du Moyen Empire, notamment *Les chants d'Isis et Nephthys*[12], on reconnaît des chants antiphonaires coptes. Les chants antiphonaires sont encore l'une des caractéristiques majeures de la musique Copte. Ils étaient également pratiqués par la communauté des Thérapeutes, qui vivait près d'Alexandrie au premier siècle BCE. Une autre caractéristique de la musique Copte pouvant avoir une origine pharaonique est l'usage des vocalises et mélismes, attesté au Moyen Empire et dans les textes gnostiques. Les anciens textes semblent être construis sur sept voyelles particulières et cette construction des mélodies se retrouve dans les chants coptes[13].

Selon Hérodote, la tradition des mélodies pathétiques remonte aux rites funéraires royaux des anciens Egyptiens. La communauté Copte est très attachée à ces mélodies par lesquelles elle commémore la Passion du Christ, et qui suscitent en elle beaucoup d'émotion.

L'influence pharaonique se retrouve encore dans certaines traditions; par exemple le service liturgique est souvent accompli par des chanteurs professionnels aveugles. Le thème du harpiste aveugle a été longuement étudié en ce qui concerne l'Égypte Ancienne et cela a perduré malgré le temps [Fig. 2]; cette tradition s'est transmise également chez les Egyptiens musulmans. L'Égypte des pharaons est également présente grâce aux percussions qui perdurent dans la musique Copte comme les *castagnettes* ou le *triangle*, qui n'est qu' une forme simplifiée du *sistre hathorique* (*zšš.t*). Enfin, certains chants folkloriques des paysans égyptiens ont des mélodies et des rythmes similaires à ceux de la musique Copte. Il y là encore un immense terrain d'étude.

II.4. Transmission

Les études réalisées récemment attestent la fiabilité de la tradition orale en Égypte, particulièrement en ce qui concerne la musique de l'Église Copte.

Certains chercheurs, comme Hans Hickmann, ont avancé l' hypothèse que des moyens mnémoniques remontant à la IVe dynastie pharaonique seraient encore en usage chez les Coptes. Il semble, en effet, que les chefs de chœurs de l'Ancienne Égypte utilisaient la *chironomie* [voir Fig. 1], c'est-à-dire qu'ils guidaient les chanteurs avec leurs doigts pour donner des consignes précises sur les notes et le rythme. Selon Ragheb Moftah, un chanteur Copte peut en effet également utiliser ses doigts pour donner des indications aux autres, mais il procède alors selon un système strictement individuel et non reçu d'une tradition définie. La transmission par la chironomie semble être alors une piste assez mince pour expliquer la fidèle transmission des chants à travers les siècles. Cela reste possible malgré tout car ils devaient nécessairement transmettre leur savoir par un moyen accessible à tous et qui ne pouvait être corrompu d'aucune manière, même si les gestes chironomiques actuellement en usage dans le chant Copte semblent plus destinés à établir un rythme qu'à déterminer les mouvements d'une mélodie donnée.

Ce n'est qu'au 20ème siècle que divers chercheurs tentèrent de noter la musique Copte avec le système occidental. Au 20ème siècle, le professeur Copte Ragheb Moftah entreprit, à l'Institut des Etudes Coptes, l'enregistrement systématique des hymnes et mélodies; il a pu ensuite établir des transcriptions, avec l'aide de spécialistes internationaux: le britannique Ernest Newlandsmith, l'allemand Hans Hickmann, les hongroises Ilona Borsai et Margit Toth, l'américaine Marian Robertson et le français René Ménard, qui découvrit qu'en passant les enregistrements au ralenti, il pouvait noter certains ornements en s'aidant pour cela des anciennes notations du chant grégorien, plus adaptées que le système occidental actuel.

Tous les chercheurs s'accordent sur le fait que la tradition musicale Copte s'est maintenue de façon remarquablement continue depuis ses origines, ce qui semble être un trait du peuple égyptien si une analogie est faite avec les canons de l'art égyptien qui n'ont pratiquement pas changé durant toute la période pharaonique exception partielle faite de l'époque amarnienne. Platon relate dans le second livre des Lois[14] que les Egyptiens ne devaient pas toucher et changer les canons de l'art y compris de la musique. Par conséquent la musique Copte, pour Hans Hickmann, constitue un lien vivant entre le passé et le présent.

II.5. Formes Musicales

D'après René Ménard et Ilona Borsai il est possible de classifier les chants coptes selon leurs structures en ce qui con-

[10] Cf. MANNICHE, 1991.

[11] Cf. art. «Coptic Music», 1732 (voir bibliographie).

[12] Cf. par exemple VERNUS, 1992: 101-19 & 193-99.

[13] Cf. HICKMANN, 1987: 80-81.

[14] 656^C; ouvrage paru aux éditions des Belles-Lettres, Paris, 1968, 43-44.

cerne les prières et les échanges entre les participants, qu'ils soient laïcs ou religieux.

Les formes musicales sont assez proches des autres Eglises orientales primitives comme l'utilisation de la litanie qui puiserait ses origines dans les temps pharaoniques et qui est utilisée dans les prières de demande ou d'intercession. Le chant responal, lui, est un dialogue entre le chœur des religieux ou la congrégation et le soliste, forme utilisée pour l'Évangile, quelques hymnes et la communion. La forme antiphonaire, quant à elle, est définie comme un dialogue entre deux parties du chœur des religieux, parfois elle peut demander la participation de laïcs notamment dans les *Psalies* dont le premier verset, porté par un lecteur, est ensuite prolongé par le chantre sur une mélodie ornée tandis que les versets suivants sont chantés alternativement par les deux parties du chœur. Les hymnes sont particulièrement employées pour les *Theotokies*, les chants pour la Mère de Dieu.

II.6. Aspects Techniques

Le chant Copte (comme le chant Byzantin), contrairement aux chants religieux grégoriens, n'est pas polyphonique mais monodique. Il est chanté *a capella* uniquement par des voix masculines et accompagné parfois de percussions telles que le triangle ou la cymbale. Les tonalités et les modes de la musique orientale ne se retrouvent pas dans le chant Copte, les intervalles sont souvent constitués de *tons* et de *demi–tons*; cependant les intervalles neutres existent, comme dans la musique arabe, mais avec des combinaisons qui n'apparaissent pas dans celle-ci.

Les demi–tons au sein des mélodies sont souvent *diatoniques*. L'*ambitus* est en général de cinq tons, avec la progression suivante: demi–ton/ton/demi–ton, aussi bien en montant qu'en descendant. Des *intervalles de tierces* existent dans la ligne mélodique, bien que la distinction entre les tierces majeures et mineures ne soit pas aussi claire que dans la musique occidentale. La seconde augmentée est rare, alors que la quarte diminuée est fréquente. Certaines fractions de ton comme les quarts de ton et les autres multiples sont d'usage extrêmement courant dans le chant Copte. L'utilisation de ces fractions de ton permet de déplacer presque imperceptiblement le centre tonal de la mélodie, ce centre tonal étant un équivalant de notre tonalité occidentale, parfois d'une tierce mineure ou même plus. Ces intervalles, comme les quarts de ton, ne peuvent être exécutés sur un instrument à clavier comme le piano ou l'orgue mais il est possible de les jouer sur des instruments à cordes frottées. Ces *micro–intervalles* ont été utilisés en Occident seulement au 20ème siècle comme musique expérimentale. En Orient ces intervalles font partie du patrimoine culturel comme en atteste les théories musicales arabes avec des octaves, un intervalle de huit notes divisé en vingt-quatre quarts[15].

Le chant Copte peut être caractérisé de plusieurs manières. *La première*, qui constitue certainement un héritage très ancien, est la prolongation d'une voyelle simple comme le son *a* pendant plusieurs phrases musicales variables en longueur et en complexité. Ceci peut se faire sous forme de vocalises, lorsque la voyelle est prolongée selon un rythme défini, ou de mélismes lorsque le rythme du chant de la voyelle est libre et indéfini. Le mélisme dure de dix à vingt secondes, tandis que la vocalise peut s'étendre sur une minute entière (exemple: le *Trisagion* du Vendredi Saint). *La deuxième* caractéristique de la musique Copte est le fait que les phrases musicales ne correspondent pas toujours aux phrases du texte chanté; ainsi, dans certaines hymnes, une cadence conclusive peut survenir même au beau milieu d'un mot. Ceci se produit en général lors des mélismes et des vocalises. Il en existe des exemples dans la liturgie de Saint Basile.

II.7. Types de Mélodies

Les Occidentaux ont longtemps cru que le chant Copte était composé de longues improvisations; les études récentes ont mis au contraire en évidence des structures bien définies, qu'il est possible de classer en trois grandes catégories.

La première catégorie concerne les chants composés de petites phrases formant des sortes de périodes facilement identifiables qui sont au nombre de trois ou quatre, et répétées avec quelques variations. Ce type de mélodies s'achève par une cadence définie. Les longues vocalises et les mélismes appartiennent à cette catégorie. Le chant *Shere Maria* en est un tel exemple [voir Fig. 3(a)].

La deuxième catégorie concerne, elle, les mélodies composées de longues phrases individuelles, complètes, dont la répétition sous forme de strophes ou de refrain suffit à élaborer des hymnes entières. C'est le cas de l'hymne *Golgotha* [voir Fig. 4].

La dernière catégorie se rapporte à certains chants qui sont constitués de lignes mélodiques et de rythmes simplifiés. Cela leur permet de suivre l'inflexion et le rythme du texte parlé. Ces mélodies sont souvent syllabiques et leur ambitus n'est que de deux ou trois tons; ex: le *Psaume 150* [voir Fig. 3(b)].

Les livres liturgiques et les manuscrits donnent, au moyen d' une terminologie très particulière, des indications sur la façon dont les textes doivent être chantés. Il existe différents types de mélodies, dont les plus courants sont *Adam* et *Batos*. Ces termes correspondent aux premiers mots des *Theotokies* du mois de *Kiyahk*, la première étant une méditation sur Adam, la seconde sur Moïse au Buisson Ardent, *batos* signifiant en Copte *buisson* (provenant de la langue hellénique). Elles se différencient par leur structure poétique, leur longueur et leur mode; il existe d'autres types de mélodies portant chacune un nom qui permet au chantre et aux chœurs de se repérer. Les hymnes classées *Adam* se chantent du dimanche au Mardi, celles appelées *Batos* sont utilisées le Vendredi et le Samedi

Le ton est également indiqué: joyeux ou pathétique, pénitentiel. Les mélodies du Grand Carême et de la Semaine Sainte ont un style pathétique très particulier, considéré par les spécialistes comme l'expression la plus ancienne et la plus sublime de la musique Copte.

III. Conclusion: L'Évolution Actuelle de la Pratique Musicale Copte

Malgré les dernières recherches effectuées sur la musique de l'Église Copte, il reste encore un immense terrain d'études

[15] DE CANDE, 1978: 155-158.

pour expliquer la transmission des textes, faire des enregistrements et des transcriptions.

L'Église d'Égypte connaît depuis une cinquantaine d'années un renouveau spectaculaire dans tous les domaines: monachisme, spiritualité, enseignement de la langue Copte, écoles du Dimanche (développement de la catéchèse), iconographie, architecture, littérature; naturellement, la musique est également concernée par ce renouveau. Deux tendances y apparaissent:

Une tendance conservatrice: les «puristes» de la musique Copte, parmi lesquels d'excellents musiciens, veillent à préserver l'héritage musical dans toute sa pureté, et à le transmettre tel quel; cette tendance est privilégiée par l'Église, et les Grands Séminaires continuent à former des chantres selon les méthodes et les usages traditionnels.

Une tendance plus moderne: les jeunes Coptes souhaitent rendre leur musique liturgique plus accessible aux chrétiens du 21ème siècle; on voit donc apparaître des tentatives d'harmonisation, de polyphonie, l'introduction d'accompagnement sur divers instruments, & c. Certaines de ces tentatives, un peu «anarchiques», dénaturent profondément la musique liturgique, suscitant des réactions de rejet de la part des conservateurs. En revanche, deux groupes de musiciens ont mérité une reconnaissance nationale et internationale, en raison de la qualité musicale de leurs interprétations et de l'intérêt de celles-ci pour l'évolution actuelle de la musique Copte: il s'agit de l'*Ensemble David*, dirigé par Georges Kyrollos, et de l'*Egyptian Coptic Choir*, dirigé par Usama Asham.

Souhaitons que la musique Copte sache prendre le tournant du 21ème siècle en préservant sa force, puisée dans son enracinement plusieurs fois millénaire, tout en restant l'expression vivante de la foi d'une communauté jeune et ouverte sur la modernité.

IV. Sources et Bibliographie Choisie

Ouvrages Généraaux

DE CANDE, ROLAND: *Histoire universelle de la musique*, **I**, Paris (Seuil) 1978.

CANNUYER CHRISTIAN: *Les Coptes* Belgique (Brepols) 1990.

Art. «Music, Coptic», *The Coptic Encyclopedia* (sous la direction d'Aziz S. Atiya), **VI**, London (MacMillan) 1991.

Le Monde Copte, Nos 1–32 , Limoges 1977-99.

Ouvrages Specialisés

BELIS, ANNIE: *Les musiciens dans l'Antiquité*, Paris (La vie quotidienne / Hachette) 1999.

BORSAI, ILONA: «Métrique et mélodie dans les Théotokies coptes», *Studia Musicologica Academia Scientarum Hungaricae*, **22**, 1980, 15-60.

GILLESPIE, JOHN: «Coptic Chant», *The Future of Coptic Studies*, Leiden (Brill / *Coptic Studies*, **1**) 1978.

HICKMANN, HANS: *Musicologie pharaonique*, Baden–Baden 1987.

LAGRANGE, FRÉDÉRIC: *Musiques d'Égypte*, Cité de la Musique (Actes Sud) 1996.

MALATY, T.Y.: *Introduction to the Coptic Orthodox Church*, Cairo 1993.

MANNICHE, LISE: *Music and Musicians in Ancient Egypt*, London (BMP) 1991.

VALENTIN, PIERRE: *Clément d'Alexandrie: Église d'hier et d'aujourd'hui*, Paris (Les éditions ouvrières) 1963.

VERNUS, PASCAL: «Les stances de la cérémonie des deux oiselles–milan», *Chants d'amour de l'Égypte Antique*, Paris (Imprimerie Nationale) 1992, 101-19 & 193-99.

FIGURE 1. Exemple d'un chironome ancien appelé Iti (*Iti*), dirigeant la harpiste appelée Hekenu (*Ḥknw*).
Relief du temple de Saqqara, datant de la Ve Dynastie, au Musée du Caire (CG 1414), d'après MANNICHE, 1991, 121: fig. 73.

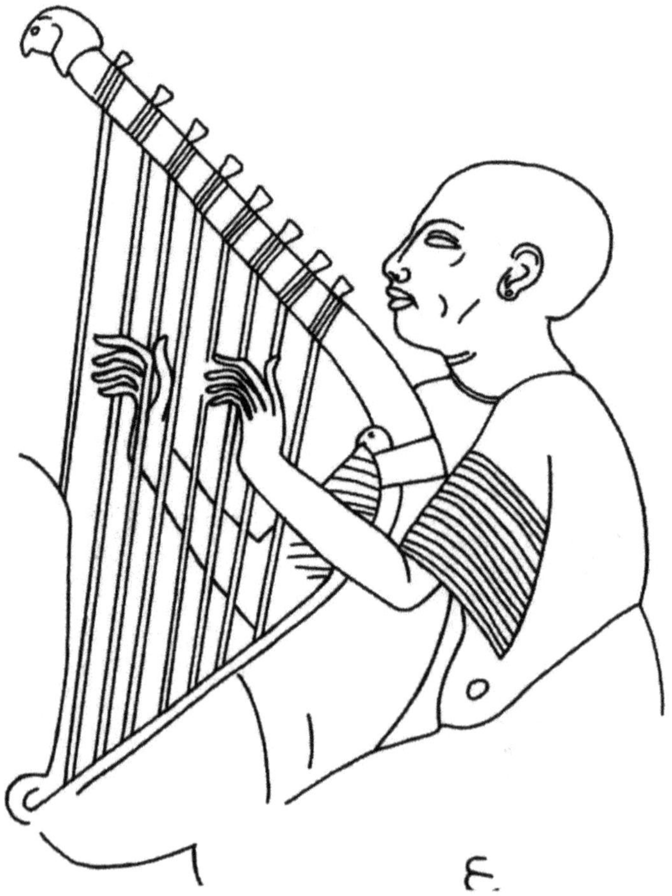

FIGURE 2. Un harpiste aveugle, jouant son instrument. Tombe de Paitenemheb (*P3-Itn-m-ḥb*) à Saqqara, datant de la XVIIIe Dynastie, au Musée van Oudheden à Leiden, d'après MANNICHE, 1991, 95: fig. 57.

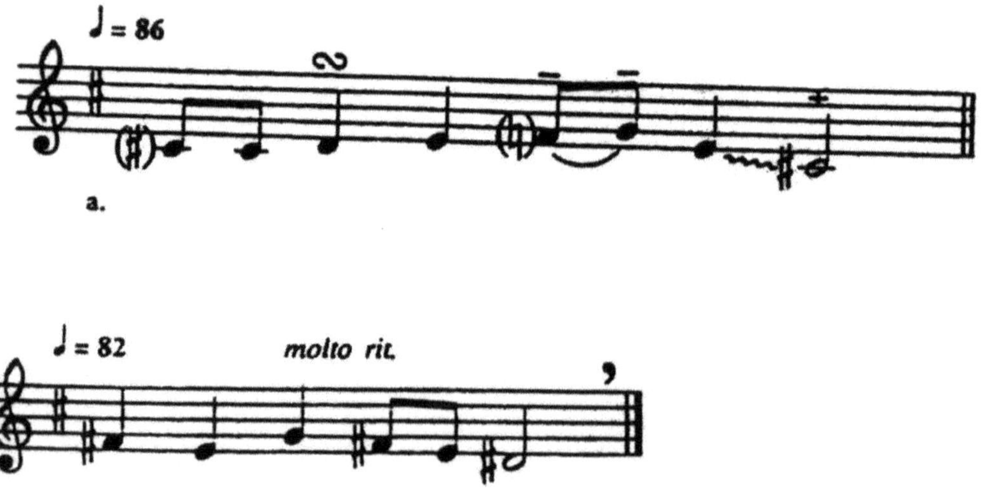

FIGURE 3. Exemples de progressions caractéristiques des intervalles (transcription de Robertson). Le signe + représente un quart de ton au-dessus de la note indiquée; le signe – un quart de ton en-dessous): (a) Extrait de l'hymne *Shere Maria*; (b) Cadence typique, extrait du *Psaume 150*.

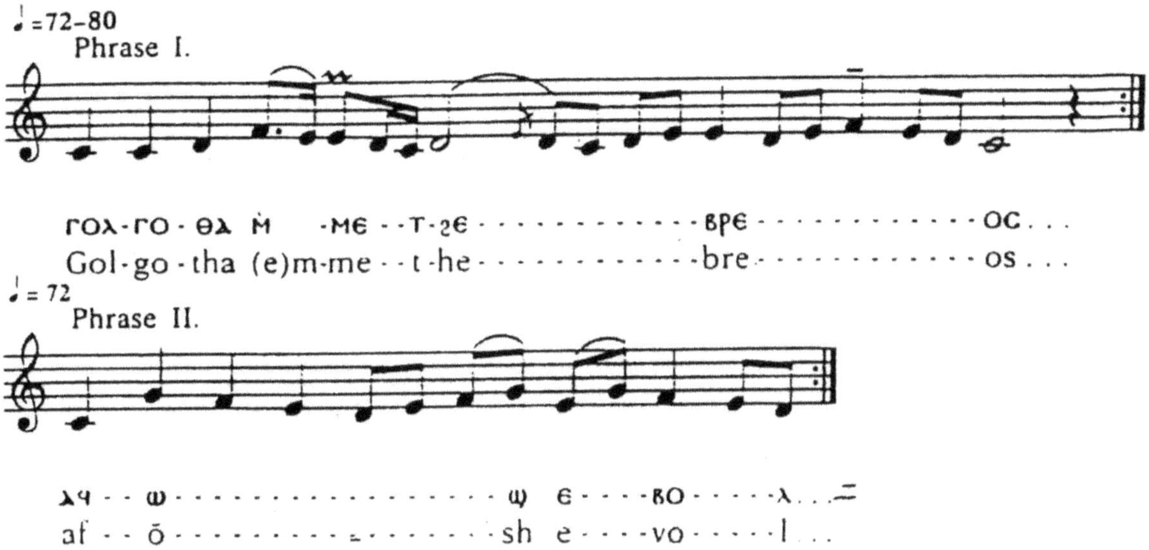

FIGURE 4. Exemple typique des phrases musicales Coptes, de l'hymne *Golgotha* (voir texte) [tiré de l'*Encyclopédie Copte*].
© Copyright Prof. Dr Ashraf–Alexandre Sadek, 2003.

FIGURE 5. Addition architecturale Copte (relief) dans le domaine du temple ancien d'Hathor à Dendara.
© Copyright Dr Amanda–Alice Maravelia, 2000.

Late Antique Textiles of the Benaki Museum with Bucolic and Mythological Iconography

Sophia Tsourinaki

Abstract

The collection of Egyptian textiles in the Benaki Museum comprises a few rare examples dating from Late Antiquity, the iconography of which is strongly influenced by the Hellenistic style. In the present paper attention will be focused on four woven pieces of garment decorations representing Dionysian scenes, comparable to the ornamentation encountered on similar textiles as well as to that on objects executed in other media. On the basis of the compositional scheme and following a thorough technical analysis of the pieces, attempt will be made to determine more precisely whether they may be classified into what appear to be three stylistic groups. The naturalistically renderd medallions in polychrome wool may derive from multicoloured mosaics and book illustrations, the black–silhouette ornamentation from black–figured mosaics and paintings of the black –figure vases, while the fragments with the simplified figures in muted colours seem to be borrowed from literary manuscript illustrations.

KEY WORDS: Late Antiquity, Hellenistic Antiquity, Textiles, Weaving Techniques, Stylistic Analysis, Hellenic Mythology, Dionysos Cycle, Benaki Museum.

I. Introduction

The Benaki Museum possesses a large collection of decorated Egyptian textiles covering a period that extends roughly from the third to the tenth century. Antonis Benaki, the founder of the Museum, was also the generous donor of the main part of the collection; the remainder has been acquired from purchases or constitutes gifts of other important donors. The attention of this paper will be focused on four rare fragments dating from Late Antiquity, which stand out for a number of reasons. To begin with, they are superb examples of the textile art. Moreover, an examination of their subject matter, style of representation and techniques attests to the tenacity of the Classical Hellenic tradition in the declining centuries of the antique world. In the present analysis, the generally used term *Coptic textiles* has been avoided. It holds implications that lessen, rather than enhance the appreciation of the different styles, artistic quality and function of the textiles. Furthermore, the term applies specifically to Egypt, and it is doubtful whether every piece of material found in that country was also made there. Hence, the more generic term *Late Antique* will be used.

The cultural diversity of Late Antiquity, an age of tremendous political, religious and cultural turmoil in the Eastern Mediterranean area[1], has been reflected in a variety of artistic forms and materials, and fabrics are no exception. Fortunately, thanks to the dry climate of Egypt thousands of samples of textiles were preserved, most of which did not come to light during scientific excavations. The surviving pieces constitute fragments of garment decorations, hangings or other domestic furnishings, although complete tunics and shawls have also been found. Their purple or multicoloured woolen ornamentation was either woven into the linen fabric, or applied. Until recently, archaeologists have traditionally tended to hold textiles in low esteem. Fragments of woven fabrics have not on the whole been considered worthy of the same kind of stylistic analysis as works in other media. However, the surviving pieces of woven material found in the Egyptian necropolises of the Late Roman and Early Byzantine era, are probably among the most interesting documents of this highly complex period. The close relationship of textiles to the general stylistic trends of Late Antiquity yields an extensive repertory of pagan motifs and themes that are also frequently encountered in other forms of art. Although mostly found in Egypt, they display an artistic style that is common to the entire Mediterranean world, as it can be seen in representations of garments and domestic furnishings adorning other media and found outside Egypt, as well as in the fabrics discovered in Dura and Palmyra[2].

II. A Comparative Study of the Textiles

Themes taken from the repertory of classical mythology were popular in Egypt[3] throughout the period that began with the founding of Alexandria in 332 BCE. The settling of Hellenic and Roman colonizers in the provincial towns favoured the wide diffusion of pagan motifs. The Indian victory of Alexander came to be identified with that of Dionysos and representation of the god's triumph was a subject of special interest[4]. Furthermore, the Ptolemies encouraged the cult of Dionysos, which was facilitated by the substitution, early on, of the Egyptian god Osiris, god of the dead and of resurrection, and 'master of wine' —as he is referred to in the *Pyramid Texts*[5]— by the Hellenic god Dionysos. Several Ptolemaic kings took the name *Neos Dionysos*, thereby proclaiming the divine legitimacy of the dynasty[6]. Ancient sources describe

[1] Trilling, J.: *The Roman Heritage: Textiles from Egypt and the Eastern Mediterranean 300 to 600 AD*, Washington D.C. (The Textile Museum) 1982, 11.

[2] For selected bibliography, see : Pfister, R. & Bellinger, L.: *The Excavations at Dura Europos Conducted by Yale University and the French Academy of Inscriptions and Letters: Final Report: IV². The Textiles*, New Haven (Yale University) 1945, pls.1, 3; *Textiles de Palmyre découverts par le Service des Antiquités du Haut Commissariat de la République Française dans la necropole de Palmyre*, Paris 1934-40, **I-III**, pl. 6. Also Forrer, R.: *Die Gräber– und Textilfunde von Achmim–Panopolis*, Strasbourg, 1891; *Die frühchristlichen Alterthümer aus dem Gräberfelde von Achmim Panopolis*, Strasbourg 1893.

[3] Hanfman, G.: 'The Continuity of Classical Art: Culture, Myth and Faith', *Age of Spirituality: A Symposium*, NY 1980.

[4] For a nice tapestry panel of the Triumph of Dionysos, probably from a ritual garment, see Marsha, H.: *Textiles in the Metropolitan Museum of Art*, NY (Metropolitan Museum) 1995, 3 and 25. For a pendant of this panel in the Hermitage Museum, St Petersburg, see Lenzen, V.–F.: *The Triumph of Dionysos on the Textiles of Late Antique Egypt*, Berkeley 1960, 24, fig. 1a & b.

[5] Rutschowscaya, M.–H.: *Tissus Coptes*, Paris (Adam Biro) 1990, 82.

[6] Ptolemy I Euergetes (246-21 BCE) claimed his descent from Dionysos and his successor Ptolemy II Philopator established the cult of the god as a state cult. He promoted it with mystery rites and claimed to be the incarnation of Dionysos. Coins of Alexandria depict the king in Dionysian costume with ivy, nebris and thyrsos. For more details on this subject, see Fraser, P.M.: *Ptolemaic Alexandria*, **I**, Oxford 1972, 202-03. Theocritos gives a vivid picture of the function of textiles in Alexandria during the time of Ptolemy II. He mentions woven 'rugs softer than the sleep', he refers to the vogue of Macedonian fashion in women clothes and gives a clear idea of the beauty of the curtains in the Ptolemaic Palace. See Theocritos: *Idylls*, 15, 78 & 125. Also Marzouk M.–A.: *History in Textile Industry in Alexandria*, Alexandria (Alexandria University Press) 1955.

the *Bakchanalia*, the spectacular processions organized by Ptolemy Philadelphos, in honour of the triumphant god, during which effigies of Dionysos[7] accompanied by the orgiastic devotees of his *Thiasos* were carried around in an atmosphere of frenzied excitement. The god of fertility and wine was the principal actor and he has been portrayed together with such attributes of his as a spotted panther[8] [Fig. 1], bunches of grapes, and the *thyrsos*, crowned by ivy and vine leaves. Dionysos' sufferings and victories had a widespread influence in the Mediterranean world of the 4th to the 6th centuries[9] and his popularity in Egypt was such that images associated with his cult[10] survived for centuries after the end of the Ptolemaic rule[11] [Figs. 2 & 3]. One source of inspiration for artists was the *Dionysiaka*, an epic, written by the Hellenic poet Nonnos, who was born at Akhmīm[12] in Middle Egypt. In the declining days of Paganism, the *Dionysiaka* through a syncretism of various Oriental and Occidental beliefs[13], presented the life of Dionysos as a sequence of struggles to surmount obstacles and thereby win admission to heaven and theophany. As late as the end of the 4th century CE, Nonnos praised the glory of the god of wine, sun and fertility in these terms: 'Speak, oh goddess, of breath which arouses the thunder of the son of Kronos, the nuptial spark which precedes the burning explosion and the lighting which was present at the union of Semelē. Speak of the dual birth of Bakchos, whom Zeus snatched still wet from the flames, the imperial product of the incomplete maternity' (see Nonnos: *Dionysiana*, Song 1, 1-5[14]).

The life cycle of the wreathed Dionysos/Bakchos is a theme repeatedly used in the magnificent textiles of Late Antiquity[15]. The god appears on monumental wall hangings with silhouette–like Bacchanalian figures (Pan playing his pipe and women dancing or playing musical instruments) framed by a row of arches. The Abegg Foundation[16] in Switzerland, the Cleveland Museum of Art[17] and the Boston's Museum of Fine Arts[18] own some of these superb examples. Another popular theme that belongs to this category of mythological representation is that of Dionysos discovering the sleeping Ariadnē[19], a scene which has been repeatedly depicted on Hellenistic, Roman and Late Antique works of art[20]. An exceptionally fine pair of woven garment elements from the Benaki collection (acc. 7131–1 and –2)[21] takes its iconography from this complex mythological theme. The tapestry woven medallions were used to decorate a tunic, the characteristic costume worn during the Late Roman and Early Byzantine Period[22]. The scene on the red ground medallion acc. 7131–2 [Fig. 4] shows Dionysos discovering the sleeping Ariadnē on the island of Naxos. It was here that according to legend, Theseus had abandoned her. The half–naked woman, reclining with her left arm behind her head, is in the foreground and closer to the viewer than her companion. Dionysos, his legs astride and standing firmly on the ground, is removing Ariadnē's *peplos*. The young god is clad a *chlamys*, an article of apparel characteristic of travelers, fastened at the right shoulder and wears short boots. Ariadnē looks more surprised than sad[23]. This scene has a counterpart in the basic iconography depicted on a neck tapestry ornament in the Boston Museum

[7] According to the accounts of Callixeamus, preserved by Athēnaios, the effigy of Dionysos was dressed in superb and luxurious textiles on this festival procession: 'A statue of Dionysos…wearing a purple tunic extending to the feet over which was a transparent saffron coat. But round his shoulder was thrown a purple mantle spangled with gold'. See Athēnaios: *The Deipnosophists*, **V**, 196B, 198C.

[8] For the fragment acc. 10342 of a bone plaque portraying the naked Dionysos beside a panther at the Benaki Museum, see Photopoulos, D. & Delivorrias, A.: *Greece at the Benaki Museum*, Athens (Benaki Museum) 1997, 155: fig. 260. **[Editor's Note:** In the magico–religious context of the funereal ceremonies in ancient Egypt, the sacral dress of the officiating *sm*–priest was a leopard skin. According to a myth it was a Sethian animal, the panther, stamped for punishment because he had threatened Osiris, that was transformed into a leopard. Into what degree the Egyptian customs may have influenced the Hellenic ones still remains an open question.]

[9] Kent J.P.C. & Painter K.S.: *Wealth of the Roman World: AD 300-700*, London 1997, 33.

[10] For a famous piece, dating from the Late Roman Antiquity (4th century CE), see Rutschowscaya: *op. cit.*, 28-29. This fabric, known as 'the veil of Antinoopolis' (Louvre), was found by Albert Gayet at Antinoopolis in 1905 and illustrates the life cycle of Dionysos. The first register depicts the birth of Dionysos while the third shows a procession of *mainades*, *silēnoi* and *satyroi* dancing or playing music and accompanying the triumphant god and his mother Semelē.

[11] For the terracotta statuette acc. 22216 and the copper–alloy figurine acc. 13819 at the Benaki Museum, see Photopoulos & Delivorrias: *op. cit.*, fig. 207, 344.

[12] In Hellenic and Roman times, Akhmīm was called *Panopolis* because of its ancient god Min, an ithyphallic god of fertility who was identified with Dionysos' cohort Pan. On this topic, see also Maravelia's & Cladaki's contribution in this volume.

[13] For a thorough discussion on this subject, see Bowersock, G.–W.: *Hellenism in Late Antiquity*, Ann Arbor MI (Univeristy of Michigan Press) 1990.

[14] Nonnos of Panopolis: *Dionysiaka* (English translation by W.H.D. Rouse), Cambridge MA 1962-63, **XXXVI**, 57; Chuvin, P.: *Mythologie et géographie dionysiaques: Recherches sur l'œuvre de Nonnos de Panopolis*, Paris (Université de Paris Sorbonne, Paris IV) 1991.

[15] For a selected bibliography, see : Lenzen, *op. cit.*, n 4; Heuk Allen, S.: 'The True Vine: Dionysian Imagery in Coptic Textiles and Later Medieval Art', *Survival of the Gods*, Providence RI 1987; Weitzman, K.: *Age of Spirituality: Late Antique Early Christian Art, Third to Seventh Century*, NY 1979.

[16] Flury–Lemberg, M.: *Textile Conservation and Research*, Bern 1988, 364-66, 370-81. ^{14}C dating to 73-380 CE; Arensberg, S.–M.: 'Dionysos: A Late Antique Tapestry', *Boston Museum Bulletin*, **75**, Boston 1977, 4 -25.

[17] Sheperd, D.: 'Late Classical Tapestry', *Bulletin of the Cleveland Museum of Art*, **63**, Cleveland 1976, 306-13.

[18] 'Abd 'el-Malek, L.–H.: 'Deities, Saints and Allegories', *Hali*, **72**, 1993-94, 83.

[19] 'Ἀριάδνη καθεύδουσα καὶ Θησεὺς ἀναγόμενος καὶ Διόνυσος ἥκων εἰς τὴν Ἀριάδνης ἁρπαγήν'. According to the accounts of Pausanias records, this scene was painted in the temple of Dionysos Elephthereus in Athens, dating from the 5th century BCE. Pausanias: ***I***, 20, 3.

[20] For a bronze crater from Derveni, depicting the sacred couple with the *Thiasos*, dated to the 4th century BCE, see Andronicos M., Chatzidakēs, M. & Karageōrgēs, V.: *The Hellenic Museums*, Athens (Ekdotikē Athēnōn) 1975, 275. For a fragment from a *trapezophoros* with Dionysos and the sleeping Ariadnē, dated from the 3rd century BCE, see Tzedakēs, G., Chrysoulakē, S., Lekka, A. & Kottaridou, A.: *Ἀπὸ τὴν Μήδεια στὴν Σαπφώ: Ἀνυπότακτες Γυναίκες στὴν ἀρχαία Ἑλλάδα: Exhibition Catalogue*, Athens (Ministry of Culture / ICOM) 1995, 106. For a Roman statue of the sleeping Ariadnē, see Richter, G.: *A Handbook of Hellenic Art*, London, (Phaidon) 1974, 169. For an ivory fragment, see Randal, R.: *Masterpieces of Ivory from the Walters Art Gallery*, NY 1985, fig. 143.

[21] Medallion acc. 7131–1 measures 6.8 x 6.4 cm; medallion acc. 7131–2 measures 6.4 x 6 cm. They are woven on a Z– plied, 2S–spun linen warp, 16 warps/cm. Wefts: S–spun undyed linen; S–spun yellow, greenish blue (blue on yellowish yarn), medium and dark blue, light blue (mixture of undyed and blue), pinkish–red, wools, 44–64 wefts/cm. Weft wrapping: soumak of S–spun undyed linen, flying shuttle of S–spun dyed wool and undyed linen. Tapestry and slit; wrapped warps; slanted wefts; weft wrapping (soumak and vertical weft brocading on borders, flying shuttle in details). Edges of the pieces have been folded under. Plying of linen warps, a solution to increase the elasticity of these threads, may suggest that they were woven on narrow loom as a separate tunic decoration.

[22] As attested by numerous monuments from the 4th century onward, the same fashion was widespread throughout the entire Roman Empire. For the decoration of tunics, see *Égyptiennes: Étoffes coptes du Nil*, Mariemont (Musée Royal de Mariemont) 1997, 89-102.

[23] According to a version of the legend, when Ariadnē awoke and saw Dionysos before her, she was overcome by surprise.

of Fine Arts, dated on the fifth century CE, in which Dionysos and Ariadnē are identified by their names in Hellenic letters woven into the background[24]. On the medallion acc. 7131 –1 [Fig. 5], Dionysos is portrayed with his beloved Ariadnē as a divine couple, depicted on the same plane of the representation. He is shown holding his *thyrsos* (the top of the staff has now worn away), while his body demonstrably exhibits feminine characteristics[25]. He is clad in a *chlamys* pinned at the right shoulder and wears short boots. His legs are crossed, the right over left. Ariadnē, wearing sumptuous jewellery (a necklace, armbands and bracelets) holds a cup of wine in a state of revel in adoration of Dionysos. The well–groomed woman gazes at the god's piercing eyes. Her wide–open eyes are characteristic of the figures on Egyptian textiles and her attitude is one of the contemplative adoration of Dionysos[26]. Green and yellow lines in her dark hair indicate a wreath, her bridal gift from Hēphaistos. Three yellow rays spring from the top of her head attesting her new divine status. Her drinking vessel (possibly a *kantharos*), another widely used Dionysian attribute[27], suggests that the scene may have been intended to convey the drunken state of the god of wine, a theme also depicted in other media[28].

The Benaki medallions belong to a special group of fine, small ornaments, portraying mythological and bucolic scenes dating from the late 5th to the early 6th century. This group, exhaustively discussed by D. Thompson[29], appears to represent a common tapestry tradition influenced by book illustrations and mosaics. Woven on linen, mostly plied warps, (which is the case with our textiles) they mainly have woolen and linen wefts[30]. They are characterized by the use of wave–crest borders, red grounds and abbreviated compositions of one or two figures[31]. The background is absent and figures appear to stand against a non–realistic red ground. They are designed to occupy the whole surface of the tapestry element and are depicted in virtually the same attitude. The scenes are obviously extracted from larger representations such as those appearing in mosaics and book illustrations. The composition on the Benaki textiles depicts figures enacting the drama in lively motion and displaying —despite the abbreviated form of the scene— considerable fidelity to the Classical style. The weaver inspired by classical prototypes, was remarkably successful in his attempt to render, by means of finely unwoven lines, some of the anatomical details of the figures. Most expressive is the swift movement of Dionysos as he unveils Ariadnē and the way that the ecstatic woman joyously adores him. The subtle touches of dyed yarn (mostly in the blue and green range) highlighting the natural tones of linen weft clearly follow the painting tradition as it appears in the mosaics and pastoral book illustrations of the late 4th to the 6th century[32]. Moreover, the extremely fine work of weaving displays certain technical and stylistic features that suggest an Egyptian work possibly derived from an Alexandrian tradition, which may be seen as testifying to the continuing vitality of literary works that were subsequently lost.

Another example of Dionysian imagery from the Benaki collection reflecting the iconography of sophisticated Late Antique Art, is the tapestry fragment acc. 7244[33] [Fig. 6]. It is one of three fragments of similar size (acc. 7242 [Fig. 7] and 7243) originally belonging to the same decorative band that was used to embellish the hem of a tunic. The three panels portray mythological figures, distributed upon their field in a manner to avoid overlapping. They are depicted between medallions enclosing quadrupeds, the greater part of which is now lost. Although the textile has suffered a fair amount of damage, figures are well preserved and their names are woven next to their heads: ΔΙΟΝΥCOC and ΑΡΙΑΤΝΗ (Dionysos and Ariadnē), ΔΑΩΓΕΝΗC and ΛΑΕΙC (Diogenēs and Lais). Despite the fact that the mythological figures of Diogenēs and Lais are of particular importance (it is a unique example with their names clearly written on the textile), our attention will be focused on the Dionysian representation. The figure of the god's female companion has unfortunately been completely lost. Only her name ΑΡΙΑΤΝΗ is preserved. The god is depicted in the 'new manner', as a 'beautiful and tender youth'[34], preserving all the essential details. His traditional attitude, a variant of the so–called *Lykeios–type* carries some of the characteristic attributes[35], as these appear on nu-

---

[24] A very rare feature in this exceptional neck decoration is the use of gold yarn wound around silk threads in parts of the weft. See Townsend, G.: 'Two Fragments of Late Hellenistic Tapestry', *Bulletin of the Museum of Fine Arts*, **XLVI**, **13**, Boston 1948, 13-18; 'Abd 'el-Malek: *op. cit.*; Weibel, A.: *Two Thousands Years of Textiles: The Figured Textiles of Europe and the East*, NY (The Detroit Institute of Arts, Pantheon ed.) 1952, 78-79, fig. 12 & 12a.

[25] Various monuments of the Late Antiquity represent Dionysos in a manner that conforms to the statement of Nonnos that the god was soft–skinned and shaped like a woman. The aspect of effeminacy attributed to Dionysos has thoroughly been discussed by Lenzen: *op. cit.*, 2-3.

[26] As F. Cumont has stated, the silent, contemplative adoration of a divinity was characteristic of the native religion of Egypt and it entered Europe through the influence of the cult of Isis. See Cumont, F.: *Les Religions orientales dans le paganisme romain*, Paris 1929, 89. The upward gaze of figures as an adoration of Dionysos has thoroughly been discussed by Lenzen: *op. cit.*, 12.

[27] On the portrayal of Ariadnē with a cup in her hand on a sculptured frieze from Ahnas 'el-Medineh, see *L'Art Copte en Égypte: 2000 ans de Christianisme*, Paris (Institut du Monde Arabe / Éditions Gallimard) 2000, 157: fig. 148. On a relief ivory pyxis in Vienna and a textile in the Metropolitan Museum of Art (NY), see Lenzen, *op. cit.*, pls. 9c and 10a.

[28] Levi, D.: *Antioch Mosaic Pavements*, **II**, Princeton 1947, and pl. 7b.

[29] Thompson, D.: *Coptic Textiles in the Brooklyn Museum*, Brooklyn (The Brooklyn Museum) 1971, 18; idem: 'Rare Coptic Textiles with Bucolic and Mythological Iconography', *Bulletin du C.I.E.T.A.*, **57-58**, Lyon 1983, 90-99.

[30] Three of the published pieces from this group contain silk in parts of the weft. See Thompson: *op. cit.*, 1983.

[31] On Roman sarcophagi, these scenes generally include other figures (*Erōtes, Satyroi, Mainades*, & c.) but on small pieces of woven material only the main figures are represented.

[32] Closest in general descriptions are the major bucolic texts of Theocritos (*Idylls*), especially popular in Alexandria, and of Virgilius Romanus. For good illustrations, see Weitzman, K.: *Late Antique and Early Christian Book Illumination*, NY 1977, pl. 11; Rosenthal, E.: *The Illuminations of the Virgilius Romanus*, Zürich 1972.

[33] Fragment acc. 7244 measures 18.6 x 15 cm. It is woven on a Z–plied, 2S–spun linen warp, 11 warps/cm. Wefts: S–spun undyed linen; Z–spun mixture of natural (?) brown, dark blue, turquoise (blue on yellowish yarn), light green (mixture of green and undyed), two shades of beige, wools, 36-62 wefts/cm. Weft wrapping: soumak 2/1 S or Z of S–spun undyed linen and Z–spun dyed wool. Tabby; weft–faced tabby; tapestry and slit; slanted wefts; weft wrapping (soumak on the borders of the medallion). The fragment retains both unreinforced selvedges. At present, it is stitched by means of ancient sewing thread (linen Z, 2S) on a plain linen ground, which might be the remains of the original tunic. Wool yarn is of fine and extra lustrous quality. Plying of linen warps suggests that it may have been woven on narrow loom as a separate tunic decoration. The designs were woven perpendicular to the warp.

[34] Diodōros: ***IV***, 5, 2: 'Δίμορφον δ' αὐτὸν δοκεῖν ὑπάρχειν διὰ τὸ δύο Διονύσους γεγονέναι, τὸν μὲν παλαιὸν καταπώγωνα διὰ τὸ τοὺς ἀρχαίους πάντας πωγωνοτροφεῖν, τὸν δὲ νεώτερον ὡραῖον καὶ τρυφερὸν καὶ νέον'.

[35] This type is generally accepted as a free adaptation of the Praxiteleian prototype of Apollōn Lykeios. In this well–known type, the god is represented in a relaxed position. For a discussion on this topic, see Marangou, L.: *Bone Carvings from Egypt*, Tübingen–Athens (Benaki Museum) 1976, 21.

merous Late Antique bone carvings[36] and other works of art. He is shown leaning on a partially preserved pillar[37] and holding a stylized cup. He wears short boots and his left leg is crossed over the right. A *chlamys* covers the left shoulder and arm. The torso forms an S–shaped twist and a halo surrounds the head, which is crowned with conventional light lines, most probably suggesting a wreath. A panther, a distinctive attribute of Dionysos, is sitting between his legs and drinking wine from his cup. An attempt has been made to render plastically the anatomical details. The figure occupies a central position in a frontally viewed situation with elements of symmetry[38], as if pausing a moment to receive the homage of the spectator. He is shown wearing a crenelated headpiece, most probably a reminiscent of Dionysos' turreted crown, provided on Eastern monuments of Late Antiquity. This headpiece does not occur in the representations of Dionysos of the Classical Hellenic and Roman period. As symbol of triumph it attests the growing influence of Oriental conceptions of divinity and imperial power. According to V. Lenzen[39], the turreted crown is a further manifestation of Orientalizing influences on the art of the Late Roman Empire.

The fragment under study comes very near in composition to a sculptured vault stone of Dionysos in the Dumbarton Oaks collections[40], to a frieze from Ahnas 'el-Medineh in the Coptic Museum[41], to a bone fragment from the Ashmolean Museum in Oxford[42], to several garment decorations from the Hermitage Museum[43] and the Musée National du Moyen Âge (Thermes de Cluny)[44] and to monumental hangings in the Abegg Foundation and the Cleeveland Museum of Art[45]. The scene however, is more abbreviated, probably due to the restricted area that the weaver had at his disposal. As a result of the spatial and technical limitations of his medium, the artist modified the design by combining two prototypes: the right side of the figure was woven as it is seen in the Abegg Foundation hanging (with the lowered hand holding a kind of *kantharos*), while the left side (with the hand leaning on a short pillar) follows the model of the other works of art mentioned above. Moreover, on the basis of technical comparisons with related textiles, the fragment presents some rare features: the very lustrous, soft Z–spun woollen yarns that may have been used as imported wefts[46], and the muted colours in parts of the weft yarn. The colours of the dyed yarns, which are intentionally muted and close to the natural hues, produce a particularly characteristic effect. The overall light brown effect created by the dark background and the brownish shades of the figures is only modified by dark blue and light green touches of colour in the outlines. Textiles woven in this range of unusual and intentionally muted colours are called 'brown–tone weavings'[47]and testify to the mutual influence between different tapestry traditions. Owing to the new directions, which were given by Oriental symbolic modes of compositions, frontality is exemplified in the Benaki fragment. Stylistic similarities with other works of art suggest that our fragment would have been made sometime between the sixth and the seventh century. However, technical characteristics that are different from most ordinary textiles displaying Dionysian images, may be indicative of a Mediterranean provenance other than Egypt. Reflecting the mythological tradition, it clearly works from the Mediterranean landscape, as this is interpreted in book illustrations of Late Antique art[48].

Among the various depictions of Dionysian imagery on textiles is a group of monochrome weavings, conventionally called *the purple and white group*. This type of composition, considered suitable for tapestry ornaments, follows the so–called dark–silhouette style, which constitutes a different time–honoured tradition. In Classical Antiquity the 'black–figure' design was used in Hellenic vase painting, while we find it in mosaics of the Archaic period long before its appearance in textiles. Roman black–silhouette floor mosaics with inner lines represented in white reached their comparatively brief period of flowering in the second century CE. This flat and two–dimensional style of decoration, which lacks the realism of a shaded representation[49], is followed in the textile acc. 7127[50] in the Benaki collection [Fig. 8]. Prominent in the decorative scheme is a scene of Dionysian celebration shaped in a pinecone arrangement[51]. A vine growing from a *kantharos* forms an almost symmetrical pattern. Two main stems open into thinner branches ending in tendrils and leaves. The field is divided into five compartments. The central part is occupied by a young figure, most probably a representation of the god Dionysos. According to the Classical models, he is shown in an approximate three–quarter view, walking to the left with his head turned backwards and holding an unidentified red object (a small sickle?). His motion

[36] Compare the corresponding details on ivory reliefs to Marangou, *op. cit.*, 153-56, fig. 1a, 3a, 4a, 4b, 7a.

[37] For parallels to this representation on textiles, see Liapounova, X.: 'L'image de Dionysos sur les tissus de l'Égypte byzantine', *Musée de l'Ermitage, Travaux du Département Oriental*, **III**, St Petersburg 1940, pl. IV. Also Lorquin, A.: *Les tissus coptes au musée national du Moyen Âge: Thermes de Cluny*, Paris (RMN) 1992, 54 & 97.

[38] Under influences from the Orient through Syria, narration in profile gave away to representation by centrality, frontality and symmetry. This type of artistic composition exemplified on textiles of the Late Antiquity contrasts with the representation in profile on Roman sarcophagi and on mosaics. It exhibits the influences that transformed Hellenistic art into the art of the Byzantine era. For a discussion on this subject, see Lenzen: *op. cit.*, 14-15.

[39] For a thorough discussion on Dionysos' representations wearing a turreted or mural crown, see Lenzen: *op. cit.*, 17-21.

[40] On this relief of Dionysos leaning on a pillar, dated in the 5th century, see Trilling: *op. cit.*, 17: n. 1 & fig. 5.

[41] See n. 27, *supra*.

[42] See Marangou: *op. cit.*, fig. 4b.

[43] See Liapounova: *op. cit.*, pl. IV.

[44] See n. 37, *supra*.

[45] See nn. 16 & 17, *supra*.

[46] De Jonghe, D., Daemen, S., Rassart–Debergh, M., De Moor, A. & Overlaet, B.: *Ancient Tapestries of the R. Pfister Collection in the Vatican Library*, Città del Vaticano (Biblioteca Apostolica Vaticana) 1999, 4.

[47] On this topic, see Thompson: *op. cit.*

[48] For a discussion on links between Late Antique brown–tone tapestries and literature, see Thompson: *op. cit.*

[49] For numerous parallels to this class of textiles see the comment by Thompson, D.: *Coptic textiles in the Brooklyn Museum*, Brooklyn (The Brooklyn Museum) 1971, 14. For textiles with the same or related type of composition, see for example: Kendrick, A.E.: *Catalogue of Textiles from Burying Grounds of Egypt*, **I**, London (Victoria and Albert Museum) 1920-1922, pl. XXIII, nos. 111, 112, 135, 136; Rutschowscaya : *op. cit.*, 80: n. 5, 91.

[50] The fragment acc. 7127 is part from a shawl decoration and measures 17.2 x 22.8 cm. It is woven on an S–spun linen warp, repp weave 2/2, 9 p. warps/cm. Wefts: S–spun undyed linen; S–spun dark blue, light green (blue on yellowish yarn), brick–red (now faded), dull yellow, wools, 40-48 wefts/cm. Weft wrapping: flying shuttle of S–spun undyed linen. Tapestry, slit and dovetailed; slanted wefts; weft wrapping (flying shuttle is used for details). The tabby ground has been completely removed. Some small fragments are pasted on the ornament in a wrong warp/weft arrangement but related technical features indicate that they belong to the same weave. Motif was woven onto the warps in sections, as if it were being drawn.

[51] For a thorough discussion of Dionysos' representation inhabiting a tree, see Apostolakē, A.: 'Διόνυσος Δενδρίτης', *Ἀρχαιολογικὴ ἐφημερίς*, 1942-44, Athens 1948, 74-83.

is indicated by his *himation* bellied in the breeze. The other four compartments formed by the branches are framing the figures of animals. At the top of the scene two polychrome birds are pecking at grapes and at the bottom, by the handles of the *kantharos*, two goats are grazing. Owing to the damage of the textile, only four grapes are still fully preserved, while the one at the bottom is partly missing. On a nearly identical ornament (acc. 1731) studied by A. Apostolakē[52] and most probably belonging to the same shawl, the young figure holds a cornucopia full of grapes. This well–known attribute of Dionysos, exhibited exultantly as a symbol of his power, has been interpreted as a source of joy and salvation to the world[53].

In terms of workmanship and weave density the fragment is a weaving of considerable quality. The mauve–blue figures of the motif are contrasted with the natural linen of the background and details are expressed by means of finely woven accents in the flying shuttle technique[54]. The human figure and the animals are set on different planes, a feature commonly seen on Late Antique textiles, due to a certain degree to the nature of the tapestry weaving process[55]. Moreover, the black–figured textile manifests features of the two previously mentioned tapestry traditions. Basically, it is a two–colour tapestry ornament originated in the classical silhouette style, which is familiar from mosaics and vase paintings. The introduction of little colours, which appears in some details (birds, grapes, sickle), thus breaking the monochrome effect, is a possible indication of a stylistic change and the mutual influence of the multicoloured tapestry tradition.

The theme of trees inhabited by gods or goddesses was an old source of inspiration for artists working in Egypt[56]. The naturalistic rendering of birds and small animals among foliage and tree scrolls[57]originated in the Hellenistic period of the late 4th and 3rd centuries, and was widely used as a favorite decorative device[58]. Liapounova and Apostolakē have set forth *the tree of life* as an ancient theme[59] of decoration represented in the art of Mesopotamia and Egypt and have cited several textiles on which Dionysos stands within the tree of life. The setting of Dionysos within the arbor or frame of vine[60] on the textiles parallels the statement of Nonnos that 'he drove the savage car of divine Kybelē...under the shadow of ivy'[61] and testifies to his status as a god of fertility[62] and regeneration[63] in Helleno–Roman Egypt. Textiles on which Dionysos is shown as a central figure accompanied with his various respective elements (vines, birds, goats and *kantharos*) represent an allegorical group and convey the concepts of fertility and abundance. Such portrayals of fruitful, divinely inhabited vines were more than mere illustrations of plenty[64]. They also functioned as magical amulets, intended to attract the prosperity they invoked[65] [Fig. 9]. The scheme of decoration, where the god inhabits a vine growing from a *kantharos*, which has traditionally been considered suitable for inwoven garment decorations, differ from portrayals of the same theme in other media. The juxtaposition of Dionysos with a *kantharos*[66], aquatic deities (personifications of rivers), fruitful vines and inhabited scrolls as multiple symbols of fertility can be seen on a complex mosaic of Nea Paphos in Cyprus[67]. The depiction of a vase containing a plant (usually a vine) is a common motif on Late Antique textiles of Hellenistic inspiration and often appears in small scale as a repeated design element[68]. As H. Maguire has stated[69], the weaver was able to compress the benefits of all of nature into these small motifs, which could be repeated several times over on a textile, like the reiteration of a charm. As selectivity and repetition characterized these compositions, it was the most important elements that were depicted [Fig. 10].

---

[52] Apostolakē, A.: *Τὰ Κοπτικὰ Ὑφάσματα τοῦ ἐν Ἀθήναις Μουσείου Κοσμητικῶν Τεχνῶν*, Athens (Hestia) 1932, fig. 83, 116-18.

[53] Grapes supported by the uplifted arm of Dionysos can be seen on the two tapestry panels of the Hermitage Museum and the Metropolitan Museum of Art at New York (see n. 4, *supra*) and on a Roman mosaic in Korinthos. See Broneer, O.: 'Excavations in Corinth 1934', *AJA*, **53**, 1935, pl. XVII, 2.

[54] This technique is apparently unique in the textiles from Egypt. The weaver used a supplementary weft thread of contrasting colour wrapped freely around the warps, to create pattern details and outlines during the course of weaving.

[55] Leipen, N.: 'Classical Tradition in Early Christian Art: A Textile Fragment in the Royal Ontario Museum', *Studies in Textile History* (Gervers, V., ed.), **I**, Toronto 1977, 168-77.

[56] For a discussion on the tree–goddesses and Hathor, see Buhl, M.L.: 'The Goddess of the Egyptian Tree Cult', *JNES*, **6**, 1947, 80-97 and Maravelia, A.-A.: 'Some Aspects of Ancient Egyptian Social Life from the Study of the Principal Love Poem's Ostraca from Deir 'al-Medina', *Egyptology at the Dawn of the 20th Century: Proceedings of the 8th International Conference of Egyptologists* (Hawass, Z., & Brock, L., eds), Cairo (The AUC Press) 2003, 281-88, especially 286. For a depiction of Mithras growing from a tree, see Apostolakē: *op. cit.*, 74-83. For the depiction of a tree inhabited by a young boy (possibly identified with Dionysos) carrying a goat, see Bötticher, C.: *Der Baumkultus der Hellenen*, Berlin 1856, f. 47.

[57] See for example, a gold diadem of the late 4th century BCE in the Metropolitan Museum of Art in New York, which displays ten small female figures playing instruments on the stems of a running acanthus *rinceau*, while Dionysos and Ariadnē are supported by the arabesques of the scroll: Richter, G.M.A.: *A Handbook of Hellenic Art*, London (The Phaidon Press) ^{5}1967, 259, fig. 381.

[58] The subject is discussed thoroughly by Toynbee, J.B.C. and Ward Perkins, J.B.: 'Peopled scrolls: A Hellenistic motif in the Imperial Art', *Papers in the British School of Archaeology at Rome*, **18**, 1950, Rome 1950, 1-43 & pls. 1-26. Textiles acc. 6930, 6940, 7103, 7016, 7149 in the Benaki collection (unpublished) depict such tender and elaborate vine or acanthus scrolls encircling fantastic mythological creatures, human figures and wild beasts. Clavus acc. 7016 consists of scroll motifs framing animals and trefoils, a type of ornament used in Mediterranean mosaics exemplified by the rinceaux ornament in the border of the Orpheus mosaic in Jerusalem. See Levi, D.: *Antioch Mosaic Pavements*, **II**, Princeton NJ (Princeton University Press) 1947, pl. 7b.

[59] Liapounova: *op. cit.*; Apostolakē: *op. cit.*

[60] For a similar setting provided for the Triumphs of Dionysos on mosaics of North Africa, see *Musées de l'Algerie et de la Tunisie: Musée Aloui*, Paris 1910, pl.XI; *Musées de Sousse*, Paris 1902, pl. VI; *Musée d'Oran*, Paris 1893, pl. VII.

[61] Nonnos: ***XVII***, 19, 21.

[62] It is to be noted that in ancient Hellenic literature numerous adjectives have been used in order to describe the fruitful attributes of the god (*Ἀνθεύς, Ἄνθιος, Κισσοφόρος, Κισσοχαίτης, Δενδρίτης, Ἔνδενδρος*), his relationship to vines (*Ληνεύς, Ὀμφακίτης, Σταφυλίτης, Εὐστάφυλος*) and to goats (*Ἐρίφιος*).

[63] Badawy, A.: *Coptic Art and Archaeology*, Cambridge (MIT) 1978, 203 & f. 3.184, 222.

[64] For a discussion on this topic, see Maguire, H.: 'Garments Pleasing to God: The Significance of Domestic Textile Designs in the Early Byzantine Period', *Dumbarton Oaks Paper*, **44**, Washington D.C. 1990.

[65] Occasionally an inscription has confirmed the visual image of this composition. For a linen curtain fragment, now at the Boston Museum of Fine arts displaying a laden tree with the inscription ΕΥΦΟΡΙ (= Flourish!), written upon its trunk, see Maguire: *op. cit.*, 217.

[66] On the portrayal of Dionysos holding a *kantharos* of Acholla in the Musée de Bardo, North Africa, on a mosaic in Korinthos and on a coin of Nikaia, see Lenzen: *op. cit.*, pls. 4a, 6a & 9a.

[67] For the new Paphos mosaics, see Daszewski, W.–A.: *Dionysos der Erlöser: Griechische Mythen im Spätantiken Cypern*, **II**, Mainz am Rheim 1985. Also Hēliadēs, G.S.: *Ὁ Οἶκος τοῦ Διονύσου: Ἡ Ἔπαυλη τῶν Μωσαϊκῶν τῆς Νέας Ἐπάφου*, Paphos 1984, 24.

[68] For example the textile acc. 7103 (unpublished) in the Benaki collection.

[69] Maguire: *op. cit.*

The cult of Dionysos, fused with the ancient myths of Osiris, Adōnis and Isis, seems to have merged with religious beliefs from the East[70]. Behind their façade of joyful games, Bakchanalia were fraught with deeper meanings: they contained allegories of the cycle of life, fertility, death and resurrection[71], which is why the festivities surrounding the grape harvest were a favorite theme derived from Dionysian imagery. The widespread use of these kinds of motifs in Late Antique textiles is not only due to their joyful significance. The harvesting of ripe grapes symbolizes the harvesting of human souls, but also the idea of sacrifice followed by resurrection, found in Christian thought. This might also be the reason why they are so frequently depicted on funerary textiles.

III. Conclusions

From the above study, the conclusion may be drawn that the four Late Antique textiles decorated with Dionysian images that have been examined here are chromatically related and stylistically affiliated to mosaics and book illustrations of that period. As the spatial and technical limitations of the medium did not allow entire scenes such as those depicted in large mosaics to be shown, a condensed image was composed by selecting a number of its components, a fairly common practice of the time. The weavers manifestly used the ingredients provided by traditional iconographic models, whose anatomy and articulated movement was fully understood. New directions were given by symbolic modes of compositions. The evident although not immediately apparent common features displayed by all these representations suggest that the scene of Dionysos and Ariadnē was most frequently portrayed and widely copied as a favourite iconographic theme in the decoration of costly textiles. Textiles, although comparatively modest products, clearly illustrate how greatly the artist depended on the Classical tradition of Hellenic art and testify to the interest in Egypt in the cult of Dionysos. Their close relationship to the general stylistic trends of Late Antiquity attests the transitional changes of Dionysian imagery and assimilates interactions and cultural exchanges in the Mediterranean World.

Aknowledgements

The author wishes to acknowledge her collaboration with Mrs Roberta Cortopassi (Musée du Louvre) and notes that the catalogue of the textiles compiled by both of them will be published shortly by the Benaki Museum.

[70] Berliner, R.: 'Tapestries from Egypt influenced by Theatrical Performances', *TMJ*, **I**[3], 1964, 35; Peter, I.: *Textilien aus Ägypten in Museum Rietberg*, Zürich 1976, 24.

[71] Jones, A.M.: *The Equestrian Motif in Coptic Textiles*, Ann Arbor (Wayne State University) 1974, 135; Badawy: *op. cit.*, 222-33.

FIGURE 1. Fragment of a bone plaque portraying a naked Dionysos beside a panther. Egypt, 2nd century CE. Benaki Museum, Athens (acc. 10342)

FIGURE 2. Copper–alloy figurine of a naked Dionysos holding a cup and reclining in the manner of a symposiast. Egypt, 4th-6th century CE. Benaki Museum, Athens (acc. 13819)
© Copyright & Courtesy of the Benaki Museum, Athens, Hellas, 2003.

FIGURE 3. Terracotta statuette of an inebriated Dionysos supported by a Silēnos. In this artless creation of late Roman times there survives an older theme introduced into Hellenistic sculpture.
Egypt, middle 3rd century CE. H. 14cm. Gift of Loukas Benaki. Benaki Museum, Athens (acc. 22216)

FIGURE 4. Tapestry medallion with the representation of Dionysos removing Ariadnē's *peplos*. Egypt, 5th-6th century CE. Tapestry. Linen and wool. Benaki Museum, Athens (acc. 7131–2)
© Copyright & Courtesy of the Benaki Museum, Athens, Hellas, 2003.

FIGURE 5. Tapestry medallion portraying the mythological scene of Dionysos and Ariadnē. Egypt, 5th-6th century CE. Tapestry. Linen and wool. Benaki Museum, Athens (acc. 7131–1)

FIGURE 6. Fragment of a tapestry band portraying Dionysos.
Egypt, 6th-7th century CE. Tapestry and tabby. Linen and wool. Benaki Museum, Athens (acc. 7244)

FIGURE 7. Fragment of a tapestry band portraying Diogenēs and Lais.
Egypt, 6th-7th century CE. Tapestry. Linen and wool. Benaki Museum, Athens (acc. 7242)

FIGURE 8. Fragment from a shawl decoration with a vine growing from a vase and scenes of grape picking. Tapestry. Linen and wool. Egypt, 4th-5th century CE. Benaki Museum, Athens (acc. 7127)
© Copyright & Courtesy of the Benaki Museum, Athens, Hellas, 2003.

FIGURE 9. Fragment from a tunic *clavus* with interlinked medallions enclosing figures and running quadrupeds. Tapestry and tabby. Linen and wool. Egypt, 4th-5th century CE. Benaki Museum, Athens (acc. 6940).

FIGURE 10. Fragment from a tunic clavus with repeated design elements of plants growing from vases. Tapestry and tabby. Linen and wool. Egypt, 4th-5th century CE. Benaki Museum, Athens (acc. 7103)
© Copyright & Courtesy of the Benaki Museum, Athens, Hellas, 2003.

Fantastic Discoveries in Archaeology: The Case of The Tomb of Alexander The Great

Harry E. Tzalas

Abstract

The mythical and the fantastic as an attempt to interpret the remains of the human past have preceded Archaeology, which as a scientific discipline is no more than two centuries old. However, ignorance coupled with fertility of mind has often brought confusion to the uninitiated general public, when ruins are arbitrarily connected to legendary palaces of mythical kings and queens. This tendency, understandable for the Dark Ages, when knowledge was the prerogative of the few, continued alas even during the 19th and the 20th centuries, although education became available to greater numbers. Tellers of fantastic discoveries are then no longer ignorant peasants or illiterate burghers. The new breed is made up of superficially educated persons with a basic knowledge, who can read and often do read profusely books of history. They tend, however, to interpret arbitrarily the remains of the past. Because of their lack of scholarly background, and moved by exaggerated ambitions, they propose naïve interpretations, irresponsible theories, formulated in an unscientific manner. Often they resort to lies and hoaxes in their frenzy to make their cause prevail. These lovers of the past and amateur researchers are found at all levels of society, from workers and clerks, to medical doctors and retired military officers. It is known that the masses are ready to accept a fantastic story, which they prefer to a historically founded fact. The story–teller whose name has not been saved to posterity but who remains known as Pseudo–Kallisthenēs is a good example: his *Alexander's Romance*, full of fantastic feats and impossible exploits prevailed during all the Middle Ages over proven historically–rooted facts. The fast spreading of information due to the expansion of the mass media, the ever–increasing necessity for a speedy, instant, transmission of the news is often detrimental to knowledge. A fantastic announcement is then transmitted without the possibility of any scientific scrutiny, and this leads the general public to side with the semi–ignorant researcher who has a fantasy discovery to report, rather than the scientist who cautiously evaluates his contribution to science. The Departments of Antiquities in various regions of the world hold in their archives an amazingly large number of incredible reports made by citizens who categorically affirm knowing the sites 'holding treasures' of the past. Others —although none of them qualified— are ready to give their own version in the interpretation of the most intricate writing and ideograms. The 'readings' of the disk of Phaestos and of the Runic inscription on the Marble Lion of Piraeus are only two of the fantastic interpretations of inscriptions that can be considered naïve at least, if not ridiculous. All means are mobilized: chance troves, secret maps, revelations in dreams and even 'psychic archaeology', a term that has lately been unashamedly advanced by a group of exalted visionaries, who nonetheless obtained permission to search in Alexandria for the tomb of Alexander the Great with the use of ... mediums. In fact, it is on the alleged discoveries of the tomb of the Great Macedonian that we will focus our attention and, more specifically, on the three most publicized and well–documented stories which have —for the last hundred and fifty years— created sensation. The dates for each story setting are different, the persons concerned have different occupations and the sites of research vary, but the pattern followed by each of the instigators is the same. An interpreter in the Consulate General of Russia in Alexandria, in the mid–19th century, an Alexandrian waiter in the mid–20th century, and an archaeologist at the end of that same century shared the same belief, with the same insistence and with the same lack of any scientific foundation. Apparently each initially believes to be the 'elected one' who will find the 'lost tomb'. As time passes, and although nothing substantiates it, the belief becomes certitude. Authorities are persuaded to grant permissions, but the visionary fails to prove his/her case and consequently further authorizations are refused. In despair the researcher claims being the victim of a plot and is appalled that the authenticity of his/her discovery is questioned. As all these cases do not fall in the field of Archaeology, knowledgeable scholars react with either silence or laconic negations, and the confusion remains in the mind of everyday people who get their information through the newspapers, radio broadcasts and television programs.

KEY WORDS: Hellenistic Egypt, Alexandria, Alexander the Great, Tomb of Alexander the Great, Fantastic and Nonsensical Discoveries, Tendentious and Forged Theories, Amvrosios Skylitsis, Stelios Koumoutsos, Liana Souvaltzi.

I. Introduction

The mythical and the fantastic as an attempt to interpret the remains of the human past have preceded Archaeology, which as a scientific discipline is less than two centuries old. However, ignorance coupled with fertility of mind has often brought confusion to the uninitiated general public, when various ruins are arbitrarily connected to legendary palaces of mythical kings and queens. This tendency, understandable for the 'Dark Ages', when knowledge was the prerogative of the few, continued —alas— even during the 19th and the 20th centuries, although education became available to greater numbers of individuals. Tellers of fantastic discoveries are then no longer ignorant peasants or illiterate burghers. The new breed is made up of superficially educated persons, with a basic knowledge, who can read, and often do read profusely books of history. They tend to interpret arbitrarily the remains of the past. Because of their lack of scholarly background, and moved by exaggerated ambitions, they propose naïve interpretations, irresponsible theories, formulated in an unscientific manner. Often they resort to lies and hoaxes in their frenzy to make their cause prevail. These lovers of the past and amateur researchers are found at all levels of society, from workers and clerks, to medical doctors and retired military officers.

It is known that the masses are ready to accept a fantastic story, which they prefer to a historically founded fact. The story–teller whose name has not been saved to posterity but who remains known as Pseudo–Kallisthenēs is a good example: his *Alexander's Romance*, full of fantastic feats and impossible exploits prevailed during all the Middle Ages over proven and historically–rooted facts.

The fast spreading of information due to the expansion of mass media, the ever–increasing necessity for a speedy, instant, transmission of the news is often detrimental to knowledge. A fantastic announcement is then transmitted without the possibility of any scientific scrutiny, and this leads the general public to side with the semi–ignorant researcher who has a fantasy discovery to report, rather than with the scientist who cautiously evaluates his/her contribution to science.

The Departments of Antiquities in various regions of the world hold in their archives an amazingly large number of incredible reports made by citizens who categorically affirm knowing the sites holding treasures of the past. Others, although none specialized, are ready to give their own version in the interpretation of the most intricate writing and ideograms. The supposed readings of the disk of Phaistos and of the Runic inscription on the Marble Lion of Piraeus are only two of the fantastic interpretations of inscriptions that can be considered naïve at the very least, if not ridiculous.

All means are mobilized: chance troves, secret maps, revelations in dreams and even 'psychic archaeology', a term that has lately been unashamedly advanced by a group of exalted visionaries, who nonetheless obtained permission to search in Alexandria for the tomb of Alexander the Great with the use of mediums[1].

In fact, it is on the alleged discoveries of the tomb of the Great Macedonian that we will focus our attention and, more specifically, on the three most publicized and well–documented stories which have, for the last hundred and fifty years, created sensation. The dates for each story setting are different, the persons concerned have different occupations and the sites of research vary; but the pattern followed by each of the instigators is the same. An interpreter in the Consulate General of Russia in Alexandria, in the mid–19th century, an Alexandrian waiter in the mid–20th century, an archaeologist at the end of that same century all share the same belief, with the same insistence and with the same lack of any scientific foundation.

Apparently each initially believes to be the 'elected one' who will find the 'lost tomb'. As time passes (and although nothing substantiates it) the belief becomes certitude. Authorities are persuaded to grant permissions for excavations, but the visionary fails to prove his/her case and consequently further authorizations are refused. In despair the researcher claims to be the victim of a plot and is appalled that the authenticity of his/her discovery is questioned. As these cases do not quite fall in the field of Archaeology, knowledgeable scholars react either with silence or laconic negations, and the confusion remains in the mind of everyday people who get their information not through specialized publications and conferences but by means of popular newspapers, radio broadcasts and low level television programs.

II. Three Nonsensical Characteristic Cases

Let me briefly summarize each of the three fantastic stories related to the supposed discovery of the tomb of Alexander the Great, while stressing that there are some one hundred persons, Alexandrians for the most part, who during the 19th and the 20th century have claimed to know where the Great Macedonian lies buried.

II.1. The Case of Amvrossios Skilitsis

We know practically nothing of this person residing in Alexandria during the mid 19th century and who was attached to the Consulate General of Russia as an interpreter. It is only through the writings of Max de Zogheb, an Alexandrian scholar that we know of Skilitsis' claim that he went down into the vault beneath the Nabi Danial mosque [Fig. 1] in 1850, whilst escorting some European travelers. He 'descended into a narrow, dark subterranean passage and reached the worm–eaten door. Looking through the cracks of the planks he saw a body with the head slightly raised lying in a crystal coffin. On the head, there was a golden diadem. Around were scattered papyri, scrolls and books. He tried to remain longer in the vault but he was pulled away by one of the monks [keepers] of the mosque, and notwithstanding his repeated attempts to return, he was forbidden the area of the crypt'[2].

This tantalizing tale conflates details from Strabōn[3] (the crystal sarcophagus), Suetonius[4] (the diadem left by Augustus), and Dio Cassius[5] (the secret books gathered there by Septimius Severus). Skilitsis may well have visited the crypt of that mosque, but the fact that he mentions papyri and books is in itself a proof that he is fabricating, such material would have certainly perished given the damp climate of Alexandria.

De Zogheb says that Skilitsis did write a letter to the Consul General of Russia[6], his superior, and to the Hellenic–Orthodox Patriarch of Alexandria[7], his spiritual leader, relating his find. Regretfully such documents were never found. In concluding Skilitsis deplores that he was not allowed to further pursue his search and that the authorities of the mosque walled two of the passages depriving him of this fantastic discovery. I have been many times in the vault and it is true that the walled passages are there, obviously obstructed by a structure much more recent than the passage walls; this may in fact be the only truth in Skilitsis' story.

Before Skilitsis' time another mosque in Alexandria had retained the attention of scholars as being the burial place of Alexander the Great. That was the ancient church of St. Athanasius transformed into a mosque after the Arab conquest[8] and known as the Attarine Mosque [Fig. 2]. French scientists of Bonaparte's Expedition had described and drawn this monument, as well as a green granite lidless sarcophagus covered with hieroglyphs and placed in the courtyard of the mosque[9] [Fig. 3]. If we believe the French scholars there was a tradition, which in fact is reported by no other traveler of the time, that this sarcophagus had contained the remains of Alexander. After the setback at the Aboukir naval battle the French had to cede this relic to the victorious British, who transported it to the British Museum where it is still exhibited.

In 1805 E.D. Clarke published this sarcophagus as 'The Tomb of Alexander'[10]. Shortly afterwards, hieroglyphs were deciphered and it became known that the sarcophagus had been made for Nektanebo II[11], the last Pharaoh of Egypt who reigned before the 2nd Persian invasion.

---

[1] Stephan A.Schwartz: *The Alexandrian Project*, NY 1983.

[2] Alexandre Max de Zogheb: *Études sur l'Ancienne Alexandrie*, Alexandria 1909.

[3] Srabōn: *Geogr.* **XVII**, C.793, 794.

[4] Suetonius: *Vit. Aug.* XVIII.

[5] Dio Cassius: **LI**, 16 and **LXX**.

[6] Correspondence of the author with the Director of the Archives of the foreign policy of the Russian Empire (1996).

[7] Such letter could not be found in the archives of the Hellenic Orthodox Patriarchate of Alexandria nor in the documents of the Patriarchal Library (1998).

[8] 'Amr 'Ibn 'El-Ass took Alexandria in 641.

[9] Saint–Genis: 'Description des antiquités d'Alexandrie et de ses environs, dans Antiquités', *Description de l'Egypte*, **II** (1818); see also Vivant Denon: *Travels in Upper and Lower Egypt*, London 1802 (this is the English edition of the French original).

[10] E.D. Clarke: *The Tomb of Alexander the Great: A Dissertation on the Sarcophagus from Alexandria and now in the British Museum*, Cambridge 1805.

[11] A strange coincidence —but purely a coincidence— this same pharaoh and magician is in the Pseudo–Kallisthenēs' *Alexander's Romance* alleged being the father of Alexander the Great. For a bibliography on the various

Although Skilitsis' hoax is very obvious, his story was widely accepted in Alexandria and for many years spread confusion among researchers. However never was an archaeologist allowed digging in the vault of Nabi Danial Mosque and never was a scholar allowed to look behind the walls of the obstructed passages. It is true that Schielmann tried hard to obtain permission but failed[12]. When two years ago I was allowed to photograph the vault and Dr Mohammad Awad, President of Alexandria's Preservation Trust, made detailed plans [Figs. 4a, 4b, 4c] we were restricted to the accessible area.

II.2. The Case of Stelios Koumoutsos

Another Alexandrian, Stelios Koumoutsos, a restaurant waiter, who for over 30 years claimed to know where Alexander's tomb was, started in the early 1960s his quest for the tomb. Although totally unversed in Archaeology and History he succeeded in obtaining permissions from the Egyptian authorities to perform at least six excavations[13].

Unaware of the topography of the ancient city his trenches were sometimes opened in locations that had been reclaimed from the sea only a few decades earlier[14] [Figs. 5a, 5b] and where there had never been land. As it is practically impossible to dig anywhere in the center of Alexandria —except if one opens a trench in what was previously the sea— without finding some ancient structures, Koumoutsos although searching at random without any preconceived plan and with only the help of an Encyclopaedia did find remains of Alexandria's past (probably water cisterns) leading him to believe that he was on the right path in his search for the tomb. The obstacles found on his underground course, such as modern foundations, which if destroyed would have put buildings at risk resulted in the authorities to stopping his work. After a number of failures, the authorities refused to grant new permissions. Koumoutsos became desperate and claimed that there was a plot to deprive him, at the very last moment, of the glory of his great discovery. Led by a real mania and failing to secure further permissions to dig, he resorted to repeated hoaxes trying desperately to get the Hellenic Ministry of Culture to intercede in his favor with the Egyptian authorities.

He forged a supposedly ancient map [Fig. 6] showing the position of the tomb in an attempt to prove its authenticity. No scholar ever took seriously this naive document, which he claimed to belong to a Hungarian musician living in Alexandria, well versed in the occult. Koumoutsos' lies culminated when, towards the end of his life he reported to an archaeologist working for the Ministry of Culture[15] that he had seen Alexander in his glass coffin from a hole made in the wall of a subterranean passage. Asked how he could be certain it was Alexander's body and not that of another king or dignitary, he candidly assured (*sic*!) that a statue set in front of the door of the tomb bore the inscription ΜΕΓΑΣ ΑΛΕΞΑΝΔΡΟΣ.

Nevertheless the fantastic stories of both Skilitsis and Koumoutsos have found their way in every study related to the tomb of Alexander the Great.

II.3. The Case of Liana Souvaltzi

The third case is more complex, as the individual involved is not a consulate interpreter nor a waiter, but a person who has studied archaeology. It is true that since the end of her studies in the late '60s Mrs Liana Souvaltzi had never lead an excavation nor did she present any paper or published any contribution to Archaeology until the day, in 1989 when she decided that she was the elected one who would find the tomb of the Macedonian conqueror not in Alexandria, but in the Western Libyan Desert at the Oasis of Siwa. Since then, Mrs Liana Souvaltzi has kept the attention of Hellenic and international mass media with her fantastic story, which is deprived of any scientific foundation. Ignoring all reliable ancient sources, which state that Alexander's mummified body was placed in the *Sōma* in Alexandria[16], although its original destination was the Oasis of Siwa[17], Souvaltzi claims without substantiating her assertion that the body was in fact buried in that oasis.

After unsuccessfully digging in the Oasis itself Souvaltzi compromised with a location distant some 20 km away, a place known as Deir el Roum[18] or Belad 'el-Roum[19]. Ancient ruins had been visible and were first reported and drawn in the early 19th century by F. Cailliaud and published by E. Jomard[20] [Fig. 7]. In 1869 the German traveler Roulfs saw the temple and describes it in his book of travels[21], but it was reduced to a heap of rubble before 1900[22], Steindorff[23] saw it in the same condition. An Egyptian archaeologist, Ahmed Fakhry visited in 1938 what was visible of this monument that he calls 'the Doric temple' and published it briefly in 1944[24]. He did also make a sketch–plan of the ancient remains in the area showing also the 'Doric Temple' [Fig. 8]. It is obvious that Souvaltzi had access to Fakhry's publication, but kept it silent and never mentioned it in her book[25]. The Egyptian archaeologist's brief report and his sketch of the temple compared with Souvaltzi's confirms that this is indeed the same monument [Figs. 9a, 9b]. Then Liana Souvaltzi proceeded in a lamentable excavation, which a few years later was to be described unanimously by the members of the

versions of the *Alexander's Romance* see H.E. Tzalas: 'The Tomb of Alexander the Great: The History and the Legend in the Helleno–Roman and Arab times' in *Graeco–Arabica*, **V**, Athens 1993, 329.

[12] Kunstchronik, **20**, Leipzig 1887/88, 323; ibid., **23**, 1887/88, 368. *La Chronique des Arts, Supplément à la Gazette des Beaux–Arts*, Paris 1888, 84.

[13] Koumoutsos performed also clandestine digs; in an instance he dug a whole night in the courtyard of St. Sabbas Monastery and when he found remains of old masonry alerted the local press claiming he was on the site of the lost tomb.

[14] One of Koumoutsos trenches was made in front of Saad Zaghloul monument, in the square that bears his name, and it is known that the sea extended until there up to the end of the 19th century.

[15] Reported to the author by the archaeologist Mrs Sophia Tarandou.

[16] Strabōn, Diodorus Siculus, Plutarchos, Zenobius, Flavius Josephus, Pausanias, Dio Cassius, Lucanus, Suetonius, Antiochus Grypus, Achilles Tatius; for references to the ancient sources see Tzalas: *supra cit.*

[17] Diodorus Siculus, 18.3.5.

[18] E. Jomard, [Deyr Roum] *Voyage à l'Oasis de Syouah, en 1819 et en 1820*, Paris, 1823.

[19] Ahmed Fakhry [Belad 'el-Roum], *The Egyptian Deserts: Siwa Oasis, Its History and Antiquities*, Cairo (Service des Antiquités de l'Egypte) 1944, 69.

[20] Jomard: *supra cit.*

[21] Roulfs, *Von Tripolis nach Alexandrien*, II. 92-93.

[22] Fakhry: *supra cit.*, 70.

[23] Steindorf's photograph of the ruins is published in Fakhry's report (see *ibid.*, 127.

[24] Fakhry: *supra cit.*, 69-71.

[25] Liana Souvaltzi: *The Tomb of Alexander the Great at the Oasis of Siwa: The History of the Excavation and the Political Background*, Athens ^{3}2002. (in Hellenic).

Supreme Council of Antiquities of Egypt (SCA) as the worse excavation ever made!

Understanding nothing about the structure of the ruined 'Doric Temple', but determined to announce that it was the tomb of Alexander, she declared that the building, which bears not even the faintest resemblance to a Macedonian tomb [Fig. 10], was in fact the long lost Mausoleum of Alexander the Great. Souvaltzi did everything possible to make her assertion prevail: lies and hoaxes were presented as facts to international mass media. The fantastic reached its zenith when she presented the macabre remains of a mummy, claiming it was one of the Macedonian soldiers guarding the tomb[26]. No one knows how this mummified head came into the possession of Souvaltzi although remains of long–looted tombs scatter the desert[27]. The fact is that it was presented to the Press with a Ptolemaic coin inserted in its mouth. Because of the henna color of the hair the head was declared to belong to a blond Macedonian guarding Alexander's tomb (*sic*!).

In 1995 Souvaltzi did find the broken parts of an ancient inscription and presented it in her book on the tomb of Alexander the Great[28], as the uncontested proof that the tomb was Alexander the Great's burial site [Figs. 11a, 11b, 11c]. It is an inscription made at the time of *Servius Sulpicius Similis*, Governor, *Praefectus Aegypti* (= Eparch of Egypt) under the reign of Trajan[29], which refers to some building dedicated 'on behalf of the Emperor's good fortune and infinite duration'[30]. The many pieces can easily be assembled and read. Similar to several other inscriptions of this type[31] [Fig. 12] it starts with the formulaic expression:ΥΠΕΡ ΑΥΤΟΚΡΑΤΟΡΟΣ ΝΕΡΟΥΑ ΤΡΑΙΑΝΟΥ ---------- ΣΕΒΑΣΤΟΥ.

As reported during a television interview by Dr Charalambos Kritzas (the director of the Epigraphic Museum of Athens, who was a member of the scientific team delegated by the Minister of Culture of Hellas to investigate Souvaltzi's alleged discovery), he explained that it was an easy matter to read and interpret the inscription which is a sole inscription and do not refer to Alexander or to his tomb as Mrs Souvaltzi erroneously claims.

Unable to correctly reassemble the broken parts of the inscription as a whole, Souvaltzi believes that there are three inscriptions. Not a word of what she insists in reading on the stone exists in real fact and one wonders how she proposes to fit such long texts in the limited space of the inscription.

I translate and quote from Mrs Souvaltzi's recently published book on the tomb of Alexander the Great at Siwa[32]:

1st inscription[33]:

ALEXANDER AMON RA
TO THE RESPECTED ONE I MADE A SACRIFICE THERE WHERE LAYS THE RECEPTACLE
IN ACCORDANCE WITH THE ORDERS OF THE GOD I TRANSPORTED THE BODY THAT WAS AS LIGHT AS A SMALL SHIELD
I WHO WAS GENERAL EPARCH OF EGYPT
I WAS ALWAYS HONOURED BY COMMON AGREEMENT
NOW THAT I AM AT THE LAST OF MY LIFE I DISCLOSE THAT I DID ALL THIS IN HIS HONOR

2nd inscription[34]:

NERVA AND TRAJAN[35] BUILT A SHRINE
AFTER HAVING PERFORMED LIBATIONS ON THE SITE
IN HONOUR OF ZEUS AND THE ETERNAL ZEUS[36]
WHO DRUNK IMPETUOUSLY THE POISON[37]
AIMING THAT THE SHRINE BE IN PUBLIC VIEW
THE SHRINE WAS BUILT WHEN SULPICIUS WAS THERE WITH ARTEMIDORUS
THE INSCRIPTION IS PRECISE BECAUSE THOSE MENTIONED [Nerva and Trajan] WERE MORAL MEN (*sic*!)

The third inscription is in fact a very small fragment, which Souvaltzi measures correctly; it is only 33 cm. x 6 cm. It reads MEXEIP, hence it is the second month of the *Winter* (*Pr.t*) according to the ancient Egyptians (later on assimilated into the Coptic) calendar as ⲙ̀ϣⲓⲣ (S) / ⲙⲉⲭⲓⲣ (B)[38], indicating probably the date when this inscription was dedicated. Souvaltzi's interpretation of these letters, is to say the least, a monument of ingenuity[39]. She declares that these are Hellenic numerals of the classical times explaining that the Oasis had 400,000 inhabitants[40], 110,000 were soldiers, among which 30,000 represented an elite guarding the tomb (*sic*!).

The archaeological authorities of Egypt have since 1996 refused to grant Mrs Liana Souvaltzi any renewal of her permission to dig. Yet far from abandoning her quest, she stubbornly insists that she is the victim of a political plot. Unbelievable as it may seem, the matter of Souvaltzi's excavations was discussed in February 1997 at the Hellenic Parliament, when deputies from different parties asked the Minister of Culture why a Hellenic archaeologist was not benefiting from the support of the Hellenic authorities[41]. Lately she regularly appears on secondary Hellenic television channels and some newspapers known for their nationalistic tendencies publish her claims.

---

[26] In the Hellenic daily newspaper *Αδέσμευτος Τύπος*, 12 April 1995.

[27] Referring to the neighboring area; the District of 'El-Maragi, Ahmed Fakhry reports that: '…there is no ridge that does not have tombs in it.' (see *supra cit.*, 71).

[28] Souvaltzi: *supra cit.*

[29] Trajan, son of Nerva, reigned from 98 to 117 CE.

[30] ΥΠΕΡ ΑΥΤΟΚΡΑΤΟΡΟΣ ΝΕΡΟΥΑ ΤΡΑΙΑΝΟΥ ΣΕΒΑΣΤΟΥ --------
ΔΑΚΙΚΟΥ [ΤΥΧΗΣ ΚΑΙ] ΑΙΩΝΙΟΥ ΔΙΑ[ΜΟΝΗΣ].

[31] A complete inscription honoring Trajan can be seen in the archaeological site of Delphi it reads:
ΑΥΤΟΚΡΑΤΟΡΑΝΕΡ
ΒΑΝΤΡΑΙΑΝΟΝΚΑΙ
ΣΑΡΑΣΕΒΑΣΤΟΝΓΕΡ
ΜΑΝΙΚΟΝΔΑΚΙΚΟΝ
ΑΡΙΣΤΟΝΑΚΑΣΣΙΟΣ
ΔΕΡΚΙΟΥΥΙΟΣΠΕΤΡΑΙ
ΟΣΕΚΤΩΝΙΔΙΩΝ.

[32] Souvaltzi: *supra cit.*

[33] *Ibid.* 157.

[34] *Ibid.*, 159.

[35] Trajan is the son of Nerva but this seems to be ignored by Mrs Souvaltzi when she refers to 'Nerva and Trajan'.

[36] Arbitrarily for Mrs Souvaltzi the eternal Zeus [Αιωνίου Διός] is Alexander. The inscription in fact reads ΑΙΩΝΙΟΥ ΔΙΑ[ΜΟΝΗΣ] 'of eternal duration'

[37] In the *Romance of Alexander* there is a version saying that Alexander was poisoned.

[38] I would like to thank Dr Amanda–Alice Maravelia for her useful remarks on the Egyptian month's names.

[39] Souvaltzi: *supra cit.*, 168-69.

[40] It should be reminded that Alexandria had in the year 60 B.C. some 300.000 citizens (Diodorus Siculus, 17.52).

[41] Report of the Deputies Mr Nikos I., Nikolopoulos (4.2.1997), Mr Stavros I. Papadopoulos (21.1.1997), and Mr Iōannēs Karakōstas (28.1.1997).

III. Conclusions

In the present paper we focused our attention on the alleged discoveries of the tomb of Alexander the Great and —more specifically— on the three most publicized and well–documented stories which have —for the last hundred and fifty years— created sensation. The dates for each story setting are different, the persons concerned have different occupations and the sites of research vary, but the pattern followed by each of the instigators is the same. An interpreter in the Consulate General of Russia in Alexandria, in the mid–19th century, an Alexandrian waiter in the mid–20th century, an archaeologist at the end of that same century shared the same belief, with the same insistence and with the same lack of any scientific foundation. Apparently each initially believes to be the 'elected one' who will find the 'lost tomb'. As time passes, and although nothing substantiates it, the belief becomes certitude. Authorities are persuaded to grant permissions, but the visionary fails to prove his/her case and consequently further authorizations are refused. In despair the researcher claims being the victim of a plot and is appalled that the authenticity of his/her discovery is questioned. As all these cases do not fall in the field of Archaeology, knowledgeable scholars react with either silence or laconic negations, and the confusion remains in the mind of everyday people who get their information through the newspapers, radio broadcasts and low level television programs.

In concluding this presentation I would like to set the problem before the competent archaeologists and ask: *how scholars should face such nonsense?*

I personally believe that in prominent cases such as the above, scientists have the obligation to step forward and inform the non–initiated general public, which obtains its information exclusively through the mass media, of where the truth stands. It should be remembered that most of scientific archaeological work is carried out with the money of taxpayers and … they deservedly have the right to know.

FIGURE 1. The Mosque Nabi Danial, view from the Kom 'el-Dikka hill. End 19th century Photograph.
© Copyright Dr Harry E. Tzalas, 2003.

FIGURE 2. The courtyard of the Attarine Mosque. The sarcophagus of Nektanebo II believed to have contained Alexander the Great's remains was placed inside the small chapel.

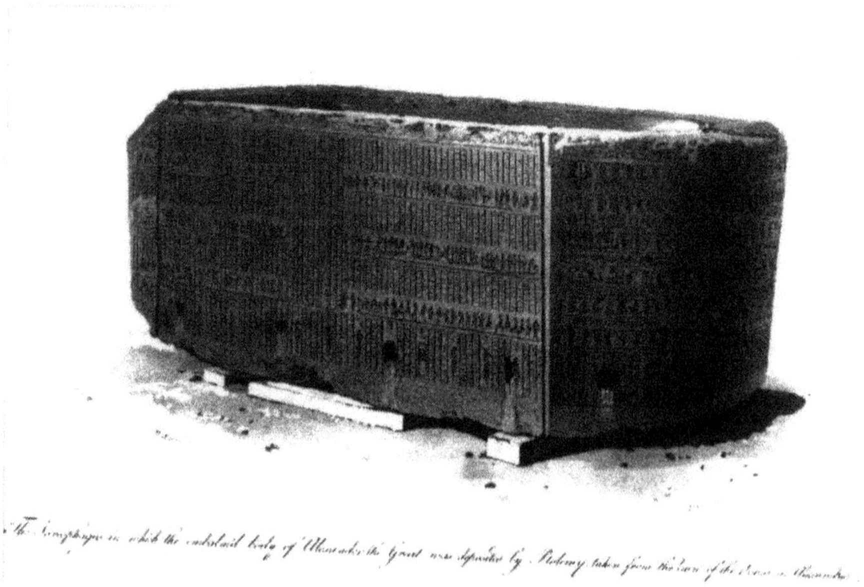

FIGURE 3. The granite sarcophagus, covered with hieroglyphs, made for Nektanebo II which is now kept in the British Museum.

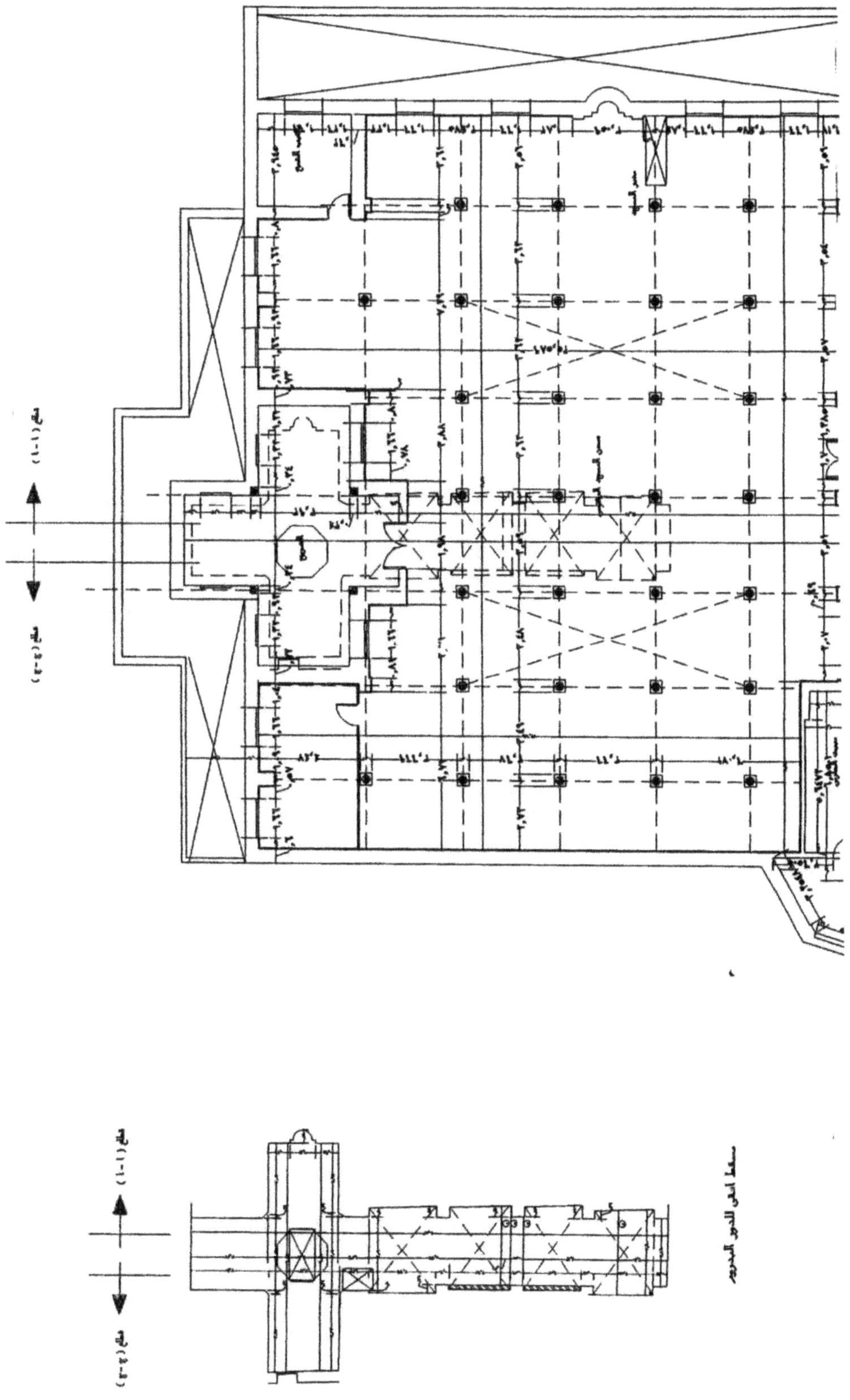

FIGURE 4(a). Plan of the vault under the Nabi Danial Mosque.
© Copyright Dr Harry E. Tzalas, 2003.

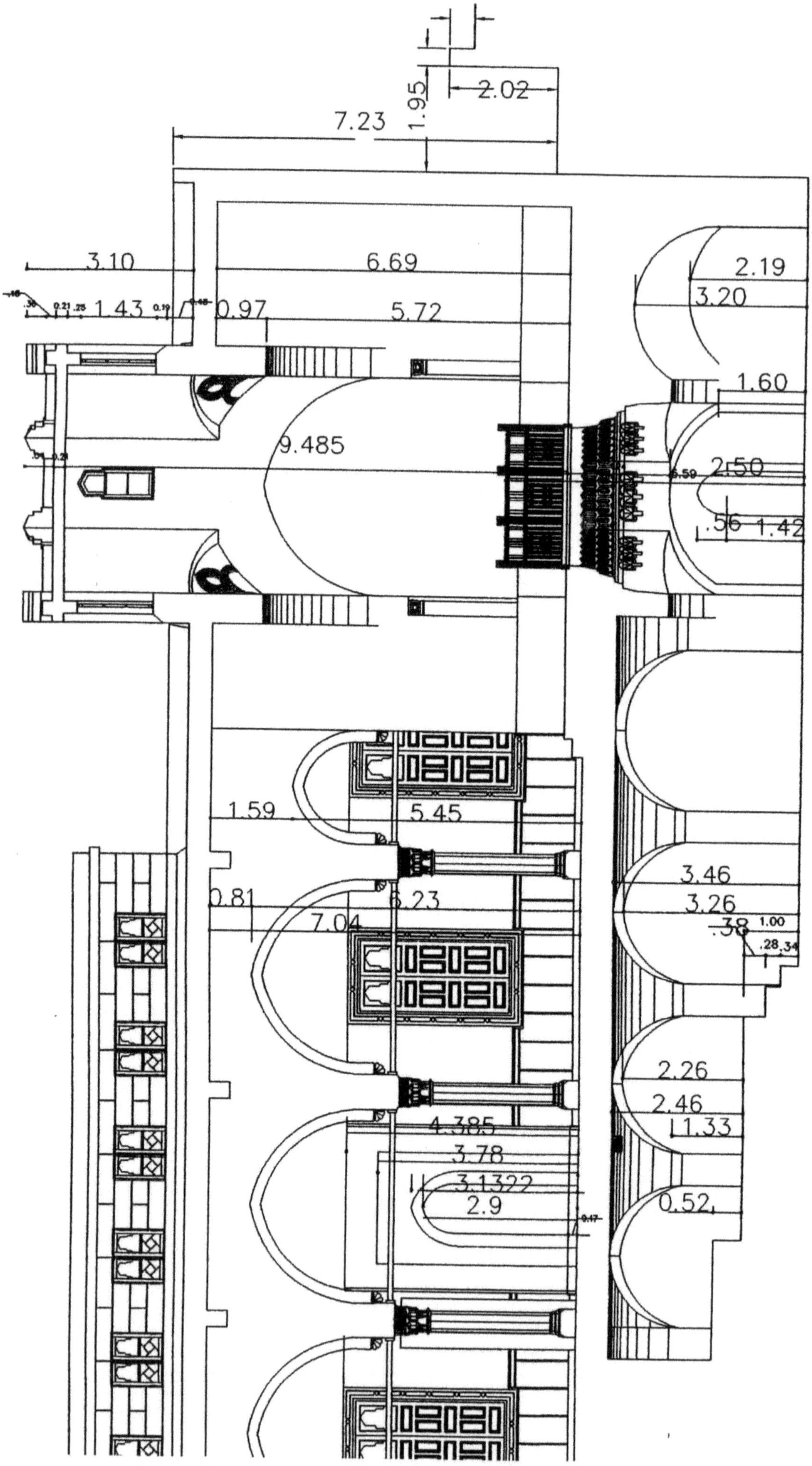

FIGURE 4(b). Same as in Fig. 4(a).
© Copyright Dr Harry E. Tzalas, 2003.

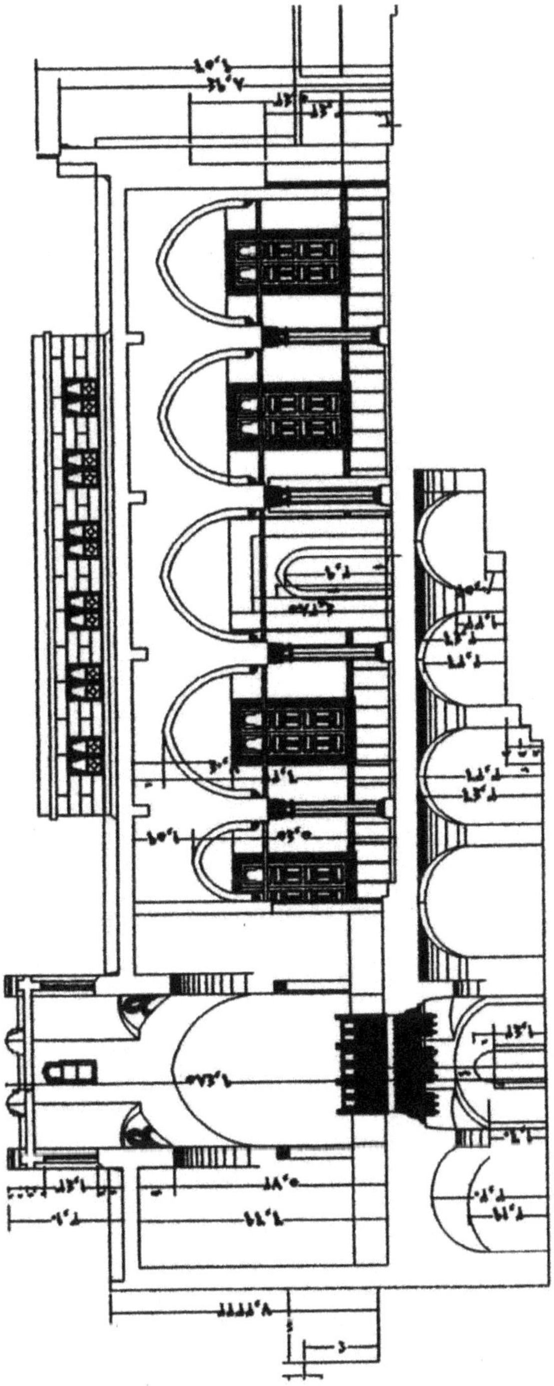

FIGURE 4(c). Same as in Fig. 4(a).

FIGURE 5(a). Stelios Koumoutsos in a trench opened in Saad Zaghloul square, Alexandria.
Note the height of the water level. Photograph archives of the Centre d'Etudes Alexandrines, Alexandria.
© Copyright Centre d'Etudes Alexandrines, Alexandria, 2003.

FIGURE 5(b). Stelios Koumoutsos' trench opened behind Saad Zaghloul statue in Alexandria.
Photograph archives of the Centre d'Etudes Alexandrines, Alexandria.

FIGURE 6. Stelios Koumoutsos plan 'showing' the tomb of Alexander the Great.
© Copyright Dr Harry E. Tzalas, 2003.

FIGURE 7. The 'Doric Temple' at Deir Roum as published by E. Jomard (1819).
© Copyright Dr Harry E. Tzalas, 2003.

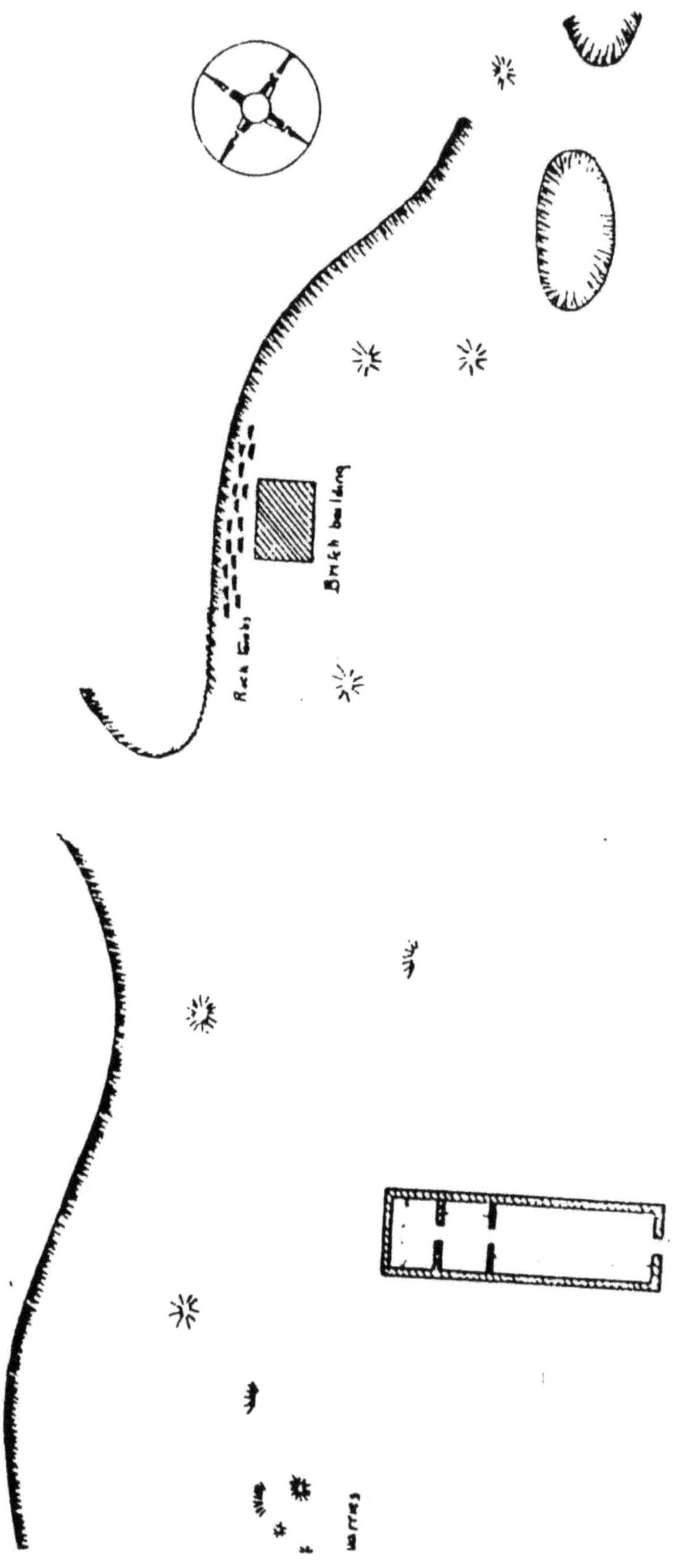

FIGURE 8. Sketch–Plan of the ancient remains at Belad 'El-Roum made by Ahmed Fakhry in 1938.
© Copyright Dr Harry E. Tzalas, 2003.

FIGURE 9(a). Ahmed Fakhry sketch–plan of the 'Doric Temple' at Belad 'El-Roum.
© Copyright Dr Harry E. Tzalas, 2003.

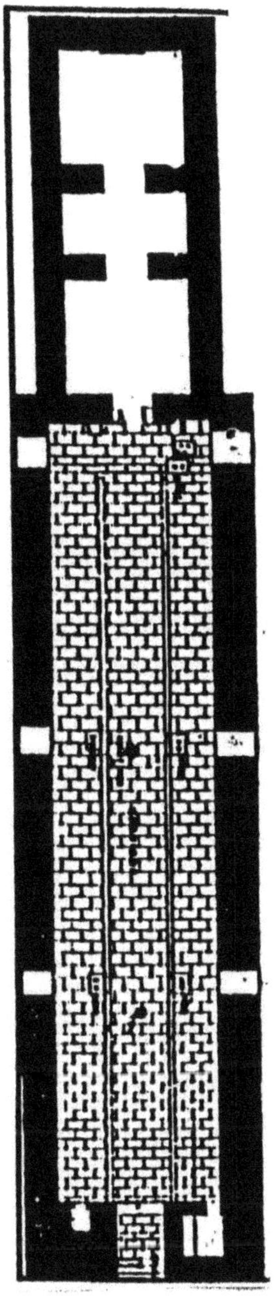

FIGURE 9(b). Liana Souvaltzi's plan of the same ruin made 60 years later and attributed to the tomb of Alexander the Great [*Εθνική Ηχώ*, Feb. 1999, 13].
© Copyright *Εθνική Ηχώ*, Athens 2003.

FIGURE 10. The present remains of the 'Doric Temple' at Deir 'El-Roum. The stones were removed by the Oasis' inhabitants during the last two centuries, and used for the construction of their houses. Photo: *Eurokinissi* Photo–Press Agency, Athens.
© Copyright *Eurokinissi* Photo–Press Agency, Athens 2003.

FIGURE 11(a). The inscription found in the 'Doric Temple' at Deir 'El-Roum, partially reassembled. Photos: Prisma – G. Karachalis, Athens (5.2.1995).
© Copyright Prisma – G. Karachalis, Athens 2003.

FIGURE 11(b). Same as in Fig. 11(a).
© Copyright Prisma – G. Karachalis, Athens 2003.

FIGURE 11(c). The inscription found in the 'Doric Temple' at Deir 'El-Roum, partially reassembled. Photo *Eurokinissi* Photo–Press Agency O.E. Athens.

FIGURE 12. The inscription of Delphi honoring emperor Trajan. Photograph by the author.
© Copyright Dr Harry E. Tzalas, 2003.

Egypt and the Great Silk Road

Tatjana A. Sherkova

Abstract

The wide popularity of Egyptian faience amulets among populations of different ethno–cultural background, belonging especially to the Helleno–Roman Period, presents a researcher with a considerable number of problems: the place of their production in Egypt itself and possible local copies; the semantics of images on these amulets outside Egypt; & c. These numerous objects make it possible to determine to a certain extent the character of continental trade and to reconstruct the meaning of the figurine for the Egyptian amulets outside Egypt. There is a notion that they were a kind of small change in the international trade. But in any case, by obtaining them the representatives of other cultures besides their aesthetic attraction appreciated their protective abilities. At present there is a vivid interest in the Great Silk Road. This conception adds the importance, which is practically identical to the system of roads that linked the Mediterranean and the Black Sea regions with India and China. As to India, it was in the sphere of sea–trade and its character differed from continental trade. Via Penjab and accordingly inner regions of Central Asia, Baktria was linked with Indian ports, through which a sea–trade with Egypt was taking place. The tracks of this trade are easily discernible due to finds of art works of the Alexandrian School of art style. A collection of such things was kept in the palace of the ruller of Capisa (the present Begram near Kabul in Afghanistan) of the Kushan Empire, which was situated in Cenral Asia from the 2nd-1st century BCE to the 2nd-3rd century CE. In the sealed treasury these valuable objects —received as gifts or confiscated by the Customs— were placed together with Chinese carved ivory and lacquers. There were glass vessels of the famous Alexandrian glass–blowers and plaster medallions, bronze figurines, the representations of Harpocratēs and Hēraklēs–Serapis being among them. The works of art of the Roman Empire were not only gods, but also samples of many local articles as well as — especially— their image–bearing series. Kushan kings used the iconography of divinities of the Helleno–Roman pantheon representing personages of the local Indo–Iranian pantheon. In the representations of their divinities on reliefs of stupa and palaces, Helleno–Roman and Egyptian iconography of gods was borrowed by the Kushans much more extensively.

KEY WORDS: Great Silk Road, Ancient Trade, Late Antiquity, Asia, India, China, Kushan Kings, Egypt, Faience Artifacts.

I. Introduction

There opened an abyss full of stars;
The stars are countless, the abyss has no bottom.

M.V. LOMONOSOV.

These lines are metaphorical to the phenomenal spread of Egyptian faience amulets added to the system of religious notions and beliefs of the ancient inhabited world during the Helleno–Roman Period[1]. The number of Egyptian amulets in many museums worldwide is countless. They are kept as a result of archaeological excavations or stray finds from England to China and from Siberia to South Africa.

With the exception of individual finds in the extremely outlying districts these objects were articles of an international trade along the brisk routes at the turn of the 1st Millennium BCE-1st Millennium CE forming a system of continental roads. The *Great Silk Road* was the main artery of this trade, and Egypt was linked with it by two roads via the Sinai peninsula.

This wide popularity of faience amulets among populations of different ethno–cultural background, belonging especially to the later historic periods, puts a number of problems before a researcher: the place of their production in Egypt itself and the possible local copies; the semantics of images on these amulets outside Egypt, & c. This article deals with Egyptian faience amulets in terms of revealing the 'darkest' sections of the Great Silk Road, which is a question of dispute in written sources. At the same time these numerous objects make it possible to determine to a certain extent the character of continental trade, and help answering the above–mentioned important questions.

II. The Great Silk Road as an Ancient Trade Route

The production of faience objects, which was taking place for a fantastically long time —from the middle of the 4th Millennium BCE to the 4th centuries of the 1st Millennium CE— was intended for all social strata. These objects combined both aesthetical aspect and content. Quite attractive and bright in outward appearance, imitating articles made of precious and semi–precious stones they represented Egyptian gods, people of great social status and numerous religious symbols. Of course, a set of figured amulets changed in one or another period of time. In the dynastic epoch from the Old and New Kingdom, Egyptian religious symbols prevailed while in the Helleno–Roman Period many of them disappeared and were substituted for those which were typical of other cultures, for example: figs, amphorae, bunches of grapes, phallic symbols, and such. However the proper Egyptian representations were preserved. They were images of Isis, Osiris, Horus, Thoth, Ptah–Sokar–Osiris and other gods, as well as sacred animals that were considered as incarnating different gods[2]: bulls, cows, scarabs, frogs, turtles, & c.

Apart from small faience objects larger objects were also produced (vessels, figurines, and even statues, shabtis, & c.). At the same time faience figurines imitated other materials, like: gold, different precious stones, crystal, chalcedony, lapis–lazuli, turquoise, & c. As a rule, amulets were worn as necklaces containing different figures, their beads being made not only of faience.

Not only the Egyptians, but inhabitants of remote countries alike —who exchanged these objects for other goods— were using such necklaces. It is possible that Egyptian faience was used as a kind of small change in the international trade. But in any case, obtaining them, the representatives of other

[1] Raschke, M.G.: 'New Studies in Roman Commerce with the East', *Aufstieg und Niedergang der römischen Welt* (Temporini, H., ed.), **II**, 1978, 9.2.B.

[2] Sherkova, T.A.: *Egipet i Kushanskoe tzarstvo (topgovie i kulturnie kontakti)*, Moscow 1991, 62 ff; 92ff; 123ff; 136 ff.

cultures, besides their esthetic attraction, they also appreciated their protective magical properties.

The closer to Egypt their adherents lived, it is more likely that the primordial (archetypal) Egyptian implication of symbolism was put into these representations. The farther these objects were taken away along caravan–routes, there are less grounds to believe that their archetypal Egyptian symbolism could be preserved. However, this scheme is not always adequate, a fact which can be explained by the character of contacts between Egypt and various other countries.

FIGURES 1-2. Terracotta statuettes of Serapis and Harpocratēs.
© Copyright Dr Tatjana A. Sherkova, 2003.

During the Helleno–Roman Period many representatives of the ancient world not only visited the remote territories of the East, but settled their occupations with trade or handicrafts. In such trading stations they continued their own distinctive way of life, including the devotion to their gods and beliefs in the magical force of amulets. Thus, the local population could learn —and learnt— their meaning, specific destination, symbolism, as well as the meaning of the represented personages on them (divinities, and such).

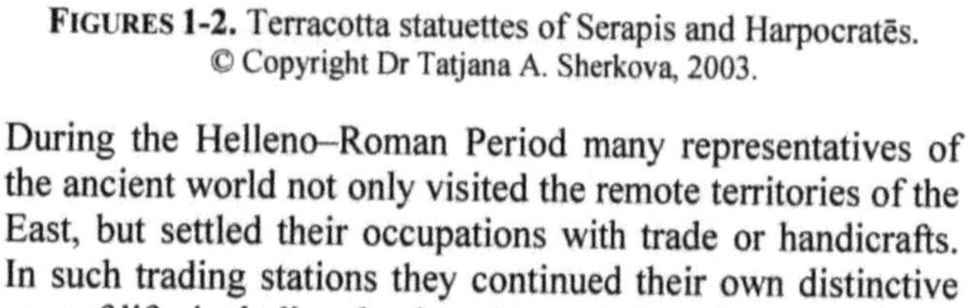

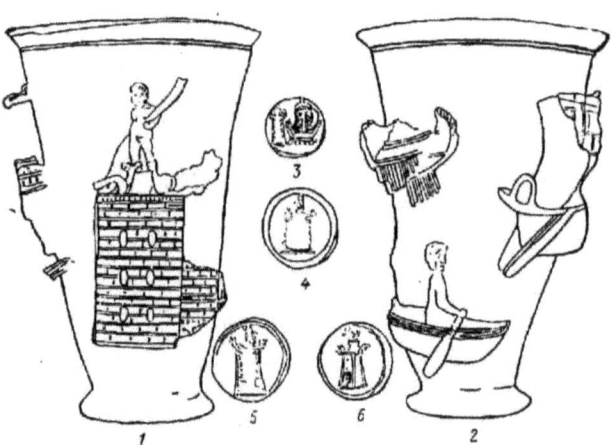

FIGURE 3. Typical examples of glass vessels, from the famous Alexandrian glass–blowers.
© Copyright Dr Tatjana A. Sherkova, 2003.

Sometimes the symbolic representations on amulets coincided with the images of local gods and symbols, and in this case the imported amulets became an integral part of the local culture. Such articles were copies and sometimes changed out of all recognition. All these transformations cover a wider layer of figurative materials, which assuredly evidence several developed trade contacts of ancient Egypt with some countries of the East (in Asia).

At present there is a great interest in the Great Silk Road. This conception adds the importance, which is practically identical to the system of roads that linked the Mediterranean and Black Sea regions with India and China. In the initial, narrower sense this road formed on the basis of the Lazuli Road or Royal Road from Asia Minor and coastal sites of Syria to Central Asia. Egypt was connected with this transcontinental route by two roads: along the eastern Mediterranean coast [Strabōn: ***XVI***, 1, 31, Plinius: ***V***, 68]; or directly via Sinai towards Petra situated on the 'road of incense' [Strabōn: ***XVI***, 4, 2; ***XVII***, 1, 30] and linked with Babylon in Mesopotamia, with Rynokolura and Gaza on the Mediterranean coast [Strabōn: ***XVI***, 4, 24], with Ela in the gulf of Aqaba [Strabōn: ***XVI***, 1, 30], as well as with Near Eastern cities Jerusalem, Jericho and Palmyra.

From the coastal Syrian cities caravans moved further to the Euphrates, to crossings on the border of Parthia. In the 1st-2nd Millennium CE the crossing took place near the site of Bambika, and then the road passed through deserted areas as far as Skena and further to Seleukia and Ktēsiphōn [Strabōn: ***XVI***, 1, 16; Plinius: ***VI***, 122].

The contacts between Egypt and Mesopotamia were traditional and Egyptian articles were numerous especially during the Roman Era. Thus, Egyptian faience and local imitations from different materials occurred in a number of the sites: in the 2nd century BCE in Palmyra, in Parthia and late Parthian archaeological layers of Dura–Eurōpos, Seleukia and Babylon. There are also similar contacts known on the territory of Iran, and in the coastal part of the Caspian Sea.

From Mesopotamia the road led towards the summer residences of Parthian kings, to Ragi via Kersmanshah and then via Apameia and Hecatompylos to the Caspian gates in Hyrcania [Strabōn: ***IX***, 9, 1; Plinius: ***VI***, 42-43]. According to the Helleno–Roman authors and Chinese dynastic chronicles, the road led to Alexandria (the present Herat), the capital of the country of Aryans. However it is not clear whether it passed through cities of Khorasan or northward, along the hills of Kopet Dagh (where the historic province of Margiana with Nissa as the capital) was situated.

In written sources this road is mentioned not earlier than the 9th century CE, while archaeological finds evidence its earlier use. Egyptian small objects belonging to different epochs are among them. As far back as in the Achaemenid Period an alabaster vessel with the inscribed name of the King Artaxerxēs was brought to Nisa.

In Uzboy (the region of the Eastern seashore of the Caspian Sea), in a burial of the first centuries CE there were found Egyptian faience amulets, including a figurine of the god Bes. It should be said that in the Middle Ages the main Amu Darya riverbed was curved towards the Caspian Sea and passed by through the present deserted Usboy; according to Strabōn, the Amu Darya was the river of various trade contacts with India.

The Chinese also knew that tradesmen and merchants lived in the Amu Darya region, and they went into land and sea trade not only with neighboring countries, but with more remote ones as well[3]. It can be supposed logically that Egyptian objects —including faience amulets— spread by this way to the cities of Khorezm, and actually the layers of the 1st century CE contain a lot of them.

But the cities of Khorezm were not the ultimate destinations of the trade going farther to the East; it was one of the branches of the Great Silk Road. The road passed to China and India via Margiana or Khorasan, and the branching took place in Baktria. It was the main part of the whole transcontinental route, the cross roads in its way on the roads leading to different directions.

The centre of these crossroads was the city of Baktria (present Balkh).The capital was located in the steppe part of the Amu Darya left bank, and from the West the road passed there through Alexandria of the Aryans. This can be confirmed by Chinese dynastic chronicles containing the description of dozens of Parthian cities.

FIGURE 4. Bronze figurine of Harpocratēs.
© Copyright Dr Tatjana A. Sherkova, 2003.

From Baktria the roads branched off: one road led to India (through this, it was possible to get to this country from Arya via Drangiana); the other road led to China. The most disputable question regarding the whole picture of the Great Silk Road is how the road passed from Baktria to China. This is described by Roman and Chinese written sources. However the toponyms mentioned there do not correspond to a geographical map if we speak only about one road.

It is most likely that in the narration of the sources the displacement of information about several roads took place, at least about three roads passing from Baktria via China: through Fergana, Karategin and the Alay valley or the southern region[4]. The area of East Turkestan (Western China) to the Southern Tjan Shan region was the point where (according to the Chinese sources) the northern road was passing.

The road of the Pamyra region led to the southern road in East Turkestan, along the spurs of Kunlun. Both the Eastern Turkestan roads met in the East in Loulan, and in Yrkend in the West.

FIGURE 5. Bronze figurine of Hēraklēs–Serapis.
© Copyright Dr Tatjana A. Sherkova, 2003.

It should be pointed out that Egyptian articles were found in the East Turkestan both in the sites along the northern road and the southern one. The articles include not only faience amulets and beads, but also terracotta figurines of Egyptian gods: Serapis [Fig. 1] and Harpocratēs [Fig. 2][5]. They could be brought by different of the above–mentioned roads passing through Central Asia.

The Egyptian objects of minor plastic arts number many dozens and even prevail over a hundred. However, if we draw the places of finds on a geographical map it seems probable that the main road through Central Asia to China passed through the Fergana region. We should remember that the Egyptian faience objects (as mass finds) were most typical of the Central Asian country between two rivers and covered the region from the middle current of the Amu Darya to Samarkand and Ferghana at least in the 1st century BCE

FIGURE 6. Another figurine of Harpocratēs.
© Copyright Dr Tatjana A. Sherkova, 2003.

That was the picture of the spread of small Egyptian faience objects along the Great Silk Road to China; they were known along its whole length. The situation to the south of Hindu Kush, on the way to India, was different. Only in Taxila, the capital city in a large bend of Indus, where the local Porus ruled when Alexander the Great conquered India, there were revealed a few Egyptian faience figurines. Egyptian amulets

[3] Velgus, V.A.: *Izvestia o stranah i narodah Afriki i mopskie svasi v basseinah Tihogo i Indijskogo okeanov*, Moscow (*Kitajskie istotchniki panee*, **XI** v) 1978, 157.

[4] Piankov, I.: *Shelkovij put ot Gierapokja v Seriku: aziatski utshastok*, Dushanbe (*Pamirovedenie*, **II**) 1985.

[5] Maillard, A.: 'A propos de deux statuettes en terre rapportées par la mission Otani: Serapis and Harpocratēs en Asia Centrale', *Journal Asiatique*, **CCLXIII**, 1975.

were also found in other royal burials in Tilla Tepa (Afghanistan)[6]. However, these are local copies made of lapis lazuli, gold and turquoise. Further information to the South on the Egyptian faience amulets is lacking.

FIGURE 7. Representations of Kushan gods, that borrowed Helleno–Roman and Egyptian iconography.
© Copyright Dr Tatjana A. Sherkova, 2003.

Judging from the above, we can conclude that the merchandise of these objects was a characteristic feature of exclusively continental trade. As to India it was in the sphere of sea–trade and its character differed from continental trade. Via Penjab (and accordingly inner regions of Central Asia) Baktria was linked with Indian ports, through which a sea–trade with Egypt was taking place. The tracks of this trade are easily distinguishable and read due to finds of artifacts of the Alexandrian School of art style.

A collection of such things was kept in the palace of the rulers of Capisa (the present Begram near Kabul in Afghanistan) of the Kushan Empire which flourished extending in most parts of Central Asia from the 1st and 2nd centuries to the 3rd century CE[7]. In the sealed treasury these valuable objects received as gifts or customs were found together with Chinese carved ivory and lacquers[8]. There were glass vessels of famous Alexandrian glass–blowers [Fig. 3] and plaster medallions, bronze figurines, and among them representations of Harpocratēs [Fig. 4] and Hēraklēs–Serapis [Fig. 5]. The representations of Harpocratēs were discovered in a palace complex of Taxila[9] [Fig. 6]. It was in the streets of the capitals and noisy markets where merchants from different countries gathered and put in motion the international trade.

Chinese written sources tell us about the prospering sea–trade between Egypt and North–Eastern India. The famous Chinese silk was brought to India through Baktria. It was taken across by sea to Egypt and from there to Rome. Undoubtedly the Chinese silk was sold along the continental route. However it is known from historical sources that there was no direct trade between China and Rome, but through Parthia which gained much profit. Kushanian kings who controlled North India tried to take the leadership by direct sea–trade with Egypt, including Chinese silk.

Finds of Roman gold and silver coins in hidden treasures of India evidence a considerable volume of Indo–Egyptian sea–trade[10]. In North India they were preserved in Buddhist stupas, sometime alongside Kushan coins. All these holy architectural objects (stupas) were situated rather densely in a large bend of the Indus river adjoining the road to Baktria, the main province of the Kushan Empire.

The works of art of the Roman Empire were not only gods but samples of many local articles as well, especially their image–bearing series. Kushan kings used iconography of the gods of the Helleno–Roman pantheon representing personages of the local Indo–Iranian pantheon. In the representations of their gods on reliefs of stupas and palaces Helleno–Roman and Egyptian iconography of gods was borrowed by the Kushans in a much broader context[11] [Fig. 7].

III. Conclusions

To sum up, the Helleno–Roman and Egyptian art became integral elements of the Kushan art and culture. We have good grounds for saying that helleno–Egyptian Serapis and Harpocratēs were also worshipped in the Kushan Kingdom.

Strictly speaking, opening an active regular sea–trade in the Indian Ocean was the result of the centuries–old searches of the shortest way from the Helleno–Roman world to India and China. A shipping route took less time and made it possible to trade rapidly; and above all, not to be trapped in the political instability on the continent.

The Parthian barrier was a reality, which should be taken into consideration. That is why the interests of the local merchant classes were limited by Mesopotamia, which traditionally had an economic and cultural propensity for the Eastern Mediterranean region, and also for the Helleno–Roman world.

Further to the East, various articles from the eastern Roman provinces and Egypt were exported by trade–agents, who had an unstable and mobile style of life. In this way objects were handed over from hand to hand towards the East.

Thus, one can say that the trade along the Great Silk Road was of interrupted distance nature. The vague character of the road on its eastern section described by Helleno–Roman authors is indicative in this respect.

In this way, passing from hand to hand, numerous Egyptian faience amulets were exported from Egypt, becoming a fact of the culture–adherent and not of the Egyptian culture.

[6] Saryanidi, V.I.: *Afghanistan: Cokrovitha tpimjannich tzarei*, Moscow 1983.

[7] Sherkova: *op. cit.*, 30-51.

[8] Hackin J.: 'Nouvelles Recherches archéologiques à Begram: 1939-1940', *MDAFA*, **XI**, 1954.

[9] Marshall, J.: *Taxila: An Illustrated Account of Archaeological Excavations*, **I–III**, Cambrige 1951.

[10] Sherkova: *op. cit*, 103 ff

[11] Rosenfield, I.M.: *The Dynastic Arts of the Kushans*, Berkeley–LA 1967, 67, tab. III/57, IX/186, 187.

The Ancient Egyptian Roots of the Phoenix Myth: On the History of the Problem

Helena G. Tolmacheva

Abstract

The classical myth of Phoenix has been under discussion since the midst of 16th century, when the humanists published a great number of authentic texts giving the possibility for the systematic study of classical heritage. The Egyptian component of the myth was not clear until 1856, when H. Brugsch proved that the Hellenic *Phoenix* has been known under the name of the Egyptian *bnw*–bird. Nevertheless the interests of the 19th century scholars were focused on Phoenix as the symbol of astronomical and chronological periods. That is why in the literature of those times this discussion is centered on such kind of correlation between the Egyptian *bnw* and the classical Phoenix. The image of *bnw*–bird had existed since the Old Kingdom until the Late Period. During more than 2000 years it was transformed from the small bird–demiurge worshipped in Heliopolis into a significant deity worshipped all over Egypt. The *bnw*–bird image was closely connected to the other supreme gods, such as Atum, Rēʿ, and Osiris. In many aspects the modifications of its functions and symbolism could be explained by the position of these gods in the Egyptian pantheon. At the time of the Old and Middle Kingdom Benu was identified with Atum–Rēʿ and had mainly solar and cosmogonical significance. On the contrary, during the New Kingdom the cult of Osiris got its major expansion. Therefore *bnw* was popularized as one of the rulers of the Netherworld. Thus the components of the myth of Phoenix, which were emphasized by A. Belluccio, could have indeed an Egyptian origin. On the other hand the Hellenic elements should not be forgotten. The image of Phoenix known from classical sources was the result of the synthesis of the Oriental and the Hellenic cultural traditions; the synthesis that was so widespread during Hellenistic times. In Coptic sources and the Early Christian literature Phoenix was considered to be the symbol of resurrection and eternal life, of revival, of the Sun, Time, Christ, Virgin Mary. According to the Coptic authors, the Phoenix appeared during the time of the first sacrifice mentioned in the *Bible*. Another text says that during the Exodus from Egypt the Phoenix appeared in the temple of Heliopolis.

KEY WORDS: Phoenix (*bnw*–bird), Phoenix Myth (Origin & Evolution), Osirian Cult, Solar Cult, Solar Deities, Heliopolis.

I. Introduction

The classical myth of Phoenix has been under discussion since the midst of 16th century, when the humanists published a great number of authentic texts giving the possibility for the systematic studies of classical heritage[1]. The Egyptian component of the myth was not clear until 1856, when H. Brugsch proved that the Hellenic φοῖνιξ has been known under the name of the Egyptian *bnw*–bird[2]. Neththertheless the interests of the 19th century scholars were focused on Phoenix as the symbol of astronomical and chronological periods. That is why in the literature of that period this discussion is centered on such kind of correlation between the Egyptian Benu and the classical Phoenix[3].

The article by A. Wiedemann on the analysis of the myth of Phoenix in ancient Egypt had great importance for studying the notions connected with Benu[4]. The author systematized all the records on Benu–Phoenix in Egyptian sources known by that time, the information about the cult of this deity, and its significance in the context of the mythological concepts of the ancient Egyptians. Despite the fact that most of Wiedemann's conclusions became obsolete and were denied by modern scholars, he offered an important contribution towards interpreting the myth of Benu.

The tradition of the identification of Benu with Phoenix was continued in the Egyptological literature of the early 20th century. The mythical *bnw*–bird was occasionally mentioned in special studies; but only the functions of Benu as the *bȝ* of Osiris and Rēʿ were presumed[5]; the mentions of Benu in the *Book of the Dead* were also quoted. K. Sethe was one of the first who studied the myth of Benu, analyzing the etymology of the name of the divine bird in a short note[6]. H. Kees attempted to describe the symbolism, the origin and the main functions of Benu in his essay on Egyptian religion[7].

Perhaps, until now there is only one complete research on the origin of the myth of Phoenix[8], namely *The Origin of the Phoenix: A Study in Egyptian Religious Symbolism* written by R.I. Clark[9]. The author studied the myth of Phoenix, which appeared in classical literature [especially Hērodotos: *II*, 73] and tried to find its strict analogies in Egyptian sources. Clark examined the components that influenced the formation of the classical conception of Phoenix. Among them are the functions of Benu as a general cosmogonical principle, belonging both to the Heliopolitan solar cult and to the Osirian cycle; the iconography of the bird, which was usually depicted perching on a tree; and the appearance of the bird in mythological themes connected with the Nile inundation.

L. Kákosy collected rich factual material on the role of Benu in ancient Egyptian religion and mythology[10]. An article by the Italian scholar Adriana Belluccio is one of the latest works on this subject[11]. This author attempted to make a parallelism between Benu and the notion of royal power, considering this deity to be a manifestation of Osiris, the first deceased king of the Earth. Belluccio suggested that: 'dans la personne du Roi se confondent comme dans un cycle éternel

[1] For further details see van Den Broek, R.: *The Myth of the Phoenix According to Classical and Early Christian Traditions*, Leiden 1972, 3.

[2] Brugsch, H.: *Nouvelles recherches sur la division de l'année des anciens égyptiens, suivies d'un mémoire sur des observations planétaires consigné dans quatre tablettes égyptiennes en écriture démotique*, Berlin 1856.

[3] Van Den Broek: *op. cit.*, 26-32.

[4] Wiedemann, A.: 'Die Phönix–Sage im alten Aegypten', *ZÄS*, **16**,1878.

[5] See Breasted, J.H.: *Development of Religion and Thought in Ancient Egypt*, London 1913, 72 (for the connection between Benu and Benben); Budge, E.A.W.: *From Fetish to God in Ancient Egypt*, London 1934, 89-90.

[6] Sethe, K.: 'Der Name der Phönix', *ZÄS*, **45**, 1908–1909, 84-85.

[7] Kees, H.: *Der Götterglaube im Alten Ägypten*, Berlin 1956, 52-53, 86-87 (for the connection between Benu and sacral willow); 217 (etymology of the Benu name); 321 (Benu as a Heracleopolitan deity).

[8] See also Clark, R.I.: 'The Legend of the Phoenix', *The University of Birmingham Historical Journal*, **2**, 1949, 105-40.

[9] This is cited by Zandee in Zandee, J: 'Clark R.I. Rundle: *The Origin of the Phoenix*', *BiOr*, **10**, 1953, 108.

[10] Kákosy, L.: art. 'Phönix', *LÄ*, **IV**, Wiesbaden 1982.

[11] Belluccio, A.: 'Le mythe du Phénix à la lumière de la consubstantialité royale du père et du fils', *Atti VI Congresso Internacionale di Egittologia*, **II**, Torino 1993, 21-39.

le début et la fin, le père et le fils, Osiris et Horus, le Phénix et le Faucon'[12].

We assume that all the works mentioned above show the tendency of identification of the Benu with the classical Phoenix. Thus, for instance, Adriana Belluccio states that all the main components of the classical myth of Phoenix existed in Egyptian sources: (i) 'la mort du Phénix et son ensevelissement par son fils, né de ses cendres; (ii) l'oeuf façonné avec des aromates, où git le Phénix défunt ; (iii) la ville d'Héliopolis, lieu de l'ensevelissement du Phénix; (iv) la naissance du Phénix des restes de son père; (v) le vol du Phénix de l'Est à l'Ouest et son éternel retour; et enfin (vi) la taille du Phénix'[13].

Besides, the Hellenic name for Phoenix itself, *φοῖνιξ* is considered as a variant of the Egyptian **boin* or **boine (bnw* or *bin.w)*[14].

R. Van Den Broek holds another opinion. He denied the pure Egyptian origin of Phoenix. In his opinion, the classical myth of Phoenix has a relation with the Egyptian one but does not derive directly from it[15]. The author has come to a conclusion that 'the classic Phoenix myth seems to have been developed on the basis of the widespread oriental conception of the 'bird of the sun'[16]. He proposed the following scheme of the correlation between Benu and Phoenix: (i) both Benu and Phoenix are solar symbols and come from Heliopolis; (ii) the core of the classical myth (death and revival of the sun–bird) was not unknown in Egypt; (iii) the self–birth is typical for both birds; (iv) the names *Benu* and *Phoenix* have something in common; (v) their appearance is different and the fusion of their iconography occurred only in Roman Egypt; (vi) the motif of a bird perching on a tree is seen in the iconography of both Benu and Phoenix. Benu is represented on a willow, Phoenix on a palm–tree; (vii) both images symbolized the revival; (viii) both Benu and Phoenix were treated as creatures belonging either to the beginning of the new world or the new era; for Benu this statement is true in the context of its role in cosmogony; for Phoenix it is connected with the Great Year conception; (ix) for the classical Phoenix it is significant that this bird appeared at the beginning of a cycle but this is not the case for the Egyptian Benu[17].

Van Den Broek proposed another etymology for the name of Phoenix. In his opinion *φοῖνιξ* goes back to Linear B, deciphered by Ventris. The Mycenaean texts contain the word *po–ni–ke* that can be translated as *palm tree* or *griffin*[18].

We hold the opinion of L. Kákosy as the most well reasoned and based on not only classical but also on Egyptian sources. The author considers that 'wichtige Elemente der Phönix–Sage [...] sind in altägypten'[19]. Kákosy also listed the typical features of the classical Phoenix myth that are reflected in Egyptian sources: (i) *Bnw* als Sonnenvogel. Verbindungen mit Heliopolis; (ii) Selbstenstandenes (*ḫpr ḏs=f*) Wessen; (iii) Tod des *Bnw*; (iv) Symbol des Fortlebens, der Überwindung des Todes und der Verjüngung (Beziehungen zu Osiris und Rē'); (v) Elemente der Perriodizität (Sonne), Beziehungen zu Zeit und Ewigkeit[20].

II. Origins and Evolution of the Phoenix Myth

Taking into account all the considerations mentioned above we shall try to trace the way of forming Benu's image in the Egyptian mythology. Since the Old Kingdom there was the cult of Benu at Heliopolis that was recorded in the *Pyramid Texts* (§ 1652)[21]. The surviving representations[22] let us identify Benu with a small bird plover that was perhaps deified as a totem ancestor and a demiurge. In the *Pyramid Texts* (Utterance 600) Benu is closely connected with the solar creator–god Atum and the ancient fetish stone obelisk Benben. The latter personified the mythical mound where Atum created the entire visible world. We also know about the so–called *Benu Temple* at Heliopolis (*Ḥw.t–Bnw*).

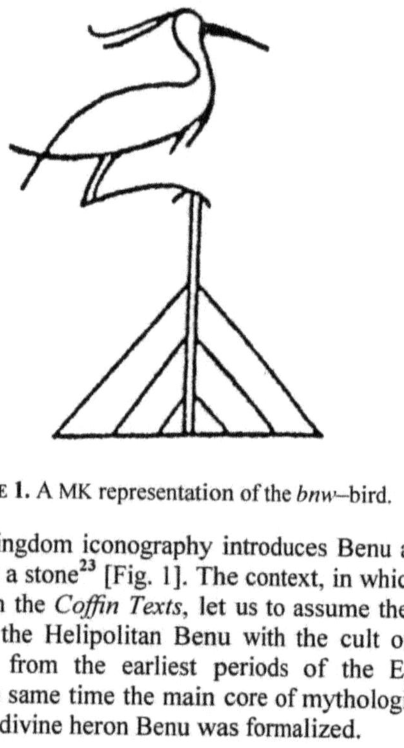

FIGURE 1. A MK representation of the *bnw*–bird.

The Middle Kingdom iconography introduces Benu as a heron perched on a stone[23] [Fig. 1]. The context, in which Benu is mentioned in the *Coffin Texts*, let us to assume the fusion of the cult of the Helipolitan Benu with the cult of heron (known to us from the earliest periods of the Egyptian history). At the same time the main core of mythological notions about the divine heron Benu was formalized.

This deity seems to be connected with the cult of Atum, falcon and Rē', i.e.: the deities of the Upper World. The 'netherworld myths cycle' correlates Benu with Anubis. The mediating function of Benu is also very important. This was the major factor for the simultaneous existence of conceptions on Benu as an 'official pantheon' deity and as a personage of the so–called *popular religion*, which was closely connected with magic[24].

[12] Belluccio: *op. cit.*, 31.
[13] Belluccio: *op. cit.*, 25.
[14] Sethe: *op. cit.*, 85; Spigelberg, W.: 'Zu dem Nomen der Phönix', *ZÄS*, **46**, 1910, 142.
[15] Van Den Broek: *op. cit.*, 25-26.
[16] Van Den Broek: *op. cit.*, 397.
[17] Van Den Broek: *op. cit.*, 25-26.
[18] Cited in van Den Broek: *op. cit.*, 62-63.
[19] Kákosy: *op. cit.*, 1037.
[20] Kákosy: *op. cit.*, 1037.
[21] We used texts published by K. Sethe (see Sethe, K.: *Die Altägyptischen Pyramidentexte, Neu herausgegeben und erläutert von Kurt Sethe*, **I-III**, Hildessheim–NY–Zürich 1987).
[22] See for instance some reliefs from the solar temple of Ny–Ouser-Rē' in Abusir in Wreszinski, W.: *Atlas zur altägyptischen Kulturgeschichte*, **III**, Leipzig 1923, 122, Tf. 60.
[23] See Spells 67f (**I**, 287), 496b (**V**, 393), & c. We used the texts published by de Buck; See de Buck, A.: *The Egyptian Coffin Texts*, **I-VII**, Chicago (The Oriental Institute) 1935-1961. **[Editor's Note:** There are more references to the Benu bird in the *CT*: **I**, 267c; 287e; **II**, 4c; **IV**, 45k; 198-199a; 198a; 340d; 341a; **VI**, 286u; 299i; 333j].
[24] For furhter details see Sadek, A.I.: *Popular Religion in Egypt during the New Kingdom*, Hildesheim (Gerstenberg Verlag, *HÄB*, **27**) 1987; Tolmache-

FIGURE 2. A NK depiction of the *bnw*–bird.

The process of coming into being of the Benu image and of formulating its functions and symbolism was finished during the time of the New Kingdom. The reliefs and paintings at tombs and temples, the vignettes from the *Book of the Dead*, and such, show the canonical iconography of Benu depicted as a heron (sp.: *ardea cinerea* or *ardea purpurea*) with two long feathers on the head [Fig. 2]. The mythological image of Benu partly differed from the natural appearance of a heron. The obligatory feature of the Benu's iconography became present in the above mentioned long crest on the back of its head. In reality such a crest is the feature of exclusively old herons. This allows us to presume that the iconography symbolized the antiquity of this divine bird, its affiliation to the mythical cosmogonical epoch, the legendary age of forefathers (*pꜣw.t tpy.t*). The plumage of the heron was usually painted light blue and/or light gray at tomb paintings or in the vignettes of papyri. In Wilkinson's opinion, this fact has a symbolic meaning: ' [...] heron, an ancient symbol of the primeval flood —and the inundation of the Nile which was an annual reminder or re–enactment of the watery origin of the world— was often painted in bright blue tones considerably different from the light gray blue of the bird's actual plumage'[25]. It is worth mentioning that in the so–called 'hunting scenes' represented on murals of the Middle and New Kingdom tombs, the plumage of the heron completely corresponds to the actual natural colors[26].

The identification of Benu with the great gods influenced the iconography of this bird. So, it is often depicted wearing the *ꜣtf*–crown of Osiris [Fig. 3][27] or the solar disc, a symbol of Rē'[28]. The representations of Benu as a heron perching on a pole (roost) in vignettes of the *Book of the Dead* testify on the one hand its identification with the *bꜥḥ*–bird, and on the other its cosmogonical symbolism[29]. The images of Benu perching the *imn.tt*–standard (cf. certain paintings at the tomb of Pashedu[30]; the coffin № 111986[31] at the Berlin Museum) show the connection of Benu and Osiris and reflect some notions about the Netherworld (*Dwꜣ.t*), which —according to the cosmological ideas of the ancient Egyptians— was located in the West.

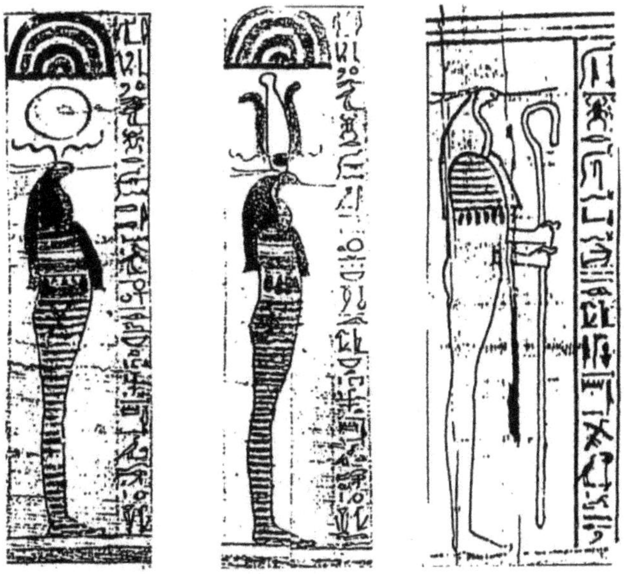

FIGURE 3. Various representations of the *bnw*–bird, as an Osirian animal–headed anthropomorphic deity.

At the end of the New Kingdom the Benu bird/divinity was occasionally depicted in human form. At Medinet Habu 'Benu, the Great God' is represented as a human with the head of a falcon[32]. In mythological papyri Benu was represented as a standing mummy with a heron's head, wearing the Osiris' crown or the disc of Rē'[33]. In some cases Benu bears another attribute of Osiris, king of the Netherworld, the *ḥkꜣ*–crook[34]. During the Ptolemaic Period the image of Benu was combined with the image of the Hellenic Phoenix and this was reflected in the iconography of Benu/Phoenix.

On the 'liturgical garment' found in one of the Saqqara tombs there is a representation of a long–legged bird that stands on a small hill and is surrounded by other deities [Fig. 4][35]. It is interesting to point out that the features of Benu's iconography (the form of a heron and its connection with the primeval mound) are consistent with the latest symbolic notions. The solar disc with dispersed rays is definitely different from the disk of Rē'. Apparently, it looks more like the nimbi of Christian saints (*mutatis mutandis*).

va, E.G.: 'Kult tsapli v Egipte v epochu Drevnego i Srednego Tsarstva: Obraz tsapli v tekstach piramid', *Voprosi istorii i economiki (sbornik aspirantskih statej)*, Moskva 2000.

25 Wilkinson, R.H.: *Symbol and Magic in Egyptian Art*, London 1994, 107.

26 See the representations of herons in the Khnum–hotep's tomb in Shedid, A.: *Die Felsengräber von Beni Hassan in Mittelägypten*, Mainz 1994, 63.

27 Desroches–Noblecourt, K.: *Egyptian Wallpaintings*, London 1962, 24; Belluccio, *op. cit.*, 1993, 38, fig.5; Piankoff, A.: *The Litany of Rē'*, NY (Princeton University Press, Bollingen Ser. **XL·4**) 1964, 90.

28 See Shedid, A.: *Das Grab des Sennedjem*, Mainz 1994, tf. 102.

29 See n. 6, *supra*. [**Editor's Note:** Cf. also Krupp, E.C.: 'Fire Bird', *Sky and Telescope*, February 2001a, 86-88].

30 Porter, B. & Moss, R.: *Topographical Bibliography of Ancient Egyptian Hieroglyphic Texts, Reliefs and Paintings: I. The Theban Necropolis*, Oxford 1994, 394.

31 Belluccio: *op. cit.*, 38 (5).

32 Kákosy: *op. cit.*, 394.

33 Piankoff: *op. cit.*, 70, 90, 92.

34 Piankoff: *op. cit.*, 70.

35 Lange, K. & Hirmer, M.: *Aegypten: Architectur Plastik Malerei in drei Jahrtausend*, München 1997, 428.

FIGURE 4. Another depiction of the *bnw*–bird, on a liturgical garment from a Saqqara tomb.

In many aspects the special place of Benu in Egyptian religion and mythology is determined by the Benu's connections with the great gods, namely Rē'–Atum, Horus, Osiris. We have mentioned that Benu, a local demiurge–god, was one of the aspects of Rē'–Atum–Khepri, who from the beginning of the Old Kingdom was considered to be an active creative force and creator of the universe. This cosmogonical conception developed in the *Coffin Texts* [cf. Spell 76, **II**, 4]. The solar nature of the heron is also emphasized in tomb reliefs and murals. Thus, on the ceiling of the tomb of Son–nedjem the deceased is represented in the bark of Rē' ferrying over the heavenly Nile to the East through the Netherworld. Son–nedjem is accompanied by the Benu, Rē' and the gods of the Great Ennead. In the vignettes of Chapter CI of the *Book of the Dead* [Fig. 5] the deceased is depicted in the boat together with Rē' and the *bnw*–bird. Benu was characterized as *the divine heart of Rē'*[36] and *the son of Rē'*[37].

FIGURE 5. A NK depiction of the *bnw*–bird from the *BD*.

The notion of Benu as 'The Ba of Rē'' is of great importance. As the *b3 of* Rē' Benu acted in Chapter XXIX of the *Book of the Dead*, one of the so–called 'heart Chapters': 'Utterance on the carnelian heart. I am Benu, Ba of Rē', the guide of the gods in Duat'[38]. In the texts of the magical *Papyri Bremner–Rind VII-IX* the Benu is mentioned again as 'the august falcon', 'sitting on the alp' and it is said of it that 'Atum is his name'[39].

As we have seen Benu was called 'the august falcon', and this connection between Benu and the falcon of Horus is really significant. It is well known that the falcon was regarded as a supreme sacral symbol of the heavenly sphere, as the solar symbol determining the semantics of the idea of *royalty* in many respects. Due to the fact that Benu was identified with Atum (bearing the epithet 'the king of the gods' and symbolizing the celestial solar bird) since the Middle Kingdom (in the *Coffin Texts*) it had been treated as closely connected with the falcon image.

In Chapter XIII of the *Book of the Dead* we find the following passage: 'I come as a falcon, I come as a *bnw*–bird, the morning star of Rē''. In addition, Chapter LXXVII of the *Book of the Dead*[40] under the title 'On the Accomplishment of Transformation into the Golden Falcon' says: 'I have shined, I have embodied as beautiful golden falcon with a *bnw*–bird head (*ḫʿ.kwi ḏmd.kwj m bik nfr n nbw tp bnw*). The appearance of 'the golden falcon with a *bnw*–bird head' seems to be highly mysterious. The grammatical structure of this sentence is puzzling: the use of the *old perfective* [**Editor's Note:** *pseudoparticiple*; cf. the Hellenic tense *parakeimenos*] (*ḫʿ.kwj, ḏmd.kwj*) stresses out the completeness and the impersonality of the action, which is approximately equal to the English present perfect tense. An adverbial predicate clause (*m bik* [...]) corresponds to epithets (attributes) *nfr* and *nbw* joined by *n*. However, following the subsequent word–combination *tp bnw* seems to be without grammatical connection to the other parts of the sentence. If we translate *tp* as *head*, the absence of a preposition or another connective makes the phrase vague. There is an alternative translation of the word *tp*. It can be translated as the preposition *on*. In this case the whole phrase becomes grammatically and syntactically correct, but the meaning of the sentence still remains obscure: 'I have shined, I have embodied as a beautiful golden falcon upon *Bnw*'. It is likely that at the time of copying of this text its sense was not clear to the scribe, who, in his turn, made a mistake. Otherwise the matter could concern not Benu but the semantically similar *bnbn*. In this case the phrase can be interpreted as a fragment of some ancient cosmogonic text dealing with the bird–demiurge, which created the word standing at the plot of land in the middle of the primeval chaos.

H. Frankfort pointed out the 'multiplicity of approaches' typical to the ancient Egyptian thought[41]. Taking into account these ideas we could interpret the passage in question as an allegorical denotation for the *b3* of Rē' or the *b3* of Osiris, i.e. 'beautiful golden falcon with *bnw*–bird head'. It is well known that according to the ancient Egyptian mythological concepts the *b3* of a god or a person was represented as a creature with the body of a falcon and a human head. In its turn Benu was regarded as the *b3* of Osiris and Rē'. Therefore the composite image of 'the beautiful golden falcon with a *bnw*–bird head' came into existence as a synthesis of two *b3*–conceptions. The first is the notion about the *b3* of Osiris

[36] *Ib n Rʿ ntry*, for which see Budge, E.A.W.: *The Mummy*, London 1894, 295.
[37] Kákosy: *op. cit.*, 1036.
[38] Hieroglyphic text according to Budge: *op. cit.*, 312.

[39] See Gardiner, A.H.: *Hieratic papyri in the British Museum*, **I**, London 1934, 75.
[40] As a rule we used the following edition of the *BD*: Budge, E.A.W. (ed.): *The Book of the Dead: Facsimiles of the Payri of Hunefer, Anhai, Kerasher and Netchemet, with Supplementary Text from the Papyrus of Nu, with Transcripts*, London 1899.
[41] Frankfort, H.: *Ancient Egyptian Religion*, NY 1948, 3-4.

and Rē', embodied in the heron Benu; and the second —the conception of the *bꜣ* mainly of mortals— as the golden falcon with human head. Hence, the previous words 'I have risen, I have gathered myself' refer to Osiris and allude to his resurrection after death and to the dismemberment of his body by Seth.

Benu was also identified with Osiris both in his aspect as the king of the Netherworld and as the god of fertility concerned with the Nile inundation. The *Coffin Texts* (Spell 335) and the so–called *Calendar Texts* of the New Kingdom convey this fact. According to the *Cairo Papyrus* composed in year 9th of Ramses II, the transformation of Osiris into Benu occurred on day 12th of the (1st month of the) *ꜣḫ.t* season. This transformation could have an unfavourable result; for this reason it was necessary to make a sacrifice on this day[42]. As Kákosy has suggested, in this case we deal with a euphemism for the death of Osiris[43]. In *Papyrus Jumilhac* Osiris acts in the form of Benu[44]. In several hymns[45] devoted to Osiris Benu is praised as his *bꜣ*. It is said about Benu in Edfu: 'le *bꜣ* august qui sort d'Osiris'[46]. Due to the connection with the heron–*bꜥḥ*, Benu was included into the Osirian circle of mythological notions as a deity of fertility, renascent nature and the Nile flood.

FIGURE 6. A related vignette from the *BD*.

The representations of Benu as a solar bird perching on a branch at the top of a tree are very popular in Egyptian sources, especially during the Late Period. The magical *Papyrus Bremner–Rind* mentions 'august Benu perching on the willow tree'[47]. We suppose that the representation of the vignette of Chapter LXIV of the *Book of the Dead* (*pNebseny*)[48] [Fig. 6] is a semantical parallel to this passage. The deceased is depicted adoring the sun disk that is at the top of a tree. The texts on the coffin of Princess 'Anch–nes–nefer–ib–Rē' say: 'She is the breath of his mouth, she is the great Benu, born on the willow at *Ḥw.t–Bnw*, belonging to the great *Ḥw.t–Sr* at Heliopolis'[49]. A *Bnw*–bird perching on a tree was also represented in the Tomb of Khaty (Dynasty XXV)[50]. In one of the representations, Benu —as the *bꜣ* of Osiris— perches on the sacral tamarisk nearby the tomb[51] [Fig. 7].

FIGURE 7. Another representation of the *bnw*–bird, perching on a tamarisk tree.

The motive of the 'bird perching on a tree' corresponds to the notions of Benu as the personification of the fructiferous sun in its creative aspect. The same idea was reflected in Chapter LXXXIV of the *Book of the Dead* saying that the *bnw*–bird 'has grown like a growing one' and 'has robed like a robed in armour' (e.g.: a turtle).

Thus the final formalization of mythological notions about the *bnw*–bird occurred as early as the New Kingdom. On funeral papyri of the *Book of the Dead* Benu is described as one of the supreme deities of the Netherworld, which owned the book containing all 'that existed and will exist' (Chapter XVIII). It is also mentioned as, 'the nose of the lord of the breath' (Chapter CXXV, l. 18, *pNu*), as 'the great god' living in Heracleopolis' (Chapter CXXV, l. 18, *pNu*). It was also thought as a personification of purity (*wꜥb*) that can be compared to the ritual purity of the deceased, who went through the Hall of Ma'at (Chapter CXXV, l. 18, *pNu*). Benu was also compared to *eternity* (*nḥḥ*) and *everlastingness* (*ḏt*) (see Chapter XVII), & c. According to Chapter LXIV of the *Book of the Dead* Benu is reported ('let to know' / '*rdi.t rḫ*') the 'situation' in the Netherworld.

III. Discussion and Conclusions

The archaic semantemes *birds–sun* and *birds–starry sky* that were already registered in the Predynastic Period and were well known from the texts of the Old and Middle Kingdom, did not lose their importance in the concepts and notions of the New Kingdom. In the so–called *astronomical texts* Benu is called the *Morning Star* (which was identified with planet Venus in mythological traditions). Here the planet corresponds to Venus of the European tradition, and was represented in the sky as a heron [Fig. 10][52]. In the same texts Benu is

[42] Troy, L.: 'Have a Nice Day! Some Reflections on the Calendars of Good and Bad Days', *The Religion of the Ancient Egyptians: Cognitive Structures and Popular Expressions*, Uppsala 1989, 133, 138, 140.
[43] Kákosy: *op. cit.*, 1035.
[44] Vandier, J.: *Le papyrus Jumilhac*, Paris 1961, 75-76.
[45] Belluccio: *op. cit.*, 29, 35.
[46] Belluccio: *op. cit.*, 29, 35.
[47] Gardiner: *op. cit.*, 75.
[48] For this vignette see Budge, E.A.W.: *Puteshestvie dushi v Tsarstve Mertvich. Egipetskaja Kniga Mertvich*, Moskva 1996, 213.
[49] Sander–Hansen, C.E.: *Die religiösen Texte auf dem Sarg der Anchnesneferibre*, Copenhagen 1937, 128.
[50] Belluccio: *op. cit.*, 38, fig. 6.
[51] Kees: *op. cit.*, 88, Abb.7.
[52] Neugebauer, O. & Parker, R.: *Egyptian Astronomical Texts: Decans, Planets, Constellations and Zodiacs / Plates*, **III**, RI (Brown University) 1965, pls. 1, 2, 3, 5, 6, 8, 9, 10, 13, 15. [**Editor's Note:** See also Krauss, R.: 'The Eye of Horus and the Planet Venus: Astronomical and Mythological

often identified with the heron–*bꜥḥ* that symbolized the notion of fertility, wealth and abundance. This stresses the connections of Benu not only to the world of gods, but also to the word of mortal humans, with the Earth in its fructiferous aspect and with plants and animals dwelling on it.

In its cosmogonic aspect known from the *Pyramid Texts* Benu acted as an astral symbol. But during the New Kingdom the notion of Benu as an ancestor and demiurge acquired its abstract (conceptual) meaning. Benu who created itself (*ḫpr ḏs=f*) and personified *eternity* and *everlastingness*, was the symbol of spatio–temporal cycles.

The complex of mythological concepts dealing with the image of *bnw*–bird was also reflected in the daily temple rituals. There are numerous evidences on the existence of a Benu cult all over Egypt. Most likely the earliest place of its worship was Heliopolis. It is also mentioned in the *Pyramid Texts*; the other sources also record the existence of *Ḥw.t–Bnw*. Thus, on the obelisk of Thutmosis III from Heliopolis 'the *išd*–tree venerated inside the *Ḥw.t–Bnw*' is mentioned [*Urk.*, **IV**, 591]. The text of the so–called *Flaminian Obelisk* erected by Sety I contains the following passage: 'Said by Rēʿ–Horakhty, the great god, lord of heaven: "He (the king) filled *Ḥw.t–Bnw* with wealth. May the Gods grant him life like Rēʿ eternally"'[53]. Probably in the Late Period *Ḥw.t–Bnw* was a part of the Heliopolitan sanctuary *Ḥw.t–Sr*. In any case the texts of 'Anch–nes–nefer–ib–Rēʿ coffin and *Metternich Stele* report: 'You are the great Benu that was born in the reeds at the great *Ḥw.t–Sr* in Heliopolis'[54].

Among the other centers of the Benu cult were Hu (Diospolis Parva) or *Pr–Bnw*, Hipnonomē (*Ḥw.t–Bnw*) (XVI nome of Upper Egypt), Hermopolis, Edfu, Philae, and Elephantine. A significant *Ḥw.t–Bnw*, in which a sanctuary of heron is recorded since the Old Kingdom, is localized between Kom 'el-Ahmar (Savaris) and Hard (Kynopolis)[55].

Later the number of Benu functions increased. Thus, Benu was identified with Amun. According to an inscription dating from the Ptolemaic Period, Amun as a primeval snake carried Benu on his back[56]. In Edfu Benu became the member of the Divine Ennead[57]. As an aspect of Horus, Benu was called the father of Hathor[58].

The latest period of the Egyptian culture is characterized by a decline ensued after the golden age of the New Kingdom. The loss of political power of royalty, as well as the spiritual crisis of society that followed, found a consequent reflection in the sphere of religion. The 'official theology' made an attempt to return to archaic cults such as the cults of solar gods. On the other hand, there was an extension of some popular beliefs, where Benu played an important role. Thus, this bird was mentioned in the conjuration against pain in the 'legs' bones'[59].

During the Hellenistic Era the most significant tendency in the evolution of the Benu image became its transformation into Phoenix, that was the symbol of the resurrection and new life known from classical sources. In the classical world Phoenix was the personification of periodic time cycles, the so–called *Phoenix Periods*. Some scholars based on the classical sources consider them to be identical to the astronomical *Sothic Periods*[60].

The image of the *bnw*–bird existed since the Old Kingdom until the Late Period. During more than 2000 years it was transformed from the small bird demiurge worshipped in Heliopolis into a significant deity worshipped all over Egypt. The *bnw*–bird image was closely connected with other supreme gods, such as Atum, Rēʿ, and Osiris. In many aspects the modifications of its functions and its inherent symbolism could be explained by the position of these gods in the Egyptian pantheon. At the time of the Old and Middle Kingdom Benu was identified with Atum–Rēʿ and had mainly solar and cosmogonic significance. On the contrary, during the New Kingdom the cult of Osiris had known its major expansion. Therefore, Benu was popularized as one of the rulers of the Netherworld.

Therefore, we conclude that the components of the myth of Phoenix, which were emphasized by A. Belluccio, could indeed have an Egyptian origin. On the other hand the Hellenic elements should not be forgotten. The image of Phoenix known from classical sources was the result of a synthesis of the Oriental and Hellenic cultural traditions; a synthesis that was so widespread during Hellenistic times.

In Coptic sources and the Early Christian literature the Phoenix was considered to be a symbol of resurrection, of eternal life and of revival in general; as well as an archetypal symbol of the Sun, Time, Christ, Virgin Mary. According to the Coptic authors, the Phoenix appeared during the time of the first sacrifice mentioned in the *Bible*[61]. Another text states that during the Exodus from Egypt the Phoenix appeared in the temple of Heliopolis[62].

Aknowledgements

The author wishes to thank Dr Galina A. Belova and Dr Tatjana A. Sherkova for their continuous support; and Dr Amanda-Alice Maravelia for her useful comments and for making her text more idiomatic in English and more rich in bibliographical references.

References', *Under One Sky: Astronomy and Mathematics in the Ancient Near East* (Steele, J.M. & Imhausen, A., eds.), Münster (Ugarit–Verlag / *Alter Orient & Altes Testament*, **Band 297**) 2002, 193-208; ibid: '*m-mitt bnw* (*pAnastasi I*, 4,5)', *JEA*, **79**, 1993, 266-67].

[53] For the hieroglyphic text see Budge, *op. cit.*, 133. **[Editor's Note:** Budge's text is incomplete; for this topic, see the thorough analysis in Lambrecht, B.: 'L'obélisque d'Hermapion (Ammien Marcellin, *Res Gestae*, XVII, 4, 17-23)', *Le Muséon*, **114**[1-2], 2001, 51-95].

[54] Sander–Hansen: *op. cit.*, 127; ibid.: *Die Texte der Metternichstele*, Copenhagen 1956, 44.

[55] For furhter details see Tolmacheva: *op. cit.*

[56] Kákosy: *op. cit.*, 1033.

[57] Kákosy: *op. cit.*, 1033.

[58] Kákosy: *op. cit.*, 1033.

[59] Kákosy: *op. cit.*, 1036.

[60] For furhter details see Van Den Broek: *op. cit.*, 26.

[61] Van Den Broek: *op. cit.*, 121.

[62] Van Den Broek: *op. cit.*, 121.

199 a

199 b

Aquileia. 199 a u.b Relief mit Hammer,Zange,Amboß und

www.ingramcontent.com/pod-product-compliance
Lightning Source LLC
Chambersburg PA
CBHW040949020526
44116CB00039B/2978